Colin Sutton.
September, 1952.

E. J. TRELAWNY

THE LAST DAYS
OF
SHELLEY AND BYRON

Being the complete text of
Trelawny's 'Recollections'
edited, with additions
from contemporary sources,
by
J. E. Morpurgo

The Folio Society
Westminster
1952

Designed and produced by The Folio Society.
Set in Baskerville type, printed and bound
by Messrs. William Clowes and Sons,
Limited, London and Beccles. Illustrations
reproduced in collotype by Messrs. Waterlow.

PRINTED IN GREAT BRITAIN

Introduction

THE son of a Trelawny and a Hawkins; the very names proclaim a brave but unquiet heredity; Edward John Trelawny spent his early manhood in a struggle against the frustrating bonds of an age already weighed down with disenchanting knowledge. In the East and in the West, in Java, India, Madagascar, the Greek Islands and the Carolinas, on board the King's ships and on board French privateers he acted out his metachronistic *picaresque*. Always he sought adventure—adventure was the inspiration of his love affairs, his politics and his travels—and when there was no adventure to be found, when he had 'nearly exhausted this planet', he turned Munchausen and invented his own: tall stories, exaggerations, lies, yet designed not to enthrall the world, but to ease his own restlessness.

In all those years of virile quest, of real and self-created excitement, Trelawny had one experience that, knowing no bounds of geography or circumstance, took precedence, in retrospect, as his greatest adventure: he met Shelley and Byron, and in a long career of bustling episodes, of thrills and disappointments, of violent loves and violent hates, of battles and of piracies, his few months of companionship with the most romantic figures of the Romantic Movement stood out as the climax of his life.

Rubbing shoulders so much with authors made him an author, but he wrote only two books: *Adventures of a Younger Son*, published in 1831, and *Recollections of the Last Days of Shelley and Byron*, published in 1858 and twenty years later amended, enlarged, emasculated, and reissued as *Records of Shelley, Byron and the Author*. Both books are built on autobiographical foundations, yet the *Younger Son* at least is so insecurely perched that it is almost impossible to raise the framework of his biography. Librarians, those stern, moralistic guardians of the literary category, are apt to hide the *Younger Son* on the crowded shelves reserved for fiction, but not even Trelawny's zest for improbabilities and his violent manipulations of historical detail can entirely discredit his bold claim, made in the year of publication, that 'my life is not a novel'. Autobiographical *facts* there are in the *Younger Son*, but, in attempting to separate them from the many fables, it is well to remember that when he came to write his first book, the months of his association with

Shelley and Byron stood, an enchantress between Trelawny and the memories of his own youth, so that history was turned to the purpose of Byronic projection and event artistically improved by Romantic exaggeration.

The *Adventures of a Younger Son* was completed eight years after the death of Shelley and six years after the death of Byron; Trelawny himself lived on until 1881 and if he had written the book at any time in the fifty lonely years that were left to him it would have sung with the same rhythms from the poets' minds. The spirit of Byron and of Shelley collaborated in his revolutionary fervour; Byron pushed Trelawny's pen through the vigorous and the angry passages; Shelley wrote in the loveliness of Zela, the Malagasy wife of the Younger Son, but though the literary influences are obvious and though certain elements of Zela's story are borrowed, in advance, from the history of Trelawny's later marriage with Tersitza, the sister of Odysseus the Greek chieftain, it is not wise to presume that this whole story (or anything else in the *Younger Son*) is just Romanticised fiction; Zela's funeral pyre is lit from the flames that blazed on August 16th, 1822, but only the greatest of artists could have dreamed the love of Zela and the Younger Son; her actual existence is hardly in doubt.

That he was born in 1792, the younger son of Charles Brereton Trelawny and of Maria Hawkins, is undisputable—it is almost the only detail of his early career which can be categorically stated. He saw some service in the Royal Navy, but the extent of his service is dubious, while his own story of desertion from a ship in Bombay, his subsequent career of piracy, his wonderful strength and marvellous courage—all these take so much blood and flesh from *Don Juan* and *The Corsair* that it is inevitable that the stripped bones should be categorised as mere lies. Inevitable, but again unjust. Byron had already used Trelawny as a model before ever they met; Trelawny saw himself in the Byronic mirror and etched in the lines of his self-portrait to fit what he saw, but the face was his own, its bronzed tone sun-earned.

Trelawny's first book ended with the promise of a sequel. The second volume was to tell of Trelawny in Europe when 'I followed the fortunes of those invincible spirits who wandered, exiled outcasts, over the world, and lent my feeble aid to unveil the frauds contained in worn-out legends which have so long deluded mankind'. With his mournful toll—'Alas! those noble beings are no more'—he rang a peal of confidence in the durability of the work of his heroes, Shelley, Byron (and Keats)—'they have left enduring monuments, and their names will live for ever'—and the very last paragraph of the *Adventures of a Younger Son* is a cry of fulfilment: ' "Methinks those who now live have survived an age of despair":

> "For freedom's battle once begun,
> Bequeathed from bleeding sire to son,
> Though baffled oft, is ever won."
>
> BYRON.'

Twenty-seven years passed before the sequel appeared. The delay is inexplicable; perhaps he was set back by his realisation that the events of 1830 were not the final victory of liberalism and then was given new confidence by the renaissance of 1848; perhaps he felt bound to wait the death of Mary Shelley (though in the days of their friendship when he had even wanted Shelley's widow as his wife, he had often discussed his project with her). But when the book appeared the accents of Shelley and Byron were unmodulated. Trelawny had seen the dead Shelley and the dead Byron but for him they had never died and in the pages of the *Recollections* he talked with them again. A great writer can reconstruct a past he has never known. Trelawny, from a distance of almost forty years, relived his only real present.

The purpose he had in mind, and the limits of his achievement, Trelawny set down with disarming frankness in the Preface of his *Recollections*:

'Any details of the lives of men whose opinions have had a marked influence upon mankind, or from whose works we have derived pleasure or profit, cannot but be interesting. This conviction induces me to record some facts regarding Shelley and Byron, two of the last of the true Poets. The matter contained in this small Volume concerning them is derived partly from notes taken and letters written at the time the events occurred, and partly from memory. I wrote what is now printed, not systematically, but just as the incidents occurred to me, thinking that with the rough draft before me it would be an easy, if not an agreeable, task to re-write the whole in a connected form; but my plan is marred by my idleness or want of literary dexterity. I therefore commit the rough draft to the printer as first written, in "most admired disorder".'

The events of the book start some six years after the last episode of the *Adventures of a Younger Son*. In re-telling his life story Trelawny had no patience for the drab years and, except for the details of a second, unhappy marriage, nothing has been discovered to throw light on his circumstances between the death of Zela and his meeting with Wordsworth. Knowing the man it seems certain that he was not still; the internal evidence of the opening chapter of the *Recollections* indicates that his travels were not all geographical—that he was already exploring the Romantic mind and seeking an opportunity for more active participation in the Romantic adventure.

John Keats, the youngest of the Romantics and the first to die, he never met and, though he always set Keats's work with Shelley's and Byron's as the epitome of Romanticism and spent much time in after years in the company of friends of Keats such as Joseph Severn and Charles Armitage Brown as if to seek through their knowledge the friendship that had been denied him, it is doubtful if Trelawny would have found pleasure in Keats, the man. Coleridge, intellectual of intellectuals, he never considered much; once he defended him to Byron, though Trelawny would have turned Jew in the moment that Byron proclaimed his devotion to Mohammed. But, in 1820 (by his own telling, in 1819), he met Wordsworth, in his person the least romantic of the Romantics, and found in him no satisfaction. Not long after, in Geneva at the house of a relative, he was introduced to Thomas Medwin who had known and admired Shelley from boyhood. Unashamedly opportunist, Trelawny seized on Medwin as his passport to the acquaintance of the two Romantics who, for themselves as well as their poetry, were most likely to prove close to his turbulence and virility, and in January 1822 he reached at last the house on the Lung 'Arno in Pisa where Shelley had a flat.

His first impression was astonishment, but astonishment gave way to awe, and as the completeness of Shelley's person and his poetry exercised its influence over his mind, awe gave way to worship. Shelley had his apostle, the Pirate was ready to stump the market-places of the world to proclaim the Poet's glory.

The next day, and in Shelley's company, Trelawny was taken to the Palazzo Lanfranchi to meet Byron. The account of this meeting in the *Recollections* is damned with memories of their subsequent acquaintanceship, but the immediate shock was no less real because it was later intensified. Byron, who, from the evidence of his work, should have been another hero such as Shelley, was instead a fool, a poseur, a snob, a villain without the greatness of true villainy. Byron, for his part, was delighted; being at that moment somewhat dissatisfied with his own work and suspicious of his own earlier honesty, nothing could be more convenient than to have, at hand for his scorn, the living parody of his own Byronic heroes. 'Trelawny was an excellent fellow,' said Byron, 'until he took to imitating my *Childe Harold* and *Don Juan*.' Even it must have seemed as if Trelawny, with so many physical advantages, was imitating the Byron that his Lordship would have wanted to be, and if Mary

Shelley within a few days of their first meeting appreciated Trelawny in Byronic terms, was excited, and pleased, Byron found the parallel at once, was excited and pleasurably angered. Byron set his snob's rudeness to the baiting of this trespasser; he posed, he teased, his arrow-humour threatened and pierced, while Trelawny could only twist in pain and disillusionment; his only defence the proof of his muscular superiority; a defence that served but to increase Byron's anger.

For both of them the position was aggravated by the presence of Shelley; Shelley who, alone among men, could make Byron feel inferior; Shelley who, above all men, could, with the simple acknowledgment of friendship, make Trelawny feel proud.

With the determination of a tourist who has at last reached Naples, of a pilgrim who has fulfilled his life's ambition to journey to Mecca, Trelawny faced the hardships of his achievement and, though he suffered from Byron and suffered from Byron's intervention in his Shelley idyll, he settled himself to increasing his knowledge of the two men. He never lost his admiration for Byron's work, but, as his belief in Shelley's mission increased with his respect for Shelley's personality and as he ceased to differentiate between the two aspects of his hero's life, so did he perceive more clearly the hideous disparity between Byron and the author of *Don Juan*. But between the two from whom he had hoped for equal gifts of romantic manna Trelawny could make no just comparisons: 'Byron and Shelley, what a contrast—the one the incarnation of rank selfishness—the other of a bountiful and loving nature'. Like another of the companions of those Pisan days, Leigh Hunt—a far more perceptive literary critic—he could not deny Byron's powers, but his criticism was sharpened by his distaste for his Lordship's manner; always his praise was qualified by dislike, his enthusiasm by hate.

There is a tragedy in the three-fold relationship that was, fortunately, never appreciated by the victim: from Shelley, for whom he would willingly have died, Trelawny received only passive, if amiable recognition: from Byron, whom at times he would willingly have killed, the recognition was fierce and active, if for the most part decidedly unamiable. Yet when Shelley died the two, Trelawny and Byron, who in their disparate manner had loved him, were together in mourning, and in their mourning tried to create a new relationship. Trelawny set himself up as nurse-maid: 'It was long my great object to get him out of Italy, and he was wearied of staying there. Exercise and excitement seemed necessary for both his body and mind, and both seemed to be declining in his long, inactive and secluded way of living in the south. He became peevish, sickly and indifferent, and discontented with everything. He acknowledged this, and I continually urged him with new plans.' Byron, for his part, at last did himself the justice of his greatness. 'He said', wrote Lady Blessington, 'that since the death of Shelley, he had become greatly attached to Mr. Trelawny; who on that melancholy occasion, had evinced such devotions to the dead and such kindness to the living, as could only spring from a fine nature', and to Trelawny Byron himself wrote: 'You must have heard that I am going to Greece. Why do you not come to me? I want your aid and am exceedingly anxious to see you . . .' And Trelawny went.

But now it was Byron who was genuine and Trelawny who acted with ponderous cunning. He would act the nurse-maid, he would act the captain, he would be the man of action, but all to show how he, and not Byron, had been worthy of Shelley's affection. As he had done at school, so again he would thrash the tutor who had bullied him. When Byron died Trelawny was thwarted. He, who has been so much praised for his Romantic exercises at Shelley's funeral, has been constantly abused for his morbid activities by Byron's death-bed, but far more vicious than his curiosity was his disappointment and his duplicity; for public consumption he wrote as a close friend was bound to write, his accents sickly with the enthusiasm of the obituary column, 'Lord Byron is dead. With all his faults I loved him truly; he is connected with every event of the most interesting years of my wandering life. His every day companion, we lived in ships, boats and houses together; we had no secrets, no reserve, and we often differed in opinions, we never quarrelled. It gave me pain, witnessing his frailties; he only wanted a little excitement to awaken and put forth virtues that redeemed them all. . . . This is no private grief, the world has lost its greatest man, I my best friend'; but to Mary Shelley he wrote the private truth, the truth of his disappointment, his disgust and his blasted revenge: 'I now feel my face burn with shame that so weak and ignoble a soul could so long have influenced me. It is a degrading reflection and ever will be. I wish he had lived a little longer that he might have witnessed how I would have soared above him here, how I would have triumphed over his mean spirit.'

With time, however, and with loneliness, his public love usurped his private hate. Byron was dead, and for Trelawny no one could take his place, for there was no one greater than Byron—except Shelley, and Shelley too was dead. He sought other heroes; he tried to find, in Mary Shelley, the spirit of her dead husband; he essayed a return to the wanderings of his youth, hurled himself despondently to the task of swimming Niagara; he settled for a while in America, like an earlier group of Romantics dreaming of 'Pantisocracy and golden days to come on earth' by the shores of the Susquehanna.

But he was lost. His Romantic being was lost among the Victorians; his bold Romantic spirit, without the power of Romantic expression, was bewildered without the two poets who had given his life its voice.

Still the old fires smouldered. Rebellion was his breath; even in the year of his death he was shouting his regrets that his age would not let him fight for the Boers in their first struggle against Britain; but rebellion faded at last: on August 13, 1881, Trelawny died at Sompting. He was buried as he had wished: by the side of Shelley.

For those who are interested in the lives of the two great poets Trelawny's *Recollections* are invaluable, but they are cursed with one particular disadvantage: Trelawny knew both men, and knew them intimately, but only for a few months at the end of their lives. He saw them both, as it were pinned to a moment of time, without appreciating very much the circumstances of heredity, environment and event which had brought them to that stage in the development of their characters and careers. Whenever he wrote of the past he wrote from rumour or conjecture, and with both men rumour and conjecture played freely. Shelley and Byron are the principal characters of the *Recollections*; almost, until after he has described the death of Shelley, they are the only characters of Trelawny's book, for the author, who is so devastatingly egotistical in the *Younger Son*, holds himself well to the background of the first half of the *Recollections*. Therefore, at risk of covering well-known ground, it is worth rehearsing the previous history of both poets.

The strains of insanity, debauchery and disquiet apparent in Byron throughout his adult years were already set for him by his heredity and upbringing; his brilliance was undeniably his own. Against his grandfather, Admiral John Byron, not much can be held save the capacity for running into storms which won him the nickname Foulweather Jack, but Byron's great-uncle, William, the Fifth Lord, from whom the poet eventually inherited the title and Newstead Abbey, gained and merited a far more sinister name: 'the Wicked Lord Byron', while Byron's father, another John (who died unmourned when his son was almost a baby), was a profligate of profligates who seduced his first wife before he married her, seduced a number of other women both before and after marriage had made it impossible for him to make seduction respectable, and spent much of his time and all of his money on women who needed no seducing.

In return for his life as a rake-hell he gained a daughter (Augusta Leigh), probably venereal disease, and certainly a vast accumulation of debts. When his first wife died he looked around for an heiress, not because he wanted to pay his debts, but because he wanted to make more. He found his heiress, Catherine Gordon of Gight in Aberdeenshire, spent much of her money, and left her soon after their child was born in 1788.

Catherine Gordon Byron may be pitied for her marriage, but in many respects she was hardly better than her husband. Certainly in the eleven years which the child spent with his mother in Aberdeen the young George Byron suffered a great deal from her tantrums and her dipsomania. 'My poor mother,' he wrote later, and even the adjective is a rare concession to pity, 'was generally in a rage every day, and used to render me sometimes almost frantic; particularly when, in her passion, she reproached me with my personal deformity.'

In 1794, on the death of a cousin, Byron became heir-presumptive to the title. In 1798 he succeeded and next year went to school at Dr. Glennie's boarding-school in Dulwich. Here he already showed that excessive pride and extravagant consciousness of position which were to make him so many enemies: the snobbishness which was to make him despise men of superior education and inferior ancestry like Leigh Hunt. Harrow, where he went in 1801, was more congenial to him. There, if his friendships were inclined to be passionate, peculiar and even erotic, they were at least with gentlemen. But neither Harrow nor Trinity College, Cambridge, made him into a scholar, though he read widely and made his first flights into poetry.

In 1807 *Hours of Idleness* appeared. Privately printed it deserved no more than to be allowed to languish and die in comparable privacy, but for some reason the *Edinburgh Review* took it upon itself to blast the young poet in a review laden with venom, rudeness and sadistic abuse. The need for revenge gave Byron inspiration. Brougham, the author of the review, had said that the verses in the *Hours of Idleness* were 'the last we shall ever have from him'. Byron would show him his folly, and did so to no mean effect in *English Bards and Scotch Reviewers*, which, published just after his twenty-first birthday, established his reputation as a satirist, gave him confidence in his ability—and, incidentally, went through five editions.

At about the same time he took his seat in the House of Lords, and made his maiden speech, on behalf of the working classes. Neither this, nor his more genuine concern with reform and libertarian movements which followed is quite so paradoxical as at first appears. If it is a paradox at all, this struggle for equality by a man who was without doubt a snob, it is a paradox quite common in English history, but in Byron's case fervour was increased by his feeling that he was himself an outcast. Aristocrat he was and inordinately proud of the fact, but that very pride filled him with a sense of political responsibility for those who, to his mind, were incapable of defending themselves. The majority, the *bourgeoisie*, had victimised him, as they victimised the poor; therefore he would attack them both as his own advocate and as advocate for the poor.

In June 1809 Byron started on the Grand Tour. In September of that year he landed in Greece for the first time, and Greece completed his education. Greece was to him, as to so many Englishmen, all that mind and heart required: adventurous, colourful, beautiful, romantic. It was, in addition, oppressed, which gave him more grounds for hating oppressors, and it still contained something of the spirit and much of the physical evidence of ancient glories.

From these experiences Byron distilled the first two cantos of *Childe Harold's Pilgrimage* and on their publication after his return to England in 1812 he 'awoke one morning and found himself famous'.

He enjoyed being lionised and found not the least of his pleasures the number of women who were prepared to lie down with the lion. Whether his half-sister, Augusta Leigh, was among their number is a matter for debate beyond the scope of these pages; whether he added the uncommon and unnatural vice of incest to his many adulteries can be neither proven nor denied. Certainly he did his best to give that impression, but Byron was twenty-five at the time when he was most often in Augusta's company, and Byron was— Byron. Many young men enjoy shocking society; in Byron's case society had grown accustomed to his more ordinary vices, but even the amoral circle in which he moved was not used to incest, and, as for the hated *bourgeoisie*, this was yet another gauntlet hurled in their faces.

In the midst of his successes, amorous and literary, Byron embarked on the most extraordinary adventure of his life. He married Annabella Milbanke, a young woman whose outstanding vice was excessive virtue, a young woman utterly incompatible with him, whose primness, moralising and reforming zeal merely drove him further into licentiousness. The reasons behind the unsuitable match are now obscure. Perhaps Byron had honest intentions of settling down, perhaps Annabella, whose conceit was no less formidable than his own, though differently directed, had hopes of persuading him to the paths of decorum. More practically, Byron had been

xi

frightened, early in 1814, by a convulsive attack and may have wished to ensure the succession to the title he prized so much, though even so it would seem surprising that he did not choose more wisely from among the many girls who would have been glad to be elected mother to the seventh Lord Byron.

At all events the marriage lasted a year; one year of unutterable misery for both husband and wife. A daughter, Augusta Ada, was born in December 1815, a month later Lady Byron left London, her husband having signified to her, in writing, 'his absolute desire that I should leave on the earliest day that I could conveniently fix'.

Society, which had idolised Byron, now ostracised him. On April 25, 1816, he left England, driven into exile, as he thought with some justice, by the unreasonableness of public opinion which condoned and even enjoyed most of his failings but which could not accept his sane decision to rid himself of the results of his most insane act.

Incidental at this moment, as most of Byron's love-affairs were incidental, but of some importance to subsequent events, was the fact that among the last of his English *amours* was a liaison with Claire Clairmont, William Godwin's step-daughter. In January 1817 she gave birth to a child, Allegra. Both Byron and Claire agreed on assuming that the child was his.

For most of 1816 Byron was in Switzerland, part of the time in the company of the Shelleys, whom he now met for the first time, and Claire Clairmont. Henceforth, though their association was intermittent and chequered, the biographies of the two poets are inextricably interwoven.

Shelley's previous career has in it some of the same features as Byron's. Like Byron, who was four years his senior, he was an aristocrat, a fact insufficiently considered by biographers who try to explain the power Shelley held over Byron's mind. Like Byron, Shelley had received the education of an English gentleman (Eton and University College, Oxford, for Byron's Harrow and Trinity College, Cambridge) which means that so far as the school-room was concerned he was almost uneducated: 'The Etonian who goes to Cambridge or Oxford has not read a single book of Herodotus, Thucydides, Xenophon, Livy, Polybius or Tacitus. He has not read a single Greek tragedy or comedy; he is utterly ignorant of mathematical or physical science . . . modern history and modern languages are of course out of the question.'

Like Byron he had taken early to the cause of reform and had suffered public condemnation, being expelled from Oxford (with his friend Hogg) for 'contumaciously refusing to answer questions proposed to them, and for also repeatedly declining to disfavour a publication entitled *The Necessity of Atheism*'. Like Byron he had made a stupid marriage, to the charming but ineffectual Harriet Westbrook, a child of sixteen, and, as Byron's, so had his marriage foundered on the sharp rocks of incompatibility.

But the similarities of circumstance in the lives of the two men, though they added to their mutual sympathy, were little more than coincidences. Between their characters as poets and as individuals there were few parallels. Shelley was in everything deeper, more earnest and more admirable than Byron. By fierce study he had made himself a scholar; even his political opinions were founded on earnest discipleship of William Godwin. Whereas Byron was a philanderer because his nature demanded change and approbation, Shelley, who was not altogether innocent of philandering, sought always in his relations with women some solid and even moral foundation. In all his activities and all his associations Shelley tried to foster the good of mankind in general and of individuals in particular, Byron was concerned for individuals, never—for mankind, sometimes—and for Lord Byron, always.

And as his motives were more unselfish, so were Shelley's failures more tragic both in implication and event. His impetuous marriage with Harriet Westbrook, for example, led first to his estrangement from his father, then to marital unhappiness, separation, and finally to the suicide of Harriet and to the revenge of her parents which deprived him of his two children. His elopement and eventual marriage with Mary Wollstonecraft Godwin, brought neither of them the content that they both coveted. His care for others, for Mary's father, William Godwin, for Godwin's step-daughter, Claire Clairmont, for Leigh Hunt—and even for Byron—brought him only difficulties, financial and personal.

And, in this unlike Byron, his work did not bring him in his lifetime even such measure of general approval as could temper the torrents of abuse that were poured upon it.

When the two first met the disparity of achievement between them was considerable, and all in favour of Byron. *The Necessity of Atheism*, published privately in 1811, had been an undergraduate protest; its dramatic consequences more violent than it deserved. *Queen Mab*, also privately printed in 1813, was hardly less juvenile, though 'midst all its philosophisings, its borrowings, and its out-politicking of Godwin's politics, there is already evidence of Shelley's superb lyrical power. (Not enough to satisfy the poet in his mature years. In 1822 he disclaimed both the poem and its thought: 'I doubt not but that it is perfectly worthless in point of literary composition; and that, in all that concerns moral and political speculation as well as in the subtler discriminations of metaphysical and religious doctrine, it is still more crude and immature. I am a devoted enemy to religious, political and domestic oppression; and I regret this publication, not so much from literary vanity as because I fear it is better fitted to injure than to serve the sacred cause of freedom . . .'.) Just a few weeks before Trelawny's two heroes came together at Geneva on May 27, 1816, Shelley had for the first time published a poem in what is now the conventional way: *Alastor, or the Spirit of Solitude*, published by Baldwin, Cradock and Jon.

But both poets were now on the verge of their mature achievement, and, if Godwin, Trelawny and Williams were all more favourably disposed to Shelley than to Byron so that all leapt to the convenient conclusion that the improvement in Byron's work from the third canto of *Childe Harold* was directly inspired by his association with Shelley (see p. 7), at least it can be argued that their contention has some substance. Shelley had much to offer Byron and little to receive in return: 'Byron was but superficial on points on which Shelley was most profound—and the latter's capacity for study, the depth of his thoughts as well as their boldness, and his superior scholarship, supplied the former with exactly what he wanted: and thus a portion of Shelley's aspirations were infused into Byron's mind.'

Above all Byron was no critic of poetry, least of all his own; Shelley was a critic, keen and well informed. Like Leigh Hunt he was both ready to *edit* Byron and capable of acting in that capacity (the difference between the two was in the great measure of personal respect and liking which Byron showed for Shelley). Already in 1816 Byron entrusted Shelley with the task of seeing through the press the third canto of *Childe Harold*, and for the rest of their association, however infuriating the one might find the other, the two were always comfortable together when discussing poetry, and, 'ready as Shelley always was with his purse or person to assist others, his purse had a limit, but his mental wealth seemed to have none . . . not only to Byron, but to anyone disposed to try his hand at literature, Shelley was ever ready to give any amount of mental labour . . .'.

The comfortable relations of their early contact could not last between them. When the Shelleys returned to the Continent, in March 1818, Shelley found himself saddled with the irksome responsibility of trying to mediate between Byron and Claire Clairmont over the custody of Allegra. Byron refused to allow Claire any rights over the child; refused even to correspond with Claire on the matter. His hard-hearted obstinacy continued to be a canker in the friendship with Shelley until the child died on April 19, 1822, nor was the situation improved by Claire's despair, which drove her to contemplate kidnapping Allegra with the assistance of Shelley, and held Shelley in a perpetual state of fear that she might carry out her mad schemes and involve him in a duel with Byron.

Byron's callousness was to have even more direct effect on the Shelleys, and again Claire was involved.

On December 27, 1818, according to Shelley's own statement in front of a Neapolitan magistrate, a daughter, Elena Adelaide Shelley, was born to Mary and Shelley. That the child was not Mary's is certain. On June 29, 1819, when Elena was still alive, Mary wrote of Clara and William as her 'two only and lovely children', in November of the same year she wrote of herself as having been childless 'for five hateful months'. That it was not Shelley's is probable; he was sufficiently quixotic to take to himself the paternity of someone else's daughter. That it was not even Claire's is at least possible, though she is known to have been ill at the time of its birth. But in the summer of 1820 a dismissed servant of the Shelleys told the wife of R. B. Hoppner, the British Consul in Venice, that this child was the daughter of Claire and Shelley, and added that while she had been in their service the two lovers had shown nothing but unkindness to Mary. The Hoppners spread the story, and among others who listened to it was Byron, who did nothing to suppress it. Even, in August 1821, not long before Trelawny's arrival, Byron revived the whole business when Shelley visited him at Ravenna.

This time his treachery was even more vile, though, perhaps fortunately, Shelley never knew of it. Mary and Shelley refuted all the charges in a letter which was to go to the Hoppners by way of Byron. That letter was found among Byron's papers after his death.

From this evidence, and from the knowledge of differences over Leigh Hunt and the *Liberal* (which will become apparent in Trelawny's *Recollections*) it seems inconceivable that the two poets could have sought each other's company. Yet their friendship survived, even if it was, as Edmund Blunden says, like 'a friendship in a play by John Webster' and, when Trelawny first appeared on the scene, the two were living in Pisa, principally for the purpose of being close to each other.

In a strange way the *Recollections* are the best of all the numerous descriptions of Shelley and Byron in Italy, and of Byron in Greece.

Leigh Hunt was a better artist, but, particularly in *Lord Byron and Some of his Contemporaries* and to a lesser extent in his *Autobiography*, his hatred of Byron betrayed him into unworthy exaggeration, while, at all events, he had mixed so much among greatness that Byron could be but one of many, and even Shelley loses something of the advantage of concentrated attention in the midst of accounts of his equals and near-equals: Coleridge, Lamb, Wordsworth, Keats. Mary Shelley loved her husband—and herself—too dearly to look wisely upon those who surrounded him, her picture is shrouded in mourning-bands for her lost Shelley and her lost happiness. Teresa Guiccioli was concerned with justifying her own relationship with Byron to a censorious world. Medwin, Parry and the many others who wrote of the Greek affair were but shambling amateurs seeking the possibility of professional reward from a much-publicised tragedy. But Trelawny was a natural writer, and Trelawny lived with his memories of the two poets until every detail of their life together, every look and every accent, took on clarity that is impossible with contemporary description.

Unfortunately, however, the actual time which Trelawny spent with Shelley and Byron was scant indeed, he had hardly arrived in Pisa before he was off ship-hunting—and then Shelley died. He went on the Greek expedition with Byron, but left him before he had set up his headquarters—and then Byron died. It is for this reason that the *Recollections* are justifiably and perhaps most satisfactorily followed with interpolations from other hands.

In this present edition Trelawny stands untouched and uncut. Where other writers intervene it is only in the hope that they will fill in the gaps which Trelawny inevitably left, and complete the pictures which Trelawny merely sketched. Trelawny was not over-scrupulous about detail; the main business of his *Recollections* was with impressions rather than with dates or incidents—where his memory failed him after almost forty years or his artistic sense won a victory over his meagre knowledge of historiography, I have attempted to correct his facts. My own interpolations, and interpolations by Trelawny's contemporaries, are set in smaller type, or where they occur in the middle of a paragraph are enclosed in square brackets, to differentiate them from Trelawny's text.

I have made no similar attempt to correct his spelling of names. This edition is based on the first edition of the *Recollections* (1858), and I feel that the haphazard Anglicising of Greek spelling is more consistent with the colourful and gloriously slapdash character of the author than is his own stolid attempt at pedantry in the *Records*.

P. B. SHELLEY

It is impossible to write on anything that concerns this period of literary history without acquiring debts. I owe much to the biographies of Shelley by Newman Ivey White and Edmund Blunden, to the edition of Shelley's *Letters* by Roger Ingpen and to the edition of his *Poems* by A. S. B. Glover. Byron biographies by Harold Nicolson, Peter Quennell and C. E. Vulliamy, have all been invaluable to me, and so have the volumes of *Letters and Journals* edited by Lord Ernle. I have gleaned much from Rosalind Glyn Grylls's many books on this group, above all from her *Trelawny*, and I have been fortunate enough to be allowed to read the manuscript of Dr. David Dakin's scholarly work on British and American Adventurers in Greece. I am grateful to the Cresset Press for permission to quote from my own edition of Leigh Hunt's *Autobiography* and to John Murray for the use of quotations from Byron's papers.

I must also acknowledge my debt of gratitude to Professor Russell B. Nye for his assistance in tracking down quotations from George Bancroft.

J. E. MORPURGO.

ACKNOWLEDGEMENTS

The portrait of E. J. Trelawny by James Kirkup is reproduced by permission of Sir John Trelawny, Bart., and of the Royal Thames Yacht Club; those of Shelley by A. Clint, Byron after R. Westall, and Leigh Hunt by S. Laurence by permission of the Trustees of the National Portrait Gallery; and those of Mary Shelley by R. Eastman and Jane Williams by G. Clint by permission of the Bodleian Library.

I

IN the summer of 1819 [in fact, the summer of 1820] I was at Ouchy, a village on the margin of the lake of Geneva, in the Canton de Vaux. The most intelligent person I could find in the neighbourhood to talk to, was a young bookseller at Lausanne, educated at a German University; he was familiar with the works of many most distinguished writers; his reading was not confined, as it generally is with men of his craft, to catalogues and indexes, for he was an earnest student, and loved literature more than lucre.

As Lausanne is one of the inland harbours of refuge in which wanderers from all countries seek shelter, his shelves contained works in all languages; he was a good linguist, and read the most attractive of them. 'The elevation of minds,' he said, 'was more important than the height of mountains (I was looking at a scale of the latter), and books are the standards to measure them by.' He used to translate for me passages from the works of Schiller, Kant, Goëthe, and others, and write comments on their paradoxical, mystical, and metaphysical theories. One morning I saw my friend sitting under the acacias on the terrace in front of the house in which Gibbon had lived, and where he wrote the *Decline and Fall*. He said, 'I am trying to sharpen my wits in this pungent air which gave such a keen edge to the great historian, so that I may fathom this book. Your modern poets, Byron, Scott, and Moore, I can read and understand as I walk along, but I have got hold of a book by one now that makes me stop to take breath and think.' It was Shelley's *Queen Mab*. As I had never heard that name or title, I asked how he got the volume. 'With a lot of new books in English, which I took in exchange for old French ones. Not knowing the names of the authors, I might not have looked into them, had not a pampered, prying priest smelt this one in my lumber-room, and, after a brief glance at the notes, exploded in wrath, shouting out "Infidel, jacobin, leveller: nothing can stop this spread of blasphemy but the stake and the faggot; the world is retrograding into accursed heathenism and universal anarchy!" When the priest had departed, I took up the small book he had thrown down, saying, "Surely there must be something here worth tasting." You know the proverb "No person throws a stone at a tree that does not bear fruit." '

'Priests do not,' I answered; 'so I, too, must have a bite of the forbidden fruit. What do you think of it?'

'To my taste,' said the bookseller, 'the fruit is crude, but well flavoured; it requires a strong stomach to digest it; the writer is an enthusiast, and has the true spirit of a poet; he aims at regenerating, not like Byron and Moore, levelling mankind. They say he is but a boy, and this his first offering: if that be true, we shall hear of him again.'

Some days after this conversation I walked to Lausanne, to breakfast at the hotel with an old friend, Captain Daniel Roberts, of the Navy. He was out, sketching, but presently came in accompanied by two English ladies, with whom he had made acquaintance whilst drawing, and whom he brought to our hotel. The husband of one of them soon followed. I saw by their utilitarian garb, as well as by the blisters and blotches on their cheeks, lips, and noses, that they were pedestrian tourists, fresh from the snow-covered mountains, the blazing sun and frosty air having acted on their unseasoned skins, as boiling water does on the lobster, by dyeing his dark coat scarlet. The man was evidently a denizen of the north, his accent harsh, skin white, of an angular and bony build, and self-confident and dogmatic in his opinions. The precision and quaintness of his language, as well as his eccentric remarks on common things, stimulated my mind. Our icy islanders thaw rapidly when they have drifted into warmer latitudes: broken loose from its anti-social system, mystic casts, coteries, sets and sects, they lay aside their purse-proud, tuft-hunting and toadying ways, and are very apt to run riot in the enjoyment of all their senses. Besides we are compelled to talk in strange company, if not from good breeding, to prove our breed, as the gift of speech is often our principal if not sole distinction from the rest of the brute animals.

To return to our breakfast. The travellers, flushed with health, delighted with their excursion, and with appetites earned by bodily and mental activity, were in such high spirits that Roberts and I caught the infection of their mirth; we

2

talked as loud and fast as if under the exhilarating influence of champagne, instead of such a sedative compound as *café au lait*. I can rescue nothing out of oblivion but a few last words. The stranger expressed his disgust at the introduction of carriages into the mountain districts of Switzerland, and at the old fogies who used them.

'As to the arbitrary, pitiless, Godless wretches,' he exclaimed, 'who have removed nature's landmarks by cutting roads through Alps and Apennines, until all things are reduced to the same dead level, they will be arraigned hereafter with the un-just: they have robbed the best specimens of what men should be, of their freeholds in the mountains; the eagle, the black cock, and the red deer they have tamed or exterminated. The lover of nature can nowhere find a solitary nook to contemplate her beauties. Yesterday,' he continued, 'at the break of day, I scaled the most rugged height within my reach; it looked in-accessible; this pleasant delusion was quickly dispelled; I was rudely startled out of a deep reverie by the accursed jarring, jingling, and rumbling of a calêche, and harsh voices that drowned the torrent's fall.'

The stranger, now hearing a commotion in the street, sprang on his feet, looked out of the window, and rang the bell violently.

'Waiter,' he said, 'is that our carriage? Why did you not tell us? Come, lasses, be stirring, the freshness of the day is gone. You may rejoice in not having to walk; there is a chance of saving the remnants of skin the sun has left on our chins and noses,—to-day we shall be stewed instead of barbecued.'

On their leaving the room to get ready for their journey, my friend Roberts told me the strangers were the poet Wordsworth, his wife and sister.

Who could have divined this? I could see no trace, in the hard features and weather-stained brow of the outer-man, of the divinity within him. In a few minutes the travellers re-appeared; we cordially shook hands, and agreed to meet again at Geneva. Now that I knew that I was talking to one of the veterans of the gentle craft, as there was no time to waste in idle ceremony, I asked him abruptly what he thought of Shelley as a poet?

'Nothing,' he replied, as abruptly.

Seeing my surprise, he added, 'A poet who has not produced

a good poem before he is twenty-five, we may conclude cannot, and never will do so.'

'The *Cenci*!' I said eagerly.

'Won't do,' he replied, shaking his head, as he got into the carriage: a rough-coated Scotch terrier followed him.

'This hairy fellow is our flea-trap,' he shouted out, as they started off.

When I recovered from the shock of having heard the harsh sentence passed by an elder bard on a younger brother of the Muses, I exclaimed:

After all, poets are but earth. It is the old story,—Envy—Cain and Abel. Professions, sects, and communities in general, right or wrong, hold together, men of the pen excepted; if one of their guild is worsted in the battle, they do as the rooks do by their inky brothers, fly from him, cawing and screaming; if they don't fire the shot, they sound the bugle to charge.

I did not then know that the full-fledged author never reads the writings of his cotemporaries, except to cut them up in a review,—that being a work of love. In after-years, Shelley being dead, Wordsworth confessed this fact; he was then induced to read some of Shelley's poems, and admitted that Shelley was the greatest master of harmonious verse in our modern literature.

2

SHORTLY after I went to Geneva. In the largest country-house (Plangeau) near that city lived a friend of mine, a Cornish baronet [Trelawny of Trelawne], a good specimen of the old school; well read, and polished by long intercourse with intelligent men of many nations. He retained a custom of the old barons, now obsolete,—his dining-hall was open to all his friends; you were welcomed at his table as often as it suited you to go there, without the ceremony of inconvenient invitations.

At this truly hospitable house, I first saw three young men, recently returned from India. They lived together at a pretty villa (*Maison aux Grenades*, signifying the House of Pomegranates), situated on the shores of the lake, and at an easy walk from the city of Geneva and the baronet's. Their names were George Jervoice, of the Madras Artillery; E. E. Williams, and Thomas Medwin, the two last, lieutenants on half-pay, late of the 8th Dragoons. Medwin was the chief medium that impressed us with a desire to know Shelley; he had known him from childhood [as had Williams who was at Eton with the poet]; he talked of nothing but the inspired boy, his virtues and his sufferings, so that, irrespective of his genius, we all longed to know him. From all I could gather from him, Shelley lived as he wrote, the life of a true poet, loving solitude, but by no means a cynic. In the two or three months I was at Geneva, I passed many agreeable days at the two villas I have mentioned. Late in the autumn I was unexpectedly called to England; Jervoice and Medwin went to Italy; the Williams's determined on passing the winter at Chalons sur Saône. I offered to drive them there, in a light Swiss carriage of my own; and in the spring to rejoin them, and to go on to Italy together in pursuit of Shelley.

Human animals can only endure a limited amount of pain or pleasure, excess of either is followed by insensibility. The Williams's, satiated with felicity at their charming villa on the cheerful lake of Geneva, resolved to leave it, and see how long they could exist deprived of everything they had been accustomed to. With such an object, a French provincial town was just the place to try the experiment. Chalons sur Saône was decided on. We commenced our journey in November, in an open carriage. After four days' drive through wind, rain, and mud, we arrived at Chalons in a sorry plight. The immense plain which surrounded the town was flooded; we took up our quarters at an hotel on the slimy banks of the Saône. What a contrast to the villa of pomegranates we had left, we all thought —but said nothing.

When I left them by the *malle poste*, on my way to Paris, I felt as a man should feel when, stranded on a barren rock, he seizes the only boat and pushes off to the nearest land, leaving his forlorn comrades to perish miserably. After a course of spare diet of soupe maigre, bouilli, sour wine, and solitary confinement had restored their senses, they departed in the spring for the south, and never looked behind them until they had crossed the Alps. They went direct to the Shelleys; and amongst Williams's letters I find his first impressions of the poet, which I here transcribe:

Pisa, April, 1821

MY DEAR TRELAWNY, We purpose wintering in Florence, and sheltering ourselves from the summer heat at a castle of a place, called Villa Poschi, at Pugnano, two leagues from hence, where, with Shelley for a companion, I promise myself a great deal of pleasure, sauntering in the shady retreats of the olive and chesnut woods that grow above our heads up the hill sides. He has a small boat building, only ten or twelve feet long, to go adventuring, as he calls it, up the many little rivers and canals that intersect this part of Italy; some of which pass through the most beautiful scenery imaginable, winding among the terraced gardens at the base of the neighbouring mountains, and opening into such lakes as Beintina, etc.

Shelley is certainly a man of most astonishing genius in appearance, extraordinarily young, of manners mild and amiable, but withal full of life and fun. His wonderful command of language, and the ease with which he speaks on what are generally considered abstruse subjects, are striking; in short, his ordinary conversation is akin to poetry, for he sees things in the most singular and pleasing lights: if he wrote as he talked, he would be popular enough. Lord Byron and others think him by far the most imaginative poet of the day. The style of his

6

lordship's letters to him is quite that of a pupil, such as asking his opinion, and demanding his advice on certain points, etc. I must tell you, that the idea of the tragedy of Manfred, and many of the philosophical, or rather metaphysical, notions interwoven in the composition of the fourth Canto of *Childe Harold*, are of his suggestion; but this, of course, is between ourselves. A few nights ago I nearly put an end to the Poet and myself. We went to Leghorn, to see after the little boat, and, as the wind blew excessively hard, and fair, we resolved upon returning to Pisa in her, and accordingly started with a huge sail, and at 10 o'clock P.M. capsized her.

I commenced this letter yesterday morning, but was prevented from continuing it by the very person of whom I am speaking, who, having heard me complain of a pain in my chest since the time of our ducking, brought with him a doctor, and I am now writing to you in bed, with a blister on the part supposed to be affected. I am ordered to lie still and try to sleep, but I prefer sitting up and bringing this sheet to a conclusion. A General R., an Englishman, has been poisoned by his daughter and her paramour, a Venetian servant, by small doses of arsenic, so that the days of the Cenci are revived, with this difference, that crimes seem to strengthen with keeping. Poor Beatrice was driven to parricide by long and unendurable outrages: in this last case, the parent was sacrificed by the lowest of human passions, the basis of many crimes. By the by, talking of Beatrice and the Cenci, I have a horrid history to tell you of that unhappy girl, that it is impossible to put on paper: you will not wonder at the act, but admire the virtue (an odd expression, you will perhaps think) that inspired the blow. Adieu. Jane desires to be very kindly remembered, and believe me, Very sincerely yours, E. E. WILLIAMS.

In a subsequent letter he gave me a foretaste of what I might expect to find in Lord Byron.

Pisa, December, 1821

MY DEAR TRELAWNY, Why, how is this? I will swear that yesterday was Christmas Day, for I celebrated it at a splendid feast given by Lord Byron to what I call his Pistol Club—*i.e.* to Shelley, Medwin, a Mr. [or Count John] Taaffe, and myself,

7

and was scarcely awake from the vision of it when your letter was put into my hands, dated 1st of *January*, 1822. Time flies fast enough, but you, in the rapidity of your motions, contrive to outwing the old fellow; rather take a plume or two from your mental pinions, and add them, like Mercury to your heels, and let us see you before another year draws upon us. Forty years hence, my lad, you will treat the present with more respect than to *ante*-date the coming one. But I hope that time with you will always fly as unheeded as it now appears to do. Lord Byron is the very spirit of this place,—that is, to those few to whom, like Mokannah,* he has lifted his veil. When you asked me, in your last letter, if it was probable to become at all intimate with him, I replied in a manner which I considered it most prudent to do, from motives which are best explained when I see you. Now, however, I know him a great deal better, and think I may safely say that that point will rest entirely with yourself. The eccentricities of an assumed character, which a total retirement from the world almost rendered a natural one, are daily wearing off. He sees none of the numerous English who are here, excepting those I have named. And of this, I am selfishly glad, for one sees nothing of a man in mixed societies. It is difficult to move him, he says, when he is once fixed, but he seems bent upon joining our party at Spezzia next summer.

I shall reserve all that I have to say about the boat until we meet at the select committee, which is intended to be held on that subject when you arrive here. Have a boat we must, and if we can get Roberts to build her, so much the better. We are settled here for the winter, perhaps many winters, for we have taken apartments and furnished them. This is a step that anchors a man at once, nay, moors him head and stern: you will find us at the Tre Palazzi, 349, Lung' Arno. Pray, remember me to Roberts; tell him he must be content to take me by the hand, though he should not discover a pipe *in* my mouth, or mustachios on it,—the first makes me sick, and the last makes Jane so.

Bring with you any new books you may have. There is a Mrs.

---

* Thomas Moore's *Lallah Rookh* includes the story of Hakem ben Aschem, or Mokannah, who wore a silver gauze veil ostensibly 'to dim the lustre of his face', but in fact to hide its repulsive ugliness.

8

B.* here, with a litter of seven daughters, she is the gayest lady, and the only one who gives dances, for the young squaws are arriving at that age, when as Lord Byron says, they must waltz for their livelihood. When a man gets on this strain, the sooner he concludes his letter the better. Addio. Believe me, Very truly yours, E. E. WILLIAMS.

To the list of Pisan intimates must be added the names of Prince Alexander Mavrocordato—who, as one of those who incited Byron to an interest in the Greek Revolution, was to play a considerable part in the lives of Byron and Trelawny—and 'the Masons'.

'Mr. and Mrs. Mason' were more particularly friends of the Shelleys. As a young girl 'Mrs. Mason' had been taught by Mary's mother, Mary Wollstonecraft. Later, after she had married Lord Mountcashell, she entertained William Godwin in Ireland and he then described her as a woman with a fine mind, a handsome face and a democratic nature. 'Mr. Mason' was the son of George William Tighe, an Irish M.P. By the time the Shelleys met them, in September 1819, these two had been living together for many years —eight of them in Italy—in an irregular but most respectable-seeming union. They immediately befriended the Shelleys and were always ready with kindly and sensible advice.

Of all the Pisan circle Count John Taafe is probably the least known. Shelley and Byron both looked upon him with the laughing condescension which one keeps for well-meaning bores. On November 16, 1821, when Taafe had already been for a year their intimate, Byron wrote to Moore: 'There is here Mr. Taafe, an Irish genius, with whom we are acquainted. He hath written a really *excellent* Commentary on Dante, full of new and true information, and much ingenuity. But his verse is such as it hath pleased God to endue him withal. Nevertheless, he is so firmly persuaded of its equal excellence, that he won't divorce the Commentary from the traduction, as I ventured delicately to hint,—not having the fear of Ireland before my eyes, and upon the presumption of having shotten very well in his presence (with common pistols too, not with my Manton's) the day before.

'But he is eager to publish all, and must be gratified, though the Reviewers will make him suffer more tortures than there are in his original. Indeed, the *Notes* are well worth publication; but he insists upon the translation for company, so that they will come out

---

* Probably Mrs. Beauclerc—the same who did Shelley 'the favour to caress me exceedingly'.

9

together, like Lady C—t chaperoning Miss —. I read a letter of yours to him yesterday, and he begs me to write to you about his Poesie. He is really a good fellow, apparently, and I dare say that his verse is very good Irish.

'Now, what shall we do for him? He says that he will risk part of the expense with the publisher. He will never rest till he is published and abused—for he has a high opinion of himself—and I see nothing left but to gratify him, so as to have him abused as little as possible; for I think it would kill him. You must write, then, to Jeffrey to beg him *not* to review him, and I will do the same to Gifford, through Murray. Perhaps they might notice the Comment without touching the text. But I doubt the dogs—the text is too tempting.'

Thomas Medwin was Shelley's cousin, and had been a companion of the poet both at Syon House, the Isleworth preparatory school, and at Eton. At Eton the two had tried combined authorship: 'We that winter [1809] wrote, in alternate chapters, the commencement of a wild and extravagant romance where a hideous witch played the principal part' (Medwin. *Revised Life of Shelley*). Later he had joined the Army, and had gone to India where he met Edward Ellerker Williams and Jane Cleveland (known to them all as Mrs. Williams). It will be seen, therefore, that if Shelley and Byron were the magnets which drew the group to Pisa, Medwin was the connecting link. The wild admiration which Shelley aroused in Medwin was hardly reciprocated. Shelley did his best to tolerate, and even to recommend Medwin's mediocre poetry, and the two made plans to study Arabic together, but before very long Shelley had come to the conclusion that Medwin was a tiresome companion— and looking back at Medwin's accounts of his relationship with the two great poets, one must admit that Shelley was probably right.

3

I WAS not accustomed to the town life I was then leading, and became as tired of society as townfolks are of solitude. The great evil in solitude is, that your brain lies idle; your muscles expand by exercise, and your wits contract from the want of it.

To obviate this evil and maintain the just equilibrium between the body and the brain, I determined to pass the coming winter in the wildest part of Italy, the Maremma, in the midst of the marshes and malaria, with my friends Roberts and Williams; keen sportsmen both—that part of the country being well stocked with woodcocks and wild fowl.* For this purpose, I shipped an ample supply of dogs, guns, and other implements of the chace to Leghorn. For the exercise of my brain, I proposed passing my summer with Shelley and Byron, boating in the Mediterranean. After completing my arrangements, I started in the autumn by the French malle-poste, from Paris to Chalons, regained possession of the horse and cabriolet I had left with Williams, and drove myself to Geneva, where Roberts was waiting for me. After a short delay, I continued my journey south with Roberts in my Swiss carriage, so that we could go on or stop, where and when we pleased. By our method of travelling, we could sketch, shoot, fish, and observe everything at our leisure. If our progress was slow, it was most pleasant. We crossed Mount Cenis, and in due course arrived at Genoa. After a long stop at that city of painted palaces, anxious to see the Poet, I drove to Pisa alone. I arrived late, and after putting up my horse at the inn and dining, hastened to the Tre Palazzi, on the Lung' Arno, where the Shelleys and Williams's lived on different flats under the same roof, as is the custom on the Continent. The Williams's received me in their earnest cordial manner; we had a great deal to communicate to each other, and were in loud and animated conversation, when I was rather put out by observing in the passage near the open door, opposite to where I sat, a pair of glittering eyes steadily fixed on mine; it was too dark to make out whom they belonged

---

* Trelawny had a private income of some £500 a year.

to. With the acuteness of a woman, Mrs. Williams's eyes followed the direction of mine, and going to the doorway, she laughingly said:

'Come in, Shelley, it's only our friend Tre just arrived.'

Swiftly gliding in, blushing like a girl, a tall thin stripling held out both his hands; and although I could hardly believe as I looked at his flushed, feminine, and artless face that it could be the Poet, I returned his warm pressure. After the ordinary greetings and courtesies he sat down and listened. I was silent from astonishment: was it possible this mild-looking, beardless boy, could be the veritable monster at war with all the world—excommunicated by the Fathers of the Church, deprived of his civil rights by the fiat of a grim Lord Chancellor, discarded by every member of his family, and denounced by the rival sages of our literature as the founder of a Satanic school? I could not believe it; it must be a hoax. He was habited like a boy, in a black jacket and trowsers, which he seemed to have outgrown, or his tailor, as is the custom, had most shamefully stinted him in his 'sizings'. Mrs. Williams saw my embarrassment, and to relieve me asked Shelley what book he had in his hand? His face brightened, and he answered briskly.

'Calderon's *Magico Prodigioso*, I am translating some passages in it.' *

'Oh, read it to us!'

Shoved off from the shore of common-place incidents that could not interest him, and fairly launched on a theme that did, he instantly became oblivious of everything but the book in his hand. The masterly manner in which he analysed the genius of the author, his lucid interpretation of the story, and the ease with which he translated into our language the most subtle and imaginative passages of the Spanish poet, were marvellous, as was his command of the two languages. After this touch of his quality I no longer doubted his identity; a dead silence ensued; looking up, I asked:

---

* At this time Shelley was much taken up with the Spanish dramatist. 'Have you read Calderon's *Magico Prodigioso*?', he wrote to John Gisborne on April 10, 1822. 'I find a striking similarity between *Faust* and this drama and if I were to acknowledge Coleridge's distinction, should say Goethe was the *greatest* philosopher, and Calderon the *greatest* poet.'

'Where is he?'

Mrs. Williams said, 'Who? Shelley? Oh, he comes and goes like a spirit, no one knows when or where.'

Presently he re-appeared with Mrs. Shelley. She brought us back from the ideal world Shelley had left us in, to the real one, welcomed me to Italy, and asked me the news of London and Paris, the new books, operas, and bonnets, marriages, murders, and other marvels. The Poet vanished, and tea appeared. Mary Woolstoncraft (the authoress), the wife of William Godwin, died in 1797, in giving birth to their only child, Mary, married to the poet Shelley; so that at the time I am speaking of Mrs. Shelley was twenty-seven. Such a rare pedigree of genius was enough to interest me in her, irrespective of her own merits as an authoress. The most striking feature in her face was her calm, grey eyes; she was rather under the English standard of woman's height, very fair and light-haired, witty, social, and animated in the society of friends, though mournful in solitude; like Shelley, though in a minor degree, she had the power of expressing her thoughts in varied and appropriate words, derived from familiarity with the works of our vigorous old writers. Neither of them used obsolete or foreign words. This command of our language struck me the more as contrasted with the scanty vocabulary used by ladies in society, in which a score of poor hackneyed phrases suffice to express all that is felt or considered proper to reveal.

The impression that Trelawny made upon Mary Shelley was considerable: 'A kind of half Arab Englishman whose life has been as changeful as that of Anastasius* and who recounts the adventures of his youth as eloquently and well as the imagined Greek . . . he is a strange web which I am endeavouring to unravel . . . he is six feet high—raven black hair which curls thickly and shortly like a Moor's —dark grey expressive eyes, overhanging brows, upturned lips and a smile which expresses good nature and kindheartedness—his shoulders are high like an Orientalist—his voice is monotonous yet emphatic and his language as he relates the events of his life energetic

---

* Thomas Hope. *Anastasius, or Memoirs of a Greek, written at the close of the Eighteenth Century*. It was of this book that Byron told Lady Blessington that it made him weep twice, first because he had not written it and secondly because Hope had.

and simple—whether the tale be one of blood and horror or of irresistible comedy. His company is delightful for he excites me to think and if any evil shade the intercourse that time will unveil—the sun will rise or night darken all.'

It is worth pausing at this stage to consider Shelley's life in Italy and his physical and mental development in the years between 1818 and 1821. Whatever Mary may have said to the contrary—'Mine own Shelley! What a horror you had of returning to this horrible country'—Shelley was not always free from homesickness. In June 1819 he had written: 'O that I could return to England! How heavy a weight when misfortune is added to exile, and solitude, as if the measure were not full, heaped high on both. O that I could return to England! I hear you say, "Desire never fails to generate capacity". Ah! but that ever-present Malthus, Necessity, has convinced Desire that even though it generated capacity, its offspring must starve.' And again in August:

'I most devoutly wish that I were living near London. I do not think I shall settle so far off as Richmond; and to inhabit any intermediate spot on the Thames would be to expose myself to the river damps; not to mention that it is not much to my taste. My inclinations point to Hampstead; but I do not know whether I should not make up my mind to something more completely suburban. What are mountains, trees, heaths, or even the glorious and ever-beautiful sky, with such sunsets as I have seen at Hampstead, to friends? Social enjoyment, in some form or other, is the alpha and omega of existence. All that I see in Italy—and from my tower window I now see the magnificent peaks of the Apennines half enclosing the plain—is nothing; it dwindles into smoke in the mind, when I think of some familiar forms of scenery, little perhaps in themselves, over which old remembrances have thrown a delightful colour. How we prize what we despised when present. So the ghosts of our dead associations rise and haunt us, in revenge for our having let them starve, and abandoned them to perish.'

And, to console himself for absence, he seemed to wish to surround himself in Italy with England as represented by his friends. Hunt, Peacock and Horace Smith all received invitations like this, written on April 20, 1820, to Hogg: 'You know that some time since we talked of visiting Italy together. At that time, as at many others, an unfortunate combination of circumstances which have now ceased to exist prevented me from enjoying your society. There is no person for whom I feel so high an esteem and value as for you, or from whom I expected to receive so great a portion of the happiness of my life;

and there is none of whose society I have been so frequently deprived by the unfortunate and almost inexplicable complexity of my situation. At this very moment perhaps when it is practicable, on my part, to put into execution the plan to which I allude, perhaps it is impossible on yours.

'But let me dwell for a moment on the other side of the question. What say you to making us a visit in Italy? How would it consist with your professional engagements?

'You could *see* but little of Italy in June and July on account of the heat, and we *must* then be at the Bagni di Lucca, which though a spot of enchanting beauty, contains none of those objects of art for which Italy is principally worth visiting. But if you are inclined seriously to think of this proposal, I would impose no other law on you than to come as soon, and return as late, as you can. Term begins, I know, in the middle of November, but how far does your business require you to be present on the first day of term? The mode of coming would be to cross France to Marseilles, from whence to Livorno there is a passage sometimes of 36 hours, but the average 3 days. Or you might engage in London for the whole journey over the Alps, but this is a very tedious and much more expensive method.

'I ought to add that Mary unites with me in wishing that we may have the pleasure of seeing you. Of course, none of my other friends will join you, but I need not say that Peacock will be welcome.'

But generally, Shelley was content enough with his surroundings. A letter to Hogg, written on August 20, 1821, gives a description of his routine and pleasures: 'Horace Smith has just sent me your letter from Paris, where his wife has persuaded a physician to assure her that the climate of Italy would destroy her. You have perhaps already heard of my iniquity in seducing Hunt over to Italy: he is coming with all his children to Pisa. What pleasure it would give me and him and all of us if you could follow his example. But law,— that disease inherited from generation to generation,—that canker in the birthright of our nation, that sieve through which our thoughts flow as fast as we pour them in, pens you in London at least for the greater part of the year. . . .

'I receive with delight your Milkwort.—It reposes between the leaves of a folio Plato, whose incredible contractions & abominable inaccuracy torment me to death, as I have only 3 vols. of my own edition as yet here. I send you a flower which grows on the mountain "perche i Pisani veder Lucca non ponno", & which when alive is very beautiful. I shall herborize myself, & will send you as I find them whatever plants are rarest or peculiar to this country. I saw a great number of the Cryptogamia genus the other day which I had never remarked in England—ferns especially. There are also curious fleshy flowers, & one that has blood and that the peasants say is alive.—

'You see the Gisbornes of course.—I read Goethe's Faust with Mr. G.—I advise you to read it—it has passages of surpassing excellence, though there are some scenes, which the fastidiousness of our taste would wish erased.—As to Botany how much more profitable and innocent an occupation is it than that absurd & un-philosophical diversion of killing birds, besides the ill taste of giving pain to sensitive & beautiful animals; this amusement of shooting familiarises people with the society of inferiors & the gross and harsh habits belonging to this sort of pursuits.

'How much I envy your walks—though I fear my health would scarcely allow me to share in them. I am glad to hear that you do not neglect the rites of the true religion. Your letter awakened my sleeping devotion, & the same evening I ascended alone the high mountain behind my house, & suspended a garland, & raised a small turf altar to the mountain-walking Pan.

'My health, in the main, is much better than when I left England, but I am weak & with much nervous irritability. My spirits also are by no means good & I feel sensibly La noia e l'affanno della passata vita—I have some thoughts, if I could get a respectable appoint-ment, of going to India, or any where where I might be compelled to active exertion, & at the same time enter into an entirely new sphere of action. But this I dare say is a mere dream; I shall probably have no opportunity of making it a reality, but finish as I have begun.

'Have you seen a poem I wrote on the death of Keats, a young Writer of bad taste, but wonderful power & promise. It is called Adonais—when you pass Ollier's you may tell him I desired you to call for one. It is perhaps the least imperfect of my pieces.

'I do not write to Peacock, who has something better to do than read scrawls, in the persuasion that you will tell him my news, & be so kind as to say, he would oblige me very much in dispatching instantly all my books to me, to the care of Messrs. Guebhard & Co. Leghorn. Gisborne will [word omitted; tell?] him how to send them, if he finds any difficulty. Of course, if you or he should wish to retain any of them they are much at your service.

'Shall I see you ever in Italy? With what pleasure I should wel-come you here I need not say, but both you & Peacock are bound to the oar—not like me by the chains of your sins. Ever most sin-cerely yours, P. B. Shelley.'

There is, in that letter, a certain deceptive warmth, an air of com-fort which is only denied in the last sentence. Shelley writes as almost

16

any cheerful exile might write to a close friend, laughing somewhat at his exile, rejoicing a little in his comfort, teasing himself for his obstinate 'nervous irritability'.

Yet his state of mind was more plagued than he admitted. Always before him was the horrible fact that he, who had had so many children, had now only one child left. His children by his first marriage had been taken from him by the harsh decision of the law; William, the child who had been so lovely that 'the Italian women used to bring each other to look at him when he was asleep', had died on June 7, 1819, the third of his children by Mary to die in childhood; and now there was only Percy Florence, born on November 12, 1819. Each time he looked at the child, Shelley tortured himself with the thought that he too might not survive.

The death of their children, far from bringing Mary and Shelley closer together, seemed to force them apart. Mary, for a while, betrayed an antagonism to her husband; antagonism almost to the point of hatred; and although their relationship recovered something of affection, the rapture had gone for ever. On August 4, 1819, Mary wrote in her journal: 'We have now lived five years together; and if all the events of the five years were blotted out, I might be happy; but to have won, and then cruelly to have lost, the association of four years is not an accident to which the human mind can bend without much suffering.'

Apathy, and particularly physical apathy, was not an attitude which Shelley could easily endure from his wife, nor were his relations with her improved by the continued demands for money made by her father, William Godwin. Depression settled upon him, and touched his work.

In 1818 and 1819 he had worked on the poem which he himself called 'my best poem', *Prometheus Unbound*, a poem of ascending and triumphant spirit; in 1820 and 1821 his work seemed overcast, though an occasional moment of comfort and delight brought forth some happy effort, such as 'The Cloud'.

He needed the inspiration which Mary no longer gave him, and, on December 5, 1820, he thought that he had found it, for it was on that date that he met the Contessina Teresa Emilia Viviani, an intelligent and beautiful girl of nineteen. Her unfortunate situation —she was kept in a convent to keep her out of the reach of her stepmother—aroused Shelley's romantic chivalrousness: 'She continues to enchant me infinitely; and I soothe myself with the idea that I make the discomfort of her captivity lighter to her by demonstration of the interest which she has awakened in me.' (Letter to Claire Clairmont, January 2, 1821.)

17

His intellectual lassitude was broken by her charm and he wrote *Epipsychidion,** one of the few poems he later regretted having published.

It is impossible to regard the Emilia affair as anything but an infatuation. Even he himself was soon over it; already by February 16, 1821, he was referring to *Epipsychidion* in a letter to Charles Ollier as 'a production of a portion of me already dead', and the advertisement of the poem deliberately ascribes it to some other person who 'died at Florence'. But even this temporary infatuation increased the estrangement from Mary, and, to add to Shelley's miseries, he was suffering badly from physical ailments: 'I have not been able to see until the last day or two. . . . I have suffered also considerably from my disease; and am already in imagination preparing to be cut for the stone. . . .' (Letter to Claire Clairmont, January 2, 1821.)

At times he was close to insanity, but the gatherings of friends around him and the thought of more friends yet to arrive, brought him a renewal of mental and physical strength. In this sense even the recovery of more-or-less comfortable relations with Byron helped him to some measure of stability 'after the dreary solitude of the understanding and imagination' from which he had suffered.

Nor was the death of Keats, and his consequent absorption with the composition of *Adonais*, without a paradoxically steadying effect. Shelley had hoped for much from a visit from Keats; deprived of that visit by the younger poet's death he poured out his grief and came through that grief to confidence not merely in the fact that Keats would transcend his calumniators but that he himself would prove greater than those who had for so long attacked him, not merely in the immortality of Keats's work but in the immortality of his own:

> 'That Light whose smile kindles the Universe,
> That Beauty in which all Things work and move,
> That Benediction which the eclipsing Curse
> Of birth can quench not, that sustaining Love
> Which through the web of being blindly wove
> By man and beast and earth and air and sea,
> Burns bright or dim, as each are mirrors of
> The fire for which all thirst; now beams on me,
> Consuming the last clouds of cold mortality.'

---

* *Epipsychidion. Verses addressed to the Noble and unfortunate Lady Emilia V, now imprisoned in the Convent of* —.

Difficulties remained, troubles and flaring passions. He found a new inspiration in Jane Williams to take the place of Emilia Viviani (see p. 50). But the Shelley who walked into Trelawny's presence on January 14, 1822, was generally more content and, despite hallucinations and occasional depression, generally more stable than he had been for two years or more.

It is well to remember this when considering the somewhat rosy pictures of Shelley in Italy painted both by Trelawny and Leigh Hunt: both saw him at his best, both approached him when the lights of optimism were more often in his mind than the gloom of frustration, hatred and lowering insanity.

4

A T two o'clock on the following day, in company with Shelley, I crossed the Ponte Vecchio, and went on the Lung' Arno to the Palazzo Lanfranchi, the residence of Lord Byron.* We entered a large marble hall, ascended a giant staircase, passed through an equally large room over the hall, and were shown into a smaller apartment which had books and a billiard-table in it. A surly-looking bull-dog (Moretto) announced us, by growling, and the Pilgrim instantly advanced from an inner chamber, and stood before us. His halting gait was apparent, but he moved with quickness; and although pale, he looked as fresh, vigorous, and animated, as any man I ever saw. His pride, added to his having lived for many years alone, was the cause I suppose that he was embarrassed at first meeting with strangers; this he tried to conceal by an affectation of ease. After the interchange of commonplace question and answer, he regained his self-possession, and turning to Shelley, said:

'As you are addicted to poesy, go and read the versicles I was delivered of last night, or rather this morning—that is, if you can. I am posed. I am getting scurrilous. There is a letter from Tom Moore; read, you are blarneyed in it ironically.'

He then took a cue, and asked me to play billiards; he struck the balls and moved about the table briskly, but neither played the game nor cared a rush about it, and chatted after this idle fashion:

'The purser of the frigate I went to Constantinople in called an officer *scurrilous* for alluding to his wig. Now, the day before I mount a wig—and I shall soon want one—I'll ride about with it on the pummel of my saddle, or stick it on my cane.

'In that same frigate, near the Dardanelles, we nearly ran down an American trader with his cargo of notions. Our captain, old Bathurst, hailed, and with the dignity of a Lord, asked

---

* 'The Casa Lanfranchi, which had been the mansion of the great Pisan family whose ancestors figure in Dante, is said to have been built by Michelangelo, and is worthy of him. It is in a bold and broad style throughout, with those harmonious graces of proportion which are sure to be found in an Italian mansion.' (Leigh Hunt. *Autobiography*.)

him where he came from, and the name of his ship. The Yankee captain bellowed:

' "You copper-bottomed sarpent, I guess you'll know when I've reported you to Congress." '

The surprise I expressed by my looks was not at what he said, but that he could register such trifles in his memory. Of course with other such small anecdotes, his great triumph at having swum from Sestos to Abydos was not forgotten. I had come prepared to see a solemn mystery, and so far as I could judge from the first act it seemed to me very like a solemn farce. I forgot that great actors when off the stage are dull dogs; and that even the mighty Prospero, without his book and magic mantle, was but an ordinary mortal. At this juncture Shelley joined us; he never laid aside his book and magic mantle; he waved his wand, and Byron, after a faint show of defiance, stood mute; his quick perception of the truth of Shelley's comments on his poem transfixed him, and Shelley's earnestness and just criticism held him captive.

I was however struck with Byron's mental vivacity and wonderful memory; he defended himself with a variety of illustrations, precedents, and apt quotations from modern authorities, disputing Shelley's propositions, not by denying their truth as a whole, but in parts, and the subtle questions he put would have puzzled a less acute reasoner than the one he had to contend with. During this discussion I scanned the Pilgrim closely.

In external appearance Byron realised that ideal standard with which imagination adorns genius. He was in the prime of life, thirty-five; of middle height, five feet eight and a half inches; regular features, without a stain or furrow on his pallid skin, his shoulders broad, chest open, body and limbs finely proportioned. His small, highly-finished head and curly hair, had an airy and graceful appearance from the massiveness and length of his throat: you saw his genius in his eyes and lips. In short, Nature could do little more than she had done for him, both in outward form and in the inward spirit she had given to animate it. But all these rare gifts to his jaundiced imagination only served to make his one personal defect (lameness) the more apparent, as a flaw is magnified in a diamond when polished;

and he brooded over that blemish as sensitive minds will brood until they magnify a wart into a wen.

His lameness certainly helped to make him sceptical, cynical, and savage. There was no peculiarity in his dress, it was adapted to the climate; a tartan jacket braided,—he said it was the Gordon pattern, and that his mother was of that ilk. A blue velvet cap with a gold band, and very loose nankeen trousers, strapped down so as to cover his feet: his throat was not bare, as represented in drawings. At three o'clock, one of his servants announced that his horses were at the door, which broke off his discussion with Shelley, and we all followed him to the hall. At the outer door, we found three or four very ordinary-looking horses; they had holsters on the saddles, and many other superfluous trappings, such as the Italians delight in, and Englishmen eschew. Shelley, and an Irish visitor just announced, mounted two of these sorry jades. I luckily had my own cattle. Byron got into a calêche, and did not mount his horse until we had cleared the gates of the town, to avoid, as he said, being stared at by the 'd—d Englishers', who generally congregated before his house on the Arno. After an hour or two of slow riding and lively talk,—for he was generally in good spirits when on horseback, —we stopped at a small *podere* on the roadside, and dismounting went into the house, in which we found a table with wine and cakes. From thence we proceeded into the vineyard at the back; the servant brought two brace of pistols, a cane was stuck in the ground and a five-paul piece, the size of half-a-crown, placed in a slit at the top of the cane. Byron, Shelley, and I, fired at fifteen paces, and one of us generally hit the cane or the coin: our firing was pretty equal; after five or six shots each, Byron pocketed the battered money and sauntered about the grounds. We then remounted. On our return homewards, Shelley urged Byron to complete something he had begun. Byron smiled and replied:

'John Murray, my patron and paymaster, says my plays won't act. I don't mind that, for I told him they were not written for the stage—but he adds, my poesy won't sell: that I do mind, for I have an "itching palm". He urges me to resume my old "Corsair style, to please the ladies".'

Shelley indignantly answered:

'That is very good logic for a bookseller, but not for an

author: the shop interest is to supply the ephemeral demand of the day. It is not for him but you "to put a ring in the monster's nose" to keep him from mischief.'

Byron smiling at Shelley's warmth, said:

'John Murray is right, if not righteous: all I have yet written has been for women-kind; you must wait until I am forty, their influence will then die a natural death, and I will show the men what I can do.'

Shelley replied:

'Do it now—write nothing but what your conviction of its truth inspires you to write; you should give counsel to the wise, and not take it from the foolish. Time will reverse the judgment of the vulgar. Cotemporary criticism only represents the amount of ignorance genius has to contend with.'

I was then and afterwards pleased and surprised at Byron's passiveness and docility in listening to Shelley—but all who heard him felt the charm of his simple, earnest manner; while Byron knew him to be exempt from the egotism, pedantry, cox-combry, and, more than all, the rivalry of authorship, and that he was the truest and most discriminating of his admirers.

Byron looking at the western sky, exclaimed:

'Where is the green your friend the Laker talks such fustian about,' meaning Coleridge:

> 'Gazing on the western sky,
> And its peculiar tint of yellow green.'
>
> *Dejection: an Ode.*

'Who ever,' asked Byron, 'saw a green sky?'

Shelley was silent, knowing that if he replied, Byron would give vent to his spleen. So I said, 'The sky in England is oftener green than blue.'

'Black, you mean,' rejoined Byron; and this discussion brought us to his door.

As he was dismounting he mentioned two odd words that would rhyme. I observed on the felicity he had shown in this art, repeating a couplet out of *Don Juan*; he was both pacified and pleased at this, and putting his hand on my horse's crest, observed:

'If you are curious in these matters, look in Swift. I will

23

send you a volume; he beats us all hollow, his rhymes are wonderful.'

And then we parted for that day, which I have been thus particular in recording, not only as it was the first of our acquaintance, but as containing as fair a sample as I can give of his appearance, ordinary habits, and conversation.

Byron, when Trelawny first met him, had reached the height of his powers in at least one aspect of his powerful life: his capacity for making enemies, and the effects of this achievement were to carry over into subsequent biographical writings so that a contributor to the *British Critic* in 1831 could write of him that 'his time was . . . pretty much divided between poetry, adultery and insurrection'.

The three were, it is true, inseparable to Byron at this time and only the poetry was of inferior quality to what had gone before. After spending 1818 in Venice, most of it in complete debauchery, Byron had settled to serious work—*Don Juan*, serious insurrection—membership in the Carbonari, and serious adultery—Teresa Guiccioli.

Trelawny is curiously reticent about Byron's relations with the Gamba family, and does not so much as mention Teresa (Gamba) Guiccioli, but however irregular their position may be in the eyes of the hypersensitive, there is no doubt that since he had become Teresa's lover, early in 1819, Byron had been almost respectable. Shelley wrote, ' Lord Byron is quite cured of his gross habits' and that he was 'becoming what he should be, a virtuous man'. Byron, himself surprised at his calmness and fidelity in adultery, wrote to Hobhouse, 'I have been an intriguer, a husband, a whoremonger, and now I am a Cavalier Servente—by the holy! it is a strange sensation.'

Medwin describes the cause of this respectability thus: 'Unlike most of the Italian women, her complexion is delicately fair. Her eyes, large, dark and languishing, are shaded by the longest eyelashes in the world. . . . Her figure is, perhaps, too much *embonpoint* for her height . . . but her bust is perfect . . .'

And Leigh Hunt fills out this description with some condescension and a dash of acid: 'Her appearance might have reminded an English spectator of Chaucer's heroine:

> Yclothed was she, fresh for to devise.
> Her yellow hair was braided in a tress
> Behind her back, a yardè long, I guess:
> And in the garden (as the sun uprist)
> She walketh up and down, where as her list:

24

and then, as Dryden has it:

> At every turn she made a little stand,
> And thrust among the thorns her lily hand.

'Madame Guiccioli, who was at that time about twenty, was hand-some and ladylike, with an agreeable manner, and a voice not par-taking of the Italian fervour too much to be gentle. She had just enough of it to give her speaking a grace. None of her graces appeared entirely free from art; nor, on the other hand, did they betray enough of it to give you an ill opinion of her sincerity and good humour. I was told that her Romagnese dialect was observable; but to me, at that time, all Italian in a lady's mouth was Tuscan pearl; and she trolled it over her lip, pure or not, with that sort of conscious grace which seems to belong to the Italian language as a matter of right. I amused her with speaking bad Italian out of Ariosto, and saying *speme* for *speranza*; in which she good-naturedly found something pleasant and *pellegrino*; keeping all the while that considerate countenance for which a foreigner has so much to be grateful. Her hair was what the poet has described, or rather *blond*, with an inclination to yellow; a very fair and delicate yellow, at all events, and within the limits of the poetical. She had regular fea-tures, of the order properly called handsome, in distinction to pretti-ness or to piquancy; being well proportioned to one another, large rather than otherwise, but without coarseness, and more harmonious than interesting. Her nose was the handsomest of the kind I ever saw; and I have known her both smile very sweetly, and look intelligently, when Lord Byron has said something kind to her.'

The whole story of the extraordinary '*affaire Guiccioli*' is perhaps told best in short space by Lady Blessington: 'She is of noble birth, being the daughter of Conte Gamba, a descendant of one of the most ancient families in Italy. Ravenna, in the vicinity of which her father possesses an estate, gave her birth. The Countess Guiccioli married, in her sixteenth year, the Conte Guiccioli, the largest landed proprietor in the north of Italy, owning the greater portion of the rich country forming the Marches of Ancona, and possessing more than one fine chateau in the Bolognese territory. The Countess is the third wife of her lord, who is said to be many years senior to her father. So great a disparity of age led to the too common result, an incompatibility of tempers; and the accidental encounter of the fair young bride, at Venice, with Lord Byron, a few months after her ill-assorted marriage, gave birth to an attachment little calcu-lated to render her more disposed to submit to ties which had been

25

previously found difficult to be borne. After having in vain combated her growing affection for Byron, who had followed her from Venice to Ravenna, and as vainly endeavoured to reconcile the conflicting feelings of duty and an unhappy passion, a separation between the Countess and her husband took place. The Pope pronounced a sentence, decreeing that a certain provision should be assigned to the lady from the vast possessions of her liege lord, and that she should reside under the roof and protection of her father. Conte Gamba, and his son Conte Pietro Gamba, being a short time after suspected of participating in the liberalism of the Carbonari, a suspicion under which Lord Byron also fell, the Gamba family were driven from Ravenna, and took refuge at Pisa. Lord Byron, as a British peer, could not on mere suspicion be compelled to leave Ravenna; and though every means were used to induce him to such a measure, and that the absence of the Gamba family, with whom the Countess Guiccioli migrated, robbed Ravenna of its attraction for him, he continued to reside there for many months after her departure; although a system of unremitting espionage was exercised towards him and his domestics. Having remained sufficiently long at Ravenna, to convince the despotic government there that he was not to be driven from it an hour sooner than he desired, he joined his friends the Gambas at Pisa, where he remained some time. Here, also, he and his friends suffered no little inconvenience from the *surveillance* directed towards them by the Tuscan government, alarmed out of its general urbanity to strangers, by the exaggerated reports of the ultra-liberalism of Byron and his friends.'

Later, in Greece, Byron discussed his membership in the Carbonari with Major William Parry, and produced a somewhat specious explanation: ' "What do they say of my politics in England?" was a question Lord Byron put to me. "I hear they call me a Carbonaro. I am one. Italy required an alteration in her government. The people were happier and more secure under Napoleon than under the Austrians; and I blame them, not for their attempt, but their failure. They don't hate the Austrians half as much as they deserve, and if they did hate them more they would sweep these intruders from their country. In wishing Italy to be free, and the Italians to be united, I am a Carbonaro." '

All this may be perfectly true, yet there is no doubt that Byron's reasons included his friendship with the Gambas.

And as she helped to make him a Carbonaro, so did Teresa help to spoil his poetry. In a sense, for a while at least, she made him too comfortable for poetry; more practically, she did not want him to go on with *Don Juan*, the poem that was still uppermost in his mind, probably because she wanted to banish for ever the profligate and cynical Byron represented in the poem.

But, poetry apart, in January 1822, Byron was calmer, happier and physically stronger than he had been for several years.

5

MEN of books, particularly Poets, are rarely men of action, their mental energy exhausts their bodily powers. Byron has been generally considered an exception to this rule, he certainly so considered himself: let us look at the facts.

In 1809, he first left England, rode on horseback through Spain and Portugal, 400 miles, crossed the Mediterranean on board a frigate, and landed in Greece; where he passed two years in sauntering through a portion of that small country: this, with a trip to Smyrna, Constantinople, Malta, and Gibraltar, generally on board our men-of-war, where you have all the ease, comfort, and most of the luxuries of your own homes; —this is the extent of the voyages and travels he was so proud of. Anything more luxurious than sailing on those seas, and riding through those lands, and in such a blessed climate, I know from experience, is not to be found in this world. Taking into account the result of these travels as shown in his works, he might well boast; he often said, if he had ever written a line worth preserving, it was Greece that inspired it. After this trip he returned to England, and remained there some years, four or five; then abandoned it for ever, passed through the Netherlands, went up the Rhine, paused for some months in Switzerland, crossed the Alps into Italy, and never left that peninsula until the last year of his life. He was never in France, for when he left England, Paris was in the hands of the Allies, and he said he could not endure to witness a country associated in his mind with so many glorious deeds of arts and arms, bullied by 'certain rascal officers, slaves in authority, the knaves of justice!'

To return, however, to his travels.* If you look at a map you will see what a narrow circle comprises his wanderings. Any man might go, and many have gone without the aid of steam, over the same ground in a few months—even if he had to walk with a knapsack, where Byron rode. The Pilgrim moved about

---

* A subject which gave Trelawny much pleasure, for it established his superiority over Lord Byron. Africa, the East and all Europe were Trelawny's province; Byron had kept pretty well to the 'tourist routes'.

like a Pasha, with a host of attendants, and all that he and they required on the journey. * So far as I could learn from Fletcher, his yeoman bold—and he had been with him from the time of his first leaving England,—Byron wherever he was, so far as it was practicable, pursued the same lazy, dawdling habits he continued during the time I knew him. He was seldom out of his bed before noon, when he drank a cup of very strong green tea, without sugar or milk. At two he ate a biscuit and drank soda-water. At three he mounted his horse and sauntered along the road—and generally the same road,—if alone, racking his brains for fitting matter and rhymes for the coming poem, he dined at seven, as frugally as anchorites are said in storybooks to have done, at nine he visited the family of Count Gamba, on his return home he sat reading or composing until two or three o'clock in the morning, and then to bed, often feverish, restless and exhausted—to dream, as he said, more than to sleep.

Something very urgent, backed by the importunity of those who had influence over him, could alone induce him to break through the routine I have described, for a day, and it was certain to be resumed on the next,—he was constant in this alone.

His conversation was anything but literary, except when Shelley was near him. The character he most commonly appeared in was of the free and easy sort, such as had been in vogue when he was in London, and George IV was Regent; and his talk was seasoned with anecdotes of the great actors on and off the stage, boxers, gamblers, duellists, drunkards, etc., etc., appropriately garnished with the slang and scandal of that day. Such things had all been in fashion, and were at that time considered accomplishments by gentlemen; and of this tribe of Mohawks the Prince Regent was the chief, and allowed to be the most perfect specimen. Byron, not knowing the tribe was extinct, still prided himself on having belonged to it; of nothing was he more indignant, than of being treated as a man of letters, instead of as a Lord and a man of fashion: this prevented

---

* 'His travelling equipage was rather a singular one . . . seven servants, five carriages, nine horses, a monkey, a bull-dog and a mastiff, two cats, three pea-fowls and some hens.' (Medwin.)

29

foreigners and literary people from getting on with him, for they invariably so offended. His long absence had not effaced the mark John Bull brands his children with; the instant he loomed above the horizon, on foot or horseback, you saw at a glance he was a Britisher. He did not understand foreigners, nor they him; and, during the time I knew him, he associated with no Italians except the family of Count Gamba.

What the Italians thought about the strange English milord is apparent from Guerrazzi's *Memorie*: 'At that time the rumour spread in Pisa that an extraordinary man had arrived there, of whom people told a hundred different tales, all contradictory and many absurd. They said that he was of royal blood, of very great wealth, of sanguine temperament, of fierce habits, masterly in knightly exercises, possessing an evil genius, but a more than human intellect. He was said to wander through the world like Job's Satan . . . It was George Byron. I wished to see him; he appeared to me like the Vatican Apollo.'

He seemed to take an especial pleasure in making a clean breast to every newcomer, as if to mock their previous conceptions of him, and to give the lie to the portraits published of him. He said to me, as we were riding together alone, shortly after I knew him:

'Now, confess, you expected to find me a "Timon of Athens", or a "Timur the Tartar"; or did you think I was a mere sing-song driveller of poesy, full of what I heard Braham at a rehearsal call "*Entusamusy*"; and are you not mystified at finding me what I am,—a man of the world—never in earnest—laughing at all things mundane.'

Then he muttered, as to himself:

'The world is a bundle of hay,
Mankind are the asses who pull.'*

Any man who cultivates his intellectual faculty so highly as to seem at times inspired, would be too much above us, if, on

---

* The world is a bundle of hay,
Mankind are the asses that pull,
Each tugs in a different way,—
And the greatest of all is John Bull.
Byron in a letter to Moore, June 22, 1812.

30

closer inspection, we should not find it alloyed with weaknesses akin to our own. Byron soon put you at your ease on this point. Godwin, in his *Thoughts on Man*, says, 'Shakespeare, amongst all his varied characters, has not attempted to draw a perfect man'; and Pope says:

'A perfect man's a thing the world ne'er saw.'

At any rate I should not seek for a model amongst men of the pen; they are too thin-skinned and egotistical. In his perverse and moody humours, Byron would give vent to his Satanic vein. After a long silence, one day on horseback, he began:

'I have a conscience, although the world gives me no credit for it; I am now repenting, not of the few sins I have committed, but of the many I have not committed. There are things, too, we should not do, if they were not forbidden. My *Don Juan* was cast aside and almost forgotten, until I heard that the pharisaic synod in John Murray's back parlour had pronounced it as highly immoral, and unfit for publication. "Because thou art virtuous thinkest thou there shall be no more cakes and ale?" Now my brain is throbbing and must have vent. I opined gin was inspiration, but cant is stronger. To-day I had another letter warning me against the Snake (Shelley). He, alone, in this age of humbug, dares stem the current, as he did to-day the flooded Arno in his skiff, although I could not observe he made any progress. The attempt is better than being swept along as all the rest are, with the filthy garbage scoured from its banks.'

Taking advantage of this panegyric on Shelley, I observed, he might do him a great service at little cost, by a friendly word or two in his next work, such as he had bestowed on authors of less merit.

Assuming a knowing look, he continued:

'All trades have their mysteries; if we crack up a popular author, he repays us in the same coin, principal and interest. A friend may have repaid money lent,—can't say any of mine have; but who ever heard of the interest being added thereto?'

I rejoined:

'By your own showing you are indebted to Shelley; some of his best verses are to express his admiration of your genius.'

'Ay,' he said, with a significant look, 'who reads them? If we puffed the Snake, it might not turn out a profitable investment. If he cast off the slough of his mystifying metaphysics, he would want no puffing.'

Seeing I was not satisfied, he added:

'If we introduced Shelley to our readers, they might draw comparisons, and they are "*odorous*".'

After Shelley's death, Byron, in a letter to Moore, of the 2nd of August, 1822, says:

'There is another man gone, about whom the world was ill-naturedly, and ignorantly, and brutally mistaken. It will, perhaps, do him justice *now*, when he can be no better for it.'

In a letter to Murray of an earlier date, he says:

'You were all mistaken about Shelley, who was without exception, the best and least selfish man I ever knew.'

And, again, he says, 'You are all mistaken about Shelley; you do not know how mild, how tolerant, how good he was [in society, and as perfect a gentleman as ever crossed a drawing-room, when he liked, and where he liked].'

What Byron says of the world, that it will, perhaps, do Shelley justice when he can be no better for it, is far more applicable to himself. If the world erred, they did so in ignorance; Shelley was a myth to them. Byron had no such plea to offer, but he was neither just nor generous, and never drew his weapon to redress any wrongs but his own.

6

Byron has been accused of drinking deeply. Our universities, certainly, did turn out more famous drinkers than scholars. In the good old times, to drink lustily was the characteristic of all Englishmen, just as tuft-hunting is now. Eternal swilling, and the rank habits and braggadocio manners which it engendered, came to a climax in George IV's reign. Since then, excessive drinking has gone out of fashion, but an elaborate style of gastronomy has come in to fill up the void; so there is not much gained. Byron used to boast of the quantity of wine he had drunk. He said, 'We young Whigs imbibed claret, and so saved our constitutions: the Tories stuck to port, and destroyed theirs and their country's.'

He bragged, too, of his prowess in riding, boxing, fencing, and even walking; but to excel in these things feet are as necessary as hands.* It was difficult to avoid smiling at his boasting and self-glorification. In the water a fin is better than a foot, and in that element he did well; he was built for floating,—with a flexible body, open chest, broad beam, and round limbs. If the sea was smooth and warm, he would stay in it for hours; but as he seldom indulged in this sport, and when he did, over-exerted himself, he suffered severely; which observing, and knowing how deeply he would be mortified at being beaten, I had the magnanimity when contending with him to give in.

He had a misgiving in his mind that I was trifling with him; and one day as we were on the shore, and the 'Bolivar' at anchor, about three miles off, he insisted on our trying conclusions; we were to swim to the yacht, dine in the sea alongside of her, treading water the while, and then to return to the shore. It was calm and hot, and seeing he would not be fobbed off, we started. I reached the boat a long time before he did; ordered the edibles to be ready, and floated until he arrived. We ate our

---

* He boasted, too, about his sailing, as witness this betting-record: 'I, E. El. Williams, do bet a wager of five crowns, that Lord Byron's boat, the "Bolivar", does not sail at the rate 11 knots within the hour, during the first month after his arrival at Leghorn. (signed) E. Trelawny. (signed) E. Ell. Williams.'

fare leisurely, from off a grating that floated alongside, drank a bottle of ale, and I smoked a cigar, which he tried to extinguish,—as he never smoked. We then put about, and struck off towards the shore. We had not got a hundred yards on our passage, when he retched violently, and, as that is often followed by cramp, I urged him to put his hand on my shoulder that I might tow him back to the schooner.

'Keep off, you villain, don't touch me. I'll drown ere I give in.'

I answered as Iago did to Roderigo:

' "A fig for drowning! drown cats and blind puppies." I shall go on board and try the effects of a glass of grog to stay my stomach.'

'Come on,' he shouted, 'I am always better after vomiting.'

With difficulty I deluded him back; I went on board, and he sat on the steps of the accommodation-ladder, with his feet in the water. I handed him a wine-glass of brandy, and screened him from the burning sun. He was in a sullen mood, but after a time resumed his usual tone. Nothing could induce him to be landed in the schooner's boat, though I protested I had had enough of the water.

'You may do as you like,' he called out, and plumped in, and we swam on shore.

He never afterwards alluded to this event, nor to his prowess in swimming, to me, except in the past tense. He was ill, and kept his bed for two days afterwards.

To return to his drinking propensities, after this digression about his gymnastic prowess: I must say, that of all his vauntings, it was, luckily for him, the emptiest—that is, after he left England and his boon companions, as I know nothing of what he did there. From all that I heard or witnessed of his habits abroad, he was and had been exceedingly abstemious in eating and drinking. When alone, he drank a glass or two of small claret or hock, and when utterly exhausted at night a single glass of grog; which when I mixed it for him I lowered to what sailors call 'water bewitched', and he never made any remark. I once, to try him, omitted the alcohol; he then said, 'Tre, have you not forgotten the creature comfort?' I then put in two spoonfuls, and he was satisfied. This does not look like an

34

habitual toper. His English acquaintances in Italy were, he said in derision, all milksops. On the rare occasions of any of his former friends visiting him, he would urge them to have a carouse with him, but they had grown wiser. He used to say that little Tommy Moore was the only man he then knew who stuck to the bottle and put him on his mettle, adding, 'But he is a native of the damp isle where men subsist by suction.'

Byron had not damaged his body by strong drinks, but his terror of getting fat was so great that he reduced his diet to the point of absolute starvation. He was of that soft, lymphatic temperament which it is almost impossible to keep within a moderate compass, particularly as in his case his lameness prevented his taking exercise. When he added to his weight, even standing was painful, so he resolved to keep down to eleven stone, or shoot himself. He said everything he swallowed was instantly converted into tallow and deposited on his ribs.

He was the only human being I ever met with who had sufficient self-restraint and resolution to resist this proneness to fatten: he did so; and at Genoa, where he was last weighed, he was ten stone and nine pounds, and looked much less. This was not from vanity about his personal appearance, but from a better motive; and as, like Justice Greedy, he was always hungry, his merit was the greater. Occasionally he relaxed his vigilance, when he swelled apace.

I remember one of his old friends saying, 'Byron, how well you are looking!' If he had stopped there it had been well, but when he added, 'You are getting fat,' Byron's brow reddened, and his eyes flashed—' Do you call getting fat looking well, as if I were a hog?' and, turning to me, he muttered, 'The beast, I can hardly keep my hands off him.' The man who thus offended him was the husband of the lady addressed as 'Genevra',* and the original of his 'Zuleika', in the *Bride of Abydos*. I don't think he had much appetite for his dinner that day, or for many days,

---

* Shelley's *Ginevra* is the story of a bride who left her wedding-breakfast to listen to the reproaches of her former lover, then went back to die in her room before ever the guests had left the house. His inspiration for the gloom associated with a wedding Shelley must have derived from his own feelings when Emilia Viviani married Luigi Bondi. But the connexion between this and Byron's *Bride of Abydos*, written in 1813, is clear only to Trelawny.

and never forgave the man who, so far from wishing to offend, intended to pay him a compliment.

Byron said he had tried all sorts of experiments to stay his hunger, without adding to his bulk. 'I swelled,' he said, 'at one time to fourteen stone, so I clapped the muzzle on my jaws, and, like the hybernating animals, consumed my own fat.'

He would exist on biscuits and soda-water for days together, then, to allay the eternal hunger gnawing at his vitals, he would make up a horrid mess of cold potatoes, rice, fish, or greens, deluged in vinegar, and gobble it up like a famished dog. On either of these unsavoury dishes, with a biscuit and a glass or two of Rhine wine, he cared not how sour, he called feasting sumptuously. Upon my observing he might as well have fresh fish and vegetables, instead of stale, he laughed and answered:

'I have an advantage over you, I have no palate; one thing is as good as another to me.'

'Nothing,' I said, 'disagrees with the natural man, he fasts and gorges, his nerves and brains don't bother him; but if you wish to live?'——

'Who wants to live?' he replied, 'not I. The Byrons are a short-lived race on both sides, father and mother: longevity is hereditary: I am nearly at the end of my tether. I don't care for death a d—n: it is her sting! I can't bear pain.'

His habits and want of exercise damaged him, not drink. It must be borne in mind, moreover, that his brain was always working at high pressure. The consequences resulting from his way of life were low or intermittent fevers; these last had fastened on him in his early travels in the Levant; and there is this peculiarity in malaria fevers, that if you have once had them, you are ever after peculiarly susceptible to a renewal of their attacks if within their reach, and Byron was hardly ever out of it. Venice and Ravenna are belted in with swamps, and fevers are rife in the autumn. By starving his body Byron kept his brains clear; no man had brighter eyes or a clearer voice; and his resolute bearing and prompt replies, when excited, gave to his body an appearance of muscular power that imposed on strangers. I never doubted, for he was indifferent to life, and prouder than Lucifer, that if he had drawn his sword in Greece, or elsewhere, he would have thrown away the scabbard.

36

7

IN the annals of authors I cannot find one who wrote under so many discouragements as Shelley; for even Bunyan's dungeon walls echoed the cheers of hosts of zealous disciples on the outside, whereas Shelley could number his readers on his fingers. He said, 'I can only print my writings by stinting myself in food!' Published, or sold openly, they were not.

The utter loneliness in which he was condemned to pass the largest portion of his life would have paralysed any brains less subtilised by genius than his were. Yet he was social and cheerful, and, although frugal himself, most liberal to others, while to serve a friend he was ever ready to make any sacrifice. It was, perhaps, fortunate he was known to so few, for those few kept him close shorn. He went to Ravenna in 1821 on Byron's business, and, writing to his wife, makes this comment on the Pilgrim's asking him to execute a delicate commission: 'But it seems destined that I am always to have some active part in the affairs of everybody whom I approach.' And so he had.

Shelley, in his elegy on the death of Keats, gives this picture of himself:

> ''Midst others of less note, came one frail Form,
> A phantom amongst men; companionless
> As the last cloud of an expiring storm,
> Whose thunder is its knell; he, as I guess,
> Had gazed on Nature's naked loveliness,
> Actæon-like, and now he fled astray
> With feeble steps o'er the world's wilderness,
> And his own thoughts, along that rugged way,
> Pursued, like raging hounds, their father and their prey.'

Every day I passed some hours with Byron, and very often my evenings with Shelley and Williams, so that when my memory summons one of them to appear, the others are sure to follow in his wake. If Byron's reckless frankness and apparent cordiality warmed your feelings, his sensitiveness, irritability, and the perverseness of his temper, cooled them. I was not then thirty, and the exigences of my now full-blown vanities were

37

unsated, and my credulity unexhausted. I believed in many things then, and believe in some now; I could not sympathise with Byron, who believed in nothing.

'As for love, friendship, and your *entusamusy*,' said he, 'they must run their course. If you are not hanged or drowned before you are forty, you will wonder at all the foolish things they have made you say and do,—as I do now.'

'I will go over to the Shelleys,' I answered, 'and hear their opinions on the subject.'

'Ay, the Snake has fascinated you; I am for making a man of the world of you; they will mould you into a Frankenstein monster: so good-night!'

Goëthe's Mephistopheles calls the serpent that tempted Eve, 'My Aunt—the renowned snake'; and as Shelley translated and repeated passages of *Faust*—to, as he said, impregnate Byron's brain,—when he came to that passage, 'My Aunt, the renowned snake', Byron said, 'Then you are her nephew', and henceforth he often called Shelley, the Snake; his bright eyes, slim figure, and noiseless movements, strengthened, if it did not suggest, the comparison. Byron was the real snake—a dangerous mischief-maker; his wit or humour might force a grim smile, or hollow laugh, from the standers by, but they savoured more of pain than playfulness, and made you dissatisfied with yourself and him. When I left his gloomy hall, and the echoes of the heavy iron-plated door died away, I could hardly refrain from shouting with joy as I hurried along the broad-flagged terrace which overhangs the pleasant river, cheered on my course by the cloudless sky, soft air, and fading light, which close an Italian day.

That Byron was always ready to gossip about Goethe is borne out by a young American, George Ticknor, who describes a conversation thus: 'He told me that M. G. Lewis once translated Goethe's *Faust* to him extemporaneously, and this accounts for the resemblance between that poem and *Manfred*, which I could not before account for, as I was aware that he did not know German.

'When I happened to tell Lord Byron that Goethe has many personal enemies in Germany, he expressed a kind of interest to know more about it that looked like Shylock's satisfaction that "other men have ill luck too"; and when I added the story of the translation of

38

the whole of a very unfair Edinburgh Review into German, directly under Goethe's nose at Jena, Byron discovered at first a singular earnestness to hear it, and then, suddenly checking himself, said, as if half in earnest, though still laughing, "And yet I don't know what sympathy I can have with Goethe unless it be that of an injured author." This was the truth, but it was evidently a little more than sympathy he felt.'

After a hasty dinner at my albergo, I hastened along the Arno to the hospitable and cheerful abode of the Shelleys. There I found those sympathies and sentiments which the Pilgrim denounced as illusions believed in as the only realities.

Shelley's mental activity was infectious; he kept your brain in constant action. Its effect on his comrade was very striking. Williams gave up all his accustomed sports for books, and the bettering of his mind; he had excellent natural ability; and the Poet delighted to see the seeds he had sown, germinating. Shelley said he was the sparrow educating the young of the cuckoo. After a protracted labour, Ned was delivered of a five-act play.* Shelley was sanguine that his pupil would succeed as a dramatic writer. One morning I was in Mrs. Williams's drawing-room, by appointment, to hear Ned read an act of his drama. I sat with an aspect as caustic as a critic who was to decide his fate. Whilst thus intent Shelley stood before us with a most woeful expression.

Mrs. Williams started up, exclaiming, 'What's the matter, Percy?'

'Mary has threatened me.'

'Threatened you with what?'

He looked mysterious and too agitated to reply.

Mrs. Williams repeated, 'With what? to box your ears?'

'Oh, much worse than that; Mary says she will have a party; there are English singers here, the Sinclairs, and she will ask them, and everyone she or you know—oh, the horror!'

We all burst into a laugh except his friend Ned.

'It will kill me.'

---

* *The Promise; or a Year, A Month and A Day.* It was never produced or published. Three acts in manuscript are in the Bodleian Library and contain many amendments in Shelley's hand.

'Music, kill you!' said Mrs. Williams. 'Why, you have told me, you flatterer, that you loved music.'

'So I do. It's the company terrifies me. For pity go to Mary and intercede for me; I will submit to any other species of torture than that of being bored to death by idle ladies and gentlemen.'

After various devices it was resolved that Ned Williams should wait upon the lady—he being gifted with a silvery tongue, and sympathising with the Poet in his dislike of fine ladies—and see what he could do to avert the threatened invasion of the Poet's solitude. Meanwhile, Shelley remained in a state of restless ecstacy; he could not even read or sit. Ned returned with a grave face; the Poet stood as a criminal stands at the bar, whilst the solemn arbitrator of his fate decides it. 'The lady,' commenced Ned, 'has set her heart on having a party, and will not be baulked'; but, seeing the Poet's despair, he added, 'It is to be limited to those here assembled, and some of Count Gamba's family; and instead of a musical feast—as we have no souls—we are to have a dinner.' The Poet hopped off, rejoicing, making a noise I should have thought whistling, but that he was ignorant of that accomplishment.

I have seen Shelley and Byron in society, and the contrast was as marked as their characters. The former, not thinking of himself, was as much at ease as in his own home, omitting no occasion of obliging those whom he came in contact with, readily conversing with all or any who addressed him, irrespective of age or rank, dress or address. To the first party I went with Byron, as we were on our road, he said:

'It's so long since I have been in English society, you must tell me what are their present customs. Does rank lead the way, or does the ambassadress pair us off into the dining-room? Do they ask people to wine? Do we exit with the women, or stick to our claret?'

On arriving, he was flushed, fussy, embarrassed, over ceremonious, and ill at ease, evidently thinking a great deal of himself and very little of others. He had learnt his manners, as I have said, during the Regency, when society was more exclusive than even now, and consequently more vulgar.

To know an author, personally, is too often but to destroy the illusion created by his works; if you withdraw the veil of your idol's sanctuary, and see him in his night-cap, you discover a querulous old crone, a sour pedant, a supercilious coxcomb, a servile tuft-hunter, a saucy snob, or, at best, an ordinary mortal. Instead of the high-minded seeker after truth and abstract knowledge, with a nature too refined to bear the vulgarities of life, as we had imagined, we find him full of egotism and vanity, and eternally fretting and fuming about trifles. As a general rule, therefore, it is wise to avoid writers whose works amuse or delight you, for when you see them they will delight you no more. Shelley was a grand exception to this rule. To form a just idea of his poetry, you should have witnessed his daily life; his words and actions best illustrated his writings. If his glorious conception of Gods and men constituted an atheist, I am afraid all that listened were little better. Sometimes he would run through a great work on science, condense the author's laboured exposition, and by substituting simple words for the jargon of the schools, make the most abstruse subject transparent. The cynic Byron acknowledged him to be the best and ablest man he had ever known. The truth was, Shelley loved everything better than himself. Self-preservation is, they say, the first law of nature, with him it was the last; and the only pain he ever gave his friends arose from the utter indifference with which he treated everything concerning himself. I was bathing one day in a deep pool in the Arno, and astonished the Poet by performing a series of aquatic gymnastics, which I had learnt from the natives of the South Seas. On my coming out, whilst dressing, Shelley said, mournfully:

'Why can't I swim, it seems so very easy?'

I answered, 'Because you think you can't. If you determine, you will; take a header off this bank, and when you rise turn on your back, you will float like a duck; but you must reverse the arch in your spine, for it's now bent the wrong way.'

He doffed his jacket and trowsers, kicked off his shoes and socks, and plunged in, and there he lay stretched out on the bottom like a conger eel, not making the least effort or struggle to save himself. He would have been drowned if I had not instantly fished him out. When he recovered his breath, he said:

'I always find the bottom of the well, and they say Truth lies there. In another minute I should have found it, and you would have found an empty shell. It is an easy way of getting rid of the body.'

'What would Mrs. Shelley have said to me if I had gone back with your empty cage?'

'Don't tell Mary—not a word!' he rejoined, and then continued, 'It's a great temptation; in another minute I might have been in another planet.'

'But as you always find the bottom,' I observed, 'you might have sunk "deeper than did ever plummet sound".'

'I am quite easy on that subject,' said the Bard. 'Death is the veil, which those who live call life: they sleep, and it is lifted. Intelligence should be imperishable; the art of printing has made it so in this planet.'

'Do you believe in the immortality of the spirit?'

He continued, 'Certainly not; how can I? We know nothing; we have no evidence; we cannot express our inmost thoughts. They are incomprehensible even to ourselves.'

'Why,' I asked, 'do you call yourself an atheist? it annihilates you in this world.'

'It is a word of abuse to stop discussion, a painted devil to frighten the foolish, a threat to intimidate the wise and good. I used it to express my abhorrence of superstition; I took up the word, as a knight took up a gauntlet, in defiance of injustice. The delusions of Christianity are fatal to genius and originality: they limit thought.'

Shelley's thirst for knowledge was unquenchable. He set to work on a book, or a pyramid of books; his eyes glistening with an energy as fierce as that of the most sordid gold-digger who works at a rock of quartz, crushing his way through all impediments, no grain of the pure ore escaping his eager scrutiny. I called on him one morning at ten, he was in his study with a German folio open, resting on the broad marble mantel-piece, over an old-fashioned fire-place, and with a dictionary in his hand. He always read standing if possible. He had promised over night to go with me, but now begged me to let him off. I then rode to Leghorn, eleven or twelve miles distant, and passed the day there; on returning at six in the evening to dine with

Mrs. Shelley and the Williams's, as I had engaged to do, I went into the Poet's room and found him exactly in the position in which I had left him in the morning, but looking pale and exhausted.

'Well,' I said, 'have you found it?'

Shutting the book and going to the window, he replied, 'No, I have lost it': with a deep sigh: 'I have lost a day.'

'Cheer up, my lad, and come to dinner.'

Putting his long fingers through his masses of wild tangled hair, he answered faintly, 'You go, I have dined—late eating don't do for me.'

'What is this?' I asked as I was going out of the room, pointing to one of his bookshelves with a plate containing bread and cold meat on it.

'That,'—colouring,—'why that must be my dinner. It's very foolish; I thought I had eaten it.'

Saying I was determined that he should for once have a regular meal, I lugged him into the dining-room, but he brought a book with him and read more than he ate. He seldom ate at stated periods, but only when hungry—and then like the birds, if he saw something edible lying about,—but the cupboards of literary ladies are like Mother Hubbard's, bare. His drink was water, or tea if he could get it, bread was literally his staff of life; other things he thought superfluous. An Italian who knew his way of life, not believing it possible that any human being would live as Shelley did, unless compelled by poverty, was astonished when he was told the amount of his income, and thought he was defrauded or grossly ignorant of the value of money. He, therefore, made a proposition which much amused the Poet, that he, the friendly Italian, would undertake for ten thousand crowns a-year to keep Shelley like a grand Seigneur, to provide his table with luxuries, his house with attendants, a carriage and opera box for my lady, besides adorning his person after the most approved Parisian style. Mrs. Shelley's toilette was not included in the wily Italian's estimates. The fact was, Shelley stinted himself to bare necessaries, and then often lavished the money, saved by unprecedented self-denial, on selfish fellows who denied themselves nothing; such as the great philosopher had in his eye, when he said, 'It is the nature of extreme self-lovers, as they will set a house on fire, an' it were only to roast their own eggs.'

Byron on our voyage to Greece, talking of England, after commenting on his own wrongs, said, 'And Shelley, too, the best and most benevolent of men; they hooted him out of his country like a mad dog, for questioning a dogma. Man is the same rancorous beast now that he was from the beginning, and if the Christ they profess to worship re-appeared, they would again crucify him.'

8

BYRON's literary was, like Alexander's military career, one great triumph; but whilst he was at the zenith of his popularity, he railed against the world's injustice. Was this insanity, or what polite doctors now call a softening of the brain? I suppose, by the 'world' he meant no more than the fashionable set he had seen squeezed together in a drawing-room, and by all the press that attacked him—the fraction of it which took its tone from some small but active clique: as to friends deserting him, that could not be, for it was his boast that he never had attempted to make any after his school hallucinations. But in the pride of his strength, and the audacity of his youth, enemies he certainly did make, and when they saw an opportunity of getting rid of a supercilious rival, they instinctively took advantage of it. As to the Poet's differences with his wife, they must have appeared absurd to men who were as indifferent to their own wives as were the majority of Byron's enemies.

When the most worldly wise and unimpassioned marry, they take a leap in the dark, and can no more foresee the consequences, than poets,—owls blinded by the light of their vain imaginations. The worldly wise, not having risked or anticipated much, stand to their bargain 'for better or worse', and say nothing about it; but the irascible tribe of songsters, when they find that marriage is not exactly what they imagined it to be, 'proclaim their griefs from the house-top', as Byron did.

Very pretty books have been written on the 'Loves of the Angels', and 'Loves of the Poets', and Love universal—but when lovers are paired and caged together in holy matrimony, the curtain is dropped, and we hear no more of them. It may be, they moult their feathers and lose their song. Byron's marriage must not be classed with those of the Poets, but of the worldly wise; he was not under the illusion of love, but of money. If he had left his wife and cut society (the last he was resolved on doing), he would have been content: that his wife and society should have cast him off, was a mortification his pride could never forgive nor forget. As to the oft-vexed question of the Poet's separation from his wife, he has told the facts in prose and verse; but omitted to state, that he treated women as things devoid of soul or sense; he would not eat, pray, walk, nor talk with them. If he had told us this, who would have marvelled that a lady, tenderly reared and richly endowed, pious, learned and prudent, deluded into marrying such a man, should have thought him mad or worse, and sought safety by flight. Within certain degrees of affinity marriages are forbidden; so they should be where there is no natural affinity of feelings, habits, tastes, or sympathies. It is very kind in the saints to ally themselves to sinners, but in ninety-nine cases out of one hundred, it turns out a failure; in Byron's case, it was signally so.

In all the transactions of his life, his intense anxiety to cut a good figure made him cruelly unjust to others. In fact, his pride and vanity mastered him, and he made no effort to conceal or to control their dominion, reckless how it marred his worldly advantages. Amidst the general homage paid to his genius, his vanity reverted to his early disappointments, when he was baffled and compelled to fly, and though Parthian-like he discharged his arrows on his pursuers, he lost the battle.

Shelley had a far loftier spirit. His pride was spiritual. When attacked, he neither fled nor stood at bay, nor altered his course, but calmly went on with heart and mind intent on elevating his species. Whilst men tried to force him down to their level, he toiled to draw their minds upwards. His words were, 'I always go on until I am stopped, and I never am stopped.' Like the Indian palms, Shelley never flourished far from water. When compelled to take up his quarters in a town, he every morning with the instinct that guides the water-birds, fled to the nearest lake, river, or sea-shore, and only returned to roost at night. If debarred from this, he sought out the most solitary places. Towns and crowds distracted him. Even the silent and half-deserted cities of Italy, with their temples, palaces, paintings and sculpture, could not make him stay, if there was a wood or water within his reach. At Pisa, he had a river under his window, and a Pine forest in the neighbourhood.

I accompanied Mrs. Shelley to this wood in search of the Poet, on one of those brilliant spring mornings we on the wrong side of the Alps are so rarely blessed with. A calêche took us out of Pisa through the gate of the Cascine; we drove through the

LORD BYRON

Cascine and onwards for two or three miles, traversing the vineyards and farms, on the Grand Ducal estate. On approaching some farm buildings, near which were a hunting-palace and chapel, we dismissed the carriage, directing the driver to meet us at a certain spot in the afternoon. We then walked on, not exactly knowing what course to take, and were exceedingly perplexed on coming to an open space, from which four roads radiated. There we stopped until I learnt from a Contadino, that the one before us led directly to the sea, which was two or three miles distant, the one on the right, led to the Serchio, and that on the left, to the Arno: we decided on taking the road to the sea. We proceeded on our journey over a sandy plain; the sun being near its zenith. Walking was not included among the number of accomplishments in which Mrs. Shelley excelled; the loose sand and hot sun soon knocked her up. When we got under the cool canopy of the pines, she stopped and allowed me to hunt for her husband. I now strode along; the forest was on my right hand and extensive pastures on my left, with herds of oxen, camels, and horses grazing thereon. I came upon the open sea at a place called Gombo, from whence I could see Via Reggio, the Gulf of Spezzia, and the mountains beyond. After bathing, seeing nothing of the Poet, I penetrated the densest part of the forest, ever and anon making the woods ring with the name of Shelley, and scaring the herons and water-birds from the chain of stagnant pools which impeded my progress.

With no landmarks to guide me, nor sky to be seen above, I was bewildered in this wilderness of pines and ponds; so I sat down, struck a light, and smoked a cigar. A red man would have known his course by the trees themselves, their growth, form, and colour; or if a footstep had passed that day, he would have hit upon its trail. As I mused upon his sagacity and my own stupidity, the braying of a brother jackass startled me. He was followed by an old man picking up pine cones. I asked him if he had seen a stranger?

'L'Inglese malincolico haunts the wood maledetta. I will show you his nest.'

As we advanced, the ground swelled into mounds and hollows. By-and-by the old fellow pointed his stick to a hat, books, and loose papers lying about, and then to a deep pool of dark glimmering water, saying 'Eccolo!' I thought he meant that Shelley was in or under the water. The careless, not to say impatient, way in which the Poet bore his burden of life, caused a vague dread amongst his family and friends that he might lose or cast it away at any moment.

The strong light streamed through the opening of the trees. One of the pines, undermined by the water, had fallen into it. Under its lee, and nearly hidden, sat the Poet, gazing on the dark mirror beneath, so lost in his bardish reverie that he did not hear my approach. There the trees were stunted and bent, and their crowns were shorn like friars by the sea breezes, excepting a cluster of three, under which Shelley's traps were lying; these overtopped the rest. To avoid startling the Poet out of his dream, I squatted under the lofty trees, and opened his books. One was a volume of his favourite Greek dramatist, Sophocles,—the same that I found in his pocket after his death —and the other was a volume of Shakespeare. I then hailed him, and, turning his head, he answered faintly:

'Hollo, come in.'

'Is this your study?' I asked.

'Yes,' he answered, 'and these trees are my books—they tell no lies. You are sitting on the stool of inspiration,' he exclaimed. 'In those three pines the weird sisters are imprisoned, and this,' pointing to the water, 'is their cauldron of black broth. The Pythian priestesses uttered their oracles from below—now they are muttered from above. Listen to the solemn music in the pine-tops—don't you hear the mournful murmurings of the sea? Sometimes they rave and roar, shriek and howl, like a rabble of priests. In a tempest, when a ship sinks, they catch the despairing groans of the drowning mariners. Their chorus is the eternal wailing of wretched men.'

'They, like the world,' I observed, 'seem to take no note of wretched women. The sighs and wailing you talk about are not those of wretched men afar off, but are breathed by a woman near at hand—not from the pine-tops, but by a forsaken lady.'

'What do you mean?' he asked.

'Why, that an hour or two ago I left your wife, Mary Shelley, at the entrance of this grove, in despair at not finding you.'

48

He started up, snatched up his scattered books and papers, thrust them into his hat and jacket pockets, sighing 'Poor Mary! her's is a sad fate. Come along; she can't bear solitude, nor I society—the quick coupled with the dead.'

He glided along with his usual swiftness, for nothing could make him pause for an instant when he had an object in view, until he had attained it. On hearing our voices, Mrs. Shelley joined us; her clear gray eyes and thoughtful brow expressing the love she could not speak. To stop Shelley's self-reproaches, or to hide her own emotions, she began in a bantering tone, chiding and coaxing him:

'What a wild-goose you are, Percy; if my thoughts have strayed from my book, it was to the opera, and my new dress from Florence—and especially the ivy wreath so much admired for my hair, and not to you, you silly fellow! When I left home, my satin slippers had not arrived. These are serious matters to gentlewomen, enough to ruffle the serenest tempered. As to you and your ungallant companion, I had forgotten that such things are; but as it is the ridiculous custom to have men at balls and operas, I must take you with me, though, from your uncouth ways, you will be taken for Valentine and he for Orson.'*

Shelley, like other students, would, when the spell that bound his faculties was broken, shut his books, and indulge in the wildest flights of mirth and folly. As this is a sport all can join in, we talked and laughed, and shrieked, and shouted, as we emerged from under the shadows of the melancholy pines and their nodding plumes, into the now cool purple twilight and open country. The cheerful and graceful peasant girls, returning home from the vineyards and olive groves, stopped to look at us. The old man I had met in the morning gathering pine cones, passed hurriedly by with his donkey, giving Shelley a wide berth, and evidently thinking that the melancholy Englishman

---

* Valentine and Orson. Twin sons of Alexander, Emperor of Constantinople, and Bellisant, they were born in a wood near Orléans, and Orson was carried off by a bear, which reared him with its cubs. When he grew up he became the Terror of France, 'The Wild Man of the Woods'. Meanwhile Valentine had also been carried off, by his uncle, King Pepin. Ultimately, according to the fifteenth-century legend, the two of them came together again, and lived in respectable nobility.

had now become a raving maniac. Sancho says, 'Blessings on the man who invented sleep'; the man who invented laughing deserves no less.

The day I found Shelley in the pine forest he was writing verses on a guitar. I picked up a fragment, but could only make out the first two lines:

> 'Ariel, to Miranda take
> This slave of music.' *

It was a frightful scrawl; words smeared out with his finger, and one upon the other, over and over in tiers, and all run together in most 'admired disorder'; it might have been taken for a sketch of a marsh overgrown with bulrushes, and the blots for wild ducks; such a dashed off daub as self-conceited artists mistake for a manifestation of genius. On my observing this to him, he answered:

'When my brain gets heated with thought, it soon boils, and throws off images and words faster than I can skim them off. In the morning, when cooled down, out of the rude sketch as you justly call it, I shall attempt a drawing. If you ask me why I publish what few or none will care to read, it is that the spirits I have raised haunt me until they are sent to the devil of a printer. All authors are anxious to breech their bantlings.'

Despite occasional domestic frictions, despite the fact that Mary was still something of a stranger to him, and despite an occasional recurrence of hallucinations and illness, Shelley was comparatively happy at this time, and the happiness was principally caused by the presence of Edward and Jane Williams. Edward was a wonderful companion, Jane 'a sort of embodied peace in the midst of our circle of tempests'.

This was no *ménage à trois*. Whereas Mary Shelley was irritable (she was again pregnant and in June 1822 suffered a miscarriage), Jane was placid; whereas Mary did not appear to understand her husband, 'from proximity and the continuity of domestic intercourse', Jane was full of sympathy for his problems and pains. Even Jane's lack of intellectual brilliance seemed in Shelley's eyes a recommendation when compared to Mary's sharp mentality. But

---

* Shelley. *With a Guitar, to Jane.*

Shelley never questioned Jane's love for Edward, not even in his poems, which were all written as it were

> 'By permission and command
> Of thine own Prince Ferdinand.'*

Nor did he attempt to break in upon it, save perhaps on one occasion, probably in May 1822, when the peacefulness of their association may have led Shelley to imagine love—and ask for more:

> 'Sweet lips, could my heart have hidden
> That its life was crushed by you,
> Ye would not have then forbidden
> The death which a heart so true
> Sought in your briny dew.'†

For the most part he was content to accept her understanding, her music, and her imagined hypnotic powers of healing.

Strangely enough, Mary Shelley, whose miseries were many, does not seem to have added to them by suspicions of the relations between her husband and Jane. On the contrary, she too regarded both the Williams as delightful companions.

---

* *With a Guitar, to Jane.*
† Lines: *We Meet Not as We Parted.*

9

ONE day I drove the poet to Leghorn. In answer to my questions, Shelley said, 'In writing the *Cenci* my object was to see how I could succeed in describing passions I have never felt, and to tell the most dreadful story in pure and refined language. The image of Beatrice haunted me after seeing her portrait. The story is well authenticated, and the details far more horrible than I have painted them. The *Cenci* is a work of art; it is not coloured by my feelings, nor obscured by my metaphysics. I don't think much of it. It gave me less trouble than anything I have written of the same length.

'I am now writing a play for the stage. It is affectation to say we write a play for any other purpose. The subject is from English history; in style and manner I shall approach as near our great dramatist as my feeble powers will permit. *King Lear* is my model, for that is nearly perfect. I am amazed at my presumption. Poets should be modest. My audacity savours of madness.

'Considering the labour requisite to excel in composition, I think it would be better to stick to one style. The clamour for novelty is leading us all astray. Yet, at Ravenna, I urged Byron to come out of the dismal "wood of error" into the sun, to write something new and cheerful. *Don Juan* is the result. The poetry is superior to *Childe Harold*, and the plan, or rather want of plan, gives scope to his astonishing natural powers.

'My friends say my *Prometheus* is too wild, ideal, and perplexed with imagery. It may be so. It has no resemblance to the Greek drama. It is original; and cost me severe mental labour. Authors, like mothers, prefer the children who have given them most trouble. Milton preferred his *Paradise Regained*, Petrarch his *Africa*, and Byron his *Doge of Venice*.

'I have the vanity to write only for poetical minds, and must be satisfied with few readers. Byron is ambitious; he writes for all, and all read his works.

'With regard to the great question, the System of the Universe, I have no curiosity on the subject. I am content to see no farther into futurity than Plato and Bacon. My mind is tranquil; I have no fears and some hopes. In our present gross material state our faculties are clouded;—when Death removes our clay coverings the mystery will be solved.'

He thought a play founded on Shakespeare's *Timon* would be an excellent mode of discussing our present social and political evils dramatically, and of descanting on them.

After we had done our business, I called on a Scotch family and lured my companion in. He abhorred forcing himself on strangers—so I did not mention his name, merely observing:

'As you said you wanted information about Italy, here is a friend of mine can give it you—for I cannot.'

The ladies—for there was no man there—were capital specimens of Scotchwomen, fresh from the land of cakes,—frank, fair, intelligent, and of course, pious. After a long and earnest talk we left them, but not without difficulty, so pressing were they for us to stop to dinner.

When I next visited them, they were disappointed at the absence of my companion; and when I told them it was Shelley, the young and handsome mother clasped her hands, and exclaimed:

'Shelley! That bright-eyed youth;—so gentle, so intelligent —so thoughtful for us. Oh, why did you not name him?'

'Because he thought you would have been shocked.'

'Shocked!—why, I would have knelt to him in penitence for having wronged him even in my thoughts. If he is not pure and good—then there is no truth and goodness in this world. His looks reminded me of my own blessed baby,—so innocent—so full of love and sweetness.'

'So is the serpent that tempted Eve described,' I said.

'Oh, you wicked scoffer!' she continued. 'But I know you love him. I shall have no peace of mind until you bring him here. You remember, sister, I said his young face had lines of care and sorrow on it—when he was showing us the road to Rome on the map and the sun shone on it;—poor boy! Oh, tell us about his wife,—is she worthy of him? She must love him dearly—and so must all who know him.'

To palliate the warm-hearted lady's admiration of the Poet —as well as my own—I must observe, that all on knowing him sang the same song; and as I have before observed, even Byron in his most moody and cynical vein, joined in the chorus, echoing my monotonous notes. The reason was, that after having heard or read the rancorous abuse heaped on Shelley by the mercenary literature of the day,—in which he was described as a monster more hideous than Caliban,—the revulsion of feeling on seeing the man was so great, that he seemed as gentle a spirit as Ariel. There never has been nor can be any true likeness of him. Desdemona says, 'I saw Othello's visage in his mind', and Shelley's 'visage' as well as his mind are to be seen in his works.

When I was at Leghorn with Shelley, I drew him towards the docks, saying:

'As we have a spare hour let's see if we can't put a girdle round about the earth in forty minutes. In these docks are living specimens of all the nationalities of the world; thus we can go round it, and visit and examine any particular nation we like, observing their peculiar habits, manners, dress, language, food, productions, arts, and naval architecture; for see how varied are the shapes, build, rigging, and decoration of the different vessels. There lies an English cutter, a French chasse marée, an American clipper, a Spanish tartan, an Austrian trabacolo, a Genoese felucca, a Sardinian zebeck, a Neapolitan brig, a Sicilian sparanza, a Dutch galleot, a Danish snow, a Russian hermaphrodite, a Turkish sackalever, a Greek bombard. I don't see a Persian dow, an Arab grab, or a Chinese junk; but there are enough for our purpose and to spare. As you are writing a poem, *Hellas*, about the modern Greeks, would it not be as well to take a look at them amidst all the din of the docks? I hear their shrill nasal voices, and should like to know if you can trace in the language or lineaments of these Greeks of the nineteenth century, A.D., the faintest resemblance to the lofty and sublime spirits who lived in the fourth century, B.C. An English merchant who has dealings with them, told me he thought these modern Greeks were, if judged by their actions, a cross between the Jews and gypsies;—but here comes the Capitano Zarita; I know him.'

So dragging Shelley with me I introduced him, and asking to see the vessel, we crossed the plank from the quay and stood on the deck of the 'San Spiridione' in the midst of her chattering irascible crew. They took little heed of the skipper, for in these trading vessels each individual of the crew is part owner, and

54

has some share in the cargo; so they are all interested in the speculation—having no wages. They squatted about the decks in small knots, shrieking, gesticulating, smoking, eating, and gambling like savages.

'Does this realise your idea of Hellenism, Shelley?' I said.

'No! but it does of Hell,' he replied.

The captain insisted on giving us pipes and coffee in his cabin, so I dragged Shelley down. Over the rudder-head facing us, there was a gilt box enshrining a flaming gaudy daub of a saint, with a lamp burning before it; this was Il Padre Santo Spiridione, the ship's godfather. The skipper crossed himself and squatted on the dirty divan. Shelley talked to him about the Greek revolution that was taking place, but from its interrupting trade the captain was opposed to it.

'Come away!' said Shelley. 'There is not a drop of the old Hellenic blood here. These are not the men to rekindle the ancient Greek fire; their souls are extinguished by traffic and superstition. Come away!'—and away we went.

'It is but a step,' I said, 'from these ruins of worn-out Greece to the New World, let's board the American clipper.'

'I had rather not have any more of my hopes and illusions mocked by sad realities,' said Shelley.

'You must allow,' I answered, 'that graceful craft was designed by a man who had a poet's feeling for things beautiful; let's get a model and build a boat like her.'

The idea so pleased the Poet that he followed me on board her. The Americans are a social, free-and-easy people, accustomed to take their own way, and to readily yield the same privilege to all others, so that our coming on board, and examination of the vessel, fore and aft, were not considered as intrusion. The captain was on shore, so I talked to the mate, a smart specimen of a Yankee. When I commended her beauty, he said:

'I do expect, now we have our new copper on, she has a look of the brass sarpent, she has as slick a run, and her bearings are just where they should be.'

I said we wished to build a boat after her model.

'Then I calculate you must go to Baltimore or Boston to get one; there is no one on this side the water can do the job. We

55

have our freight all ready, and are homeward-bound; we have elegant accommodation, and you will be across before your young friend's beard is ripe for a razor. Come down, and take an observation of the state cabin.'

It was about seven and a half feet by five; 'plenty of room to live or die comfortably in,' he observed, and then pressed us to have a chaw of real old Virginian cake, *i.e.* tobacco, and a cool drink of peach brandy. I made some observation to him about the Greek vessel we had visited.

'Crank as an eggshell,' he said; 'too many sticks and top hamper, she looks like a bundle of chips going to hell to be burnt.'

I seduced Shelley into drinking a wine-glass of weak grog, the first and last he ever drank. The Yankee would not let us go until we had drunk, under the star-spangled banner, to the memory of Washington, and the prosperity of the American commonwealth.

'As a warrior and statesman,' said Shelley, 'he was righteous in all he did, unlike all who lived before or since; he never used his power but for the benefit of his fellow-creatures:

> "He fought,
> For truth and wisdom, foremost of the brave;
> Him glory's idle glances dazzled not;
> 'Twas his ambition, generous and great,
> A life to life's great end to consecrate." '

'Stranger,' said the Yankee, 'truer words were never spoken; there is dry rot in all the main timbers of the Old World, and none of you will do any good till you are docked, refitted, and annexed to the New. You must log that song you sang; there ain't many Britishers that will say as much of the man that whipped them; so just set these lines down in the log, or it won't go for nothing.'

Shelley wrote some verses in the book, but not those he had quoted; and so we parted.

It was now time to return to Pisa. I never lost an opportunity of thus giving the dreamy bard glimpses of rough life. He disliked it, but could not resist my importunity. He had seen no more of the working-day world than a girl at a boarding-school, and his habit of eternally brooding on his own thoughts, in

56

solitude and silence, damaged his health of mind and body. Like many other over-sensitive people, he thought everybody shunned him, whereas it was he who stood aloof. To the few who sought his acquaintance, he was frank, cordial, and, if they appeared worthy, friendly in the extreme; but he shrank like a maiden from making the first advances. At the beginning of his literary life, he believed all authors published their opinions as he did his from a deep conviction of their truth and importance, after due investigation. When a new work appeared, on any subject that interested him, he would write to the authors expressing his opinion of their books, and giving his reasons for his judgment, always arguing logically, and not for display; and, with his serene and imperturbable temper, variety of knowledge, tenacious memory, command of language, or rather of all the languages of literature, he was a most subtle critic; but, as authors are not the meekest or mildest of men, he occasionally met with rude rebuffs, and retired into his own shell.

In this way he became acquainted with Godwin, in early life; and in his first work, *Queen Mab*, or rather in the notes appended to that poem, the old philosopher's influence on the beardless boy is strongly marked. For publishing these notes Shelley was punished as the man is stated to have been who committed the first murder: 'every man's hand was against him'. Southey, Wordsworth, Coleridge, Keats, and others he had either written to, corresponded with, or personally known; but in their literary guild he found little sympathy; their enthusiasm had burnt out whilst Shelley's had waxed stronger. Old Rothschild's sage maxim perhaps influenced them, 'Never connect yourself with an unlucky man.' However that may be, all intercourse had long ceased between Shelley and any of the literary fraternity of the day, with the exception of Peacock, Keats, Leigh Hunt, and the Brothers Smith, of the *Rejected Addresses*.

I will now return to our drive home from visiting the ships in the docks of Leghorn. Shelley was in high glee, and full of fun, as he generally was after these 'distractions', as he called them. The fact was his excessive mental labour impeded, if it did not paralyse, his bodily functions. When his mind was fixed on a subject, his mental powers were strained to the utmost. If not writing or sleeping, he was reading; he read, whilst eating,

57

walking, or travelling—the last thing at night, and the first thing in the morning—not the ephemeral literature of the day, which requires little or no thought, but the works, of the old sages, metaphysicians, logicians, and philosophers, of the Grecian and Roman poets, and of modern scientific men, so that anything that could diversify or relax his overstrained brain was of the utmost benefit to him. Now he talked of nothing but ships, sailors, and the sea; and, although he agreed with Johnson that a man who made a pun would pick a pocket, yet he made several in Greek, which he at least thought good, for he shrieked with laughter as he uttered them. Fearing his phil-Hellenism would end by making him serious, as it always did, I brought his mind back by repeating some lines of Sedley's, beginning

> Love still has something of the sea
> From whence his mother rose. *

During the rest of our drive we had nothing but sea yarns. He regretted having wasted his life in Greek and Latin, instead of learning the useful arts of swimming and sailoring. He resolved to have a good-sized boat forthwith. I proposed we should form a colony at the Gulf of Spezzia, and I said—'You get Byron to join us, and with your family and the Williams', and books, horses, and boats, undisturbed by the botherations of the world, we shall have all that reasonable people require.'

This scheme enchanted him. 'Well,' I said, 'propose this to Byron to-morrow.'

'No!' he answered, 'you must do that. Byron is always influenced by his last acquaintance. You are the last man, so do you pop the question.'

'I understand that feeling,' I observed. 'When well known neither men nor women realise our first conception of them, so we transfer our hopes to the new men or women who make a sign of sympathy, only to find them like those who have gone before, or worse.' I quoted his own lines as exemplifying my meaning:

> Where is the beauty, love, and truth we seek,
> But in our minds!†

---

* Sir Charles Sedley. *Love still has Something.*
† 'Where is the love, beauty and truth we seek'—Shelley, *Julian and Madallo.*

Byron, too, visited an American ship at about this time. In 1822, a young Harvard graduate, George Bancroft, was in Italy, and in his journal Bancroft, later famous as a historian of the United States, wrote on May 21st: 'Leghorn: Joined Major Stith in a visit to the "Constitution". Lord Byron came on board. We were presented to him. From the "Constitution" he went to the "Ontario", where Captain Chauncy received him with most distinguished civility. A salute was fired, the yards were manned: and three cheers given in most glorious and clear union.'

This short description is supplemented by information contained in a letter from Bancroft to Samuel A. Eliot: '. . . I must begin a new period to tell you what else I've seen: what do you think now: I went on board the Commodore's ship, Sir! the Constitution or Old Ironsides as she hath been rightly termed: Well! Is that all? Not quite. A short time after I had been on board a man, who wore his hair very long, with full fat cheeks, a healthy lively pair of dark eyes, a cheerful forehead, a man of gentle manners though of a misshapen foot, a man of rank and some note in our small world, came on board. Whom do you guess it was? Prince Borghese? No, the fat old goat I do not mean. The Tuscan Duke? No, for he is a good fellow to be sure, quite a radical, an honest man, who wears a blue coat and a white hat, and is drawn about by six horses. 'Tis not he I mean. Who was it then? Why, nothing but a poet; yet it was a pleasure to have a poet on board an American Squadron, and to have been presented to Lord Byron anywhere else, would not have given me half so much pleasure as it did to meet him on American boards and beneath the American flag. I was out to see him afterwards, and was treated by him with more civility than I have ever been by any man in Europe. I hardly know if I ever talked with a man so frankly. He is very gay and fashionable in his way of talking, will converse of duels and horses, rows and swimming and good principles of Liberty, and in short is one of the pleasantest men in the world. Of himself he spoke with the utmost openness, of his success and his enemies. I was taken into a room of his villa: as I believed to enjoy the prospect toward the West: when my eyes were suddenly dazzled by beauty almost more than human and my ears soothed by the sweetest Italian accents from sweet Italian lips. Who was the lady? I know not. It was a beautiful apparition, and why attach harsh ideas and harsher words to one who looked so innocent and conversed so purely?'

. This courtesy, surprising from the U.S. Navy to a man who had neither military nor political position, added to Bancroft's desire to know Byron better. He wrote for an interview and next day saw

Byron. His journal for that day repeats some of Byron's comments: ' "The British speak of me as one they deem incorrigible." He spoke of the king as of one determined to persecute him. "I never went to court," said B., "and one evening at a ball was presented to the king at the king's own request." And yet the king complains of B.'s having written eight lines against him after having been treated so civilly. "The lines," added B., "were written before I was presented to him."

'I mentioned Goethe's comparison of *Faust* and *Manfred*: and Byron observed, evidently in earnest, that he deemed it honor enough to have his work mentioned with *Faust*. As to its origin, Lord B. said that some time before he had conceived the idea of his piece, Monk Lewis had translated to him some of the scenes and had given him an idea of the plan of the piece.

'Speaking of the immorality of his works, he said: "Why what are Fielding and Smollett and those authors?" He seemed to think there were worse things in Smollett than in anything he had written. What would they say, too, to the introduction to Goethe's *Faust*? Many of his friends, he said, in Italy as well as in England, had entreated him not to go on with *Don Juan*.

'He had dedicated one of his late works to Goethe; but for some reason or other his publisher had omitted to print it.

'Shelley is translating *Faust*: "Shelley of whom you may have heard many foolish stories, of his being a man of no principles, an atheist and all that: but he is not."

'Lord Byron related to me the late scrape, into which he or his servant got at Pisa [see p. 77].

'He laughed at the story Goethe tells of his murdering a man at Florence—hopes Goethe may not hear of this affair at Pisa, lest he should make a famous story out of it.

'He asked me if I had come on foot, offering me his carriage or his horse to return with.

'I was taken into another room, without knowing that I was doing anything more than going to enjoy new views from the pleasant villa where Byron resides. I was astonished to find myself in the same room with a most exquisitely beautiful lady, of apparently twenty-five. She was on the sopha. I had the seat nearest her. Conversation was now carried on in Italian, of music, of the fine pianofortes made in Germany, of Berlin and the love of Berlin ladies for music, of *Lalla Rookh*, of France and Italy, in short of the things which are proper to be discussed in the company of a very pretty woman. Lord Byron speaks Italian perfectly, the lady with the sweetest pronunciation in the world. She is of a delicate style of beauty: has a fine neck, a lovely complexion, on her cheeks the richest vermillion colour; a fine white forehead, a sweet little mouth, a graceful nose, good teeth; she is tall and her waist beautifully small. Innocence and repose seem the leading expression of her countenance. Her smile is heavenly; her dark eyes have a calm and gentle expression: and though I have seen more splendid beauty, I have seldom seen any, who produced on me a pleasanter impression.

'Lord Byron says he left Ravenna because all his friends were exiled. The priests stuck up an affiche threatening him with I know not what. The young men of Italy, Lord B. thinks, are in a good way: they long for liberty. Let them get that, and then afterwards study politics and understand it.*

'Lord B. wishes to go to America. He could judge it impartially: till now none had been there but spectators: he would go unprejudiced; at least with no prepossessions for his mother country.'

---

* See also quotation from Parry, p. 26, on Byron as a Carbonaro.

10

THE following morning I told Byron our plan. Without any suggestion from me he eagerly volunteered to join us, and asked me to get a yacht built for him, and to look out for a house as near the sea as possible. I allowed some days to pass before I took any steps in order to see if his wayward mind would change. As he grew more urgent I wrote to an old naval friend, Captain Roberts, then staying at Genoa, a man peculiarly fitted to execute the order, and requested him to send plans and estimates of an open boat for Shelley, and a large decked one for Byron. Shortly after, Williams and I rode along the coast to the Gulf of Spezzia. Shelley had no pride or vanity to provide for, yet we had the greatest difficulty in finding any house in which the humblest civilised family could exist.

On the shores of this superb bay, only surpassed in its natural beauty and capability by that of Naples, so effectually has tyranny paralysed the energies and enterprise of man, that the only indication of human habitation was a few most miserable fishing villages scattered along the margin of the bay. Near its centre, between the villages of Sant'Arenzo and Lerici, we came upon a lonely and abandoned building called the Villa Magni, though it looked more like a boat- or bathing-house than a place to live in. It consisted of a terrace or ground-floor unpaved, and used for storing boat-gear and fishing-tackle, and of a single storey over it divided into a hall or saloon and four small rooms which had once been whitewashed; there was one chimney for cooking. This place, we thought the Shelleys might put up with for the summer. The only good thing about it was a verandah facing the sea, and almost over it. So we sought the owner and made arrangements, dependent on Shelley's approval, for taking it for six months. As to finding a palazzo grand enough for a Milordo Inglese, within a reasonable distance of the bay, it was out of the question.

Williams returned to Pisa; I rode on to Genoa, and settled with Captain Roberts about building the boats. He had already, with his usual activity, obtained permission to build them in the government dock-yards, and had his plans and estimates made

MARY SHELLEY

out. I need hardly say that though the Captain was a great arithmetician, this estimate, like all the estimates as to time and cost that were ever made, was a mere delusion, which made Byron wroth, but did not ruffle Shelley's serenity.

On returning to Pisa I found the two Poets going through the same routine of habits they had adopted before my departure; the one getting out of bed after noon, dawdling about until two or three, following the same road on horseback, stopping at the same Podere, firing his pop-guns, and retracing his steps at the same slow pace;—his frugal dinner followed by his accustomed visit to an Italian family, and then—the midnight lamp, and the immortal verses.

The other was up at six or seven, reading Plato, Sophocles, or Spinoza, with the accompaniment of a hunch of dry bread; then he joined Williams in a sail on the Arno, in a flat-bottomed skiff, book in hand, and from thence he went to the pine-forest, or some out-of-the-way place. When the birds went to roost he returned home, and talked and read until midnight. The monotony of this life was only broken at long intervals by the arrival of some old acquaintances of Byron's: Rogers, Hobhouse, Moore, Scott*—not Sir Walter,—and these visits were brief. John Murray, the publisher, sent out new books, and wrote amusing gossiping letters, as did Tom Moore and others. These we were generally allowed to read, or hear read, Byron archly observing, 'My private and confidential letters are better known than any of my published works.'

Shelley's boyish eagerness to possess the new toy, from which he anticipated never-failing pleasure in gliding over the azure seas, under the cloudless skies of an Italian summer, was pleasant to behold. His comrade Williams was inspired by the same spirit. We used to draw plans on the sands of the Arno of the

---

* Samuel Rogers (1763–1855): Banker, poet and philanthropist. John Cam Hobhouse (1786–1869): Byron's companion in Albania in 1813, he became a distinguished Liberal politician and, in 1851, first Lord Broughton. Thomas Moore (1779–1852): The Irish poet; in his lifetime his poetry was as popular as Byron's. Byron's 'official' biographer. John Scott (1783–1821): First Editor of the *London Magazine*. He was killed by J. G. Lockhart's second in a duel arising out of an attack he had made on Lockhart and *Blackwood's*.

exact dimensions of the boat, dividing her into compartments (the forepart was decked for stowage), and then, squatting down within the lines, I marked off the imaginary cabin. With a real chart of the Mediterranean spread out before them, and with faces as grave and anxious as those of Columbus and his companions, they held councils as to the islands to be visited, coasts explored, courses steered, the amount of armament, stores, water and provisions which would be necessary. Then we would narrate instances of the daring of the old navigators, as when Diaz discovered the Cape of Good Hope in 1446, with two vessels each of fifty tons burthen; or when Drake went round the world, one of his craft being only thirty tons; and of the extraordinary runs and enterprises accomplished in open boats of equal or less tonnage, than the one we were building from the earliest times to those of Commodore Bligh. Byron with the smile of a Mephistophiles standing by, asked me the amount of salvage we, the salvors, should be entitled to in the probable event of our picking up and towing Shelley's water-logged craft into port.

The Shelleys and the Williams had plans to spend the summer on the coast, and these plans were accelerated by political uncertainty occasioned by the affair of Serjeant-Major Masi which Trelawny refers to later (on p. 77). On April 15, 1822, Claire Clairmont arrived in Pisa, probably with the intention of accompanying the two families to the sea-side. It was decided that she should go with the Williams to Spezia to look for a suitable house.

While they were away news came that Allegra, Byron's daughter by that 'damned Bitch' Claire Clairmont, had died of typhus fever in her convent school at Bagnacavallo. Shelley determined that Claire should be away from Byron when the news was broken to her. He was not to be gainsaid. Like 'a torrent hurrying everything in its course' he pushed Mary, Claire and Trelawny off to San Terenzo on April 26.

Claire was told of her child's death on May 2, and, like an insane creature, wrote viciously to Byron, accusing him of murdering Allegra. Nor, in her later life, was she ever to achieve calmness on this tragedy—even Mary and Shelley were excoriated in her journals for their part in the business.

In fact the death of his five-year-old daughter affected Byron as deeply as any personal loss could affect him. On hearing the news

(April 23, 1822) he had written to Shelley: 'The blow was stunning and unexpected; for I thought the danger over, by the long interval between her stated amelioration and the arrival of the express. But I have borne up against it as I best can, and so far successfully, that I can go about the usual business of life with the same appearance of composure, and even greater. There is nothing to prevent your coming to-morrow; but, perhaps, to-day, and yester-evening, it was better not to have met. I do not know that I have anything to reproach in my conduct, and certainly nothing in my feelings and intentions towards the dead. But it is a moment when we are apt to think that, if this or that had been done, such event might have been prevented,—though every day and hour shows us that they are the most natural and inevitable. I suppose that Time will do his usual work—Death has done his. Yours, ever, N.B.'

A few days later he wrote to Sir Walter Scott: 'My dear Sir Walter,—Your account of your family is very pleasing; would that I "could answer this comfort with the like!" but I have just lost my natural daughter, Allegra, by a fever. The only consolation, save time, is the reflection that she is either at rest or happy; for her few years (only five) prevented her from having incurred any sin, except what we inherit from Adam.'

As the world spun round, the sandy plains of Pisa became too hot to be agreeable, and the Shelleys, longing for the sea breezes, departed to their new abode. Byron could not muster energy enough to break through his dawdling habits, so he lingered on under the fair plea of seeing the Leigh Hunts settled in his ground-floor, which was prepared for them.* I rode on to Genoa to hasten the completion and despatch of the long-promised boat-flotilla. I found Captain Roberts had nearly finished Shelley's boat. Williams had brought with him, on leaving England, the section of a boat as a model to build from, designed by a naval officer, and the two friends had so often sat contemplating this toy, believing it to be a marvel of nautical architecture, that nothing would satisfy them but that their craft should be built exactly on the same lines. Roberts, and the builder at Genoa, not approving, protested against it. You might as well have attempted to persuade a young man after a season of boating, or hunting, that he was not a thorough

---

* Some account of the relationship between Hunt and Byron will be found on p. 106 *et seq.*

seaman and sportsman; or a youngster flushed with honours from a university that he was not the wisest of men. Williams was on ordinary occasions as humble-minded as Shelley, but having been two or three years in the navy, and then in the cavalry, he thought there was no vanity in his believing that he was as good a judge of a boat or horse as any man. In these small conceits we are all fools at the beginning of life, until time, with his sledge hammer, has let the daylight into our brain-boxes; so the boat was built according to his cherished model. When it was finished, it took two tons of iron ballast to bring her down to her bearings, and then she was very crank in a breeze, though not deficient in beam. She was fast, strongly built, and Torbay rigged. I despatched her under charge of two steady seamen, and a smart sailor lad, aged eighteen, named Charles Vivian. Shelley sent back the two sailors and only retained the boy; they told me on their return to Genoa, that they had been out in a rough night, that she was a ticklish boat to manage, but had sailed and worked well, and with two good seamen she would do very well; and that they had cautioned the gents accordingly. I shortly after received the following letter from Shelley:

Lerici, May 16, 1822

MY DEAR TRELAWNY, The 'Don Juan' is arrived, and nothing can exceed the admiration she has excited; for we must suppose the name to have been given her during the equivocation of sex which her godfather suffered in the harem. Williams declares her to be perfect, and I participate in his enthusiasm, inasmuch as would be decent in a landsman. We have been out now several days, although we have sought in vain for an opportunity of trying her against the feluccas or other large craft in the bay; she passes the small ones as a comet might pass the dullest planet of the heavens. When do you expect to be here in the 'Bolivar'? If Roberts's 50*l.* grow into a 500*l.*, and his ten days into months, I suppose I may expect that I am considerably in your debt, and that you will not be round here until the middle of the summer. I hope that I shall be mistaken in the last of these conclusions; as to the former, whatever may be the result, I have little reason and less inclination to complain of

66

my bargain. I wish you could express from me to Roberts, how excessively I am obliged to him for the time and trouble he has expended for my advantage, and which I wish could be as easily repaid as the money which I owe him, and which I wait your orders for remitting.

I have only heard from Lord Byron once, and solely upon that subject. Tita* is with me, and I suppose will go with you in the schooner to Leghorn. We are very impatient to see you, and although we cannot hope that you will stay long on your *first* visit, we count upon you for the latter part of the summer, as soon as the novelty of Leghorn is blunted. Mary desires her best regards to you, and unites with me in a sincere wish to renew an intimacy from which we have already experienced so much pleasure. Believe me, my dear Trelawny, Your very sincere friend, P. B. SHELLEY.

Lerici, June 18, 1822

MY DEAR TRELAWNY, I have written to Guelhard [sic],† to pay you 154 Tuscan crowns, the amount of the balance against me according to Roberts's calculation, which I keep for your satisfaction, deducting sixty, which I paid the aubergiste at Pisa, in all 214. We saw you about eight miles in the offing this morning; but the abatement of the breeze leaves us little hope that you can have made Leghorn this evening. Pray write us a full, true, and particular account of your proceedings, etc.—How Lord Byron likes the vessel; what are your arrangements and intentions for the summer; and when we may expect to see you or him in this region again; and especially whether there is any news of Hunt.

Roberts and Williams are very busy in refitting the 'Don Juan'; they seem determined that she shall enter Leghorn in style. I am no great judge of these matters; but am excessively obliged to the former, and delighted that the latter should find amusement, like the sparrow, in educating the cuckoo's young.

---

* 'Tita the Venetian is here, and operates as my valet; a fine fellow, with a prodigious black beard, and who has stabbed two or three people, and is one of the most good-natured looking fellows I ever saw.' (Shelley to Mary, August 9, 1821.)

† Guebhard & Co., Shelley's bankers at Leghorn.

You, of course, enter into society at Leghorn: should you meet with any scientific person, capable of preparing the *Prussic Acid, or essential oil of bitter almonds*, I should regard it as a great kindness if you could procure me a small quantity. It requires the greatest caution in preparation, and ought to be highly concentrated; I would give any price for this medicine; you remember we talked of it the other night, and we both expressed a wish to possess it; my wish was serious, and sprung from the desire of avoiding needless suffering. I need not tell you I have no intention of suicide at present, but I confess it would be a comfort to me to hold in my possession that golden key to the chamber of perpetual rest. *The Prussic Acid* is used in medicine in infinitely minute doses; but that preparation is weak, and has not the concentration necessary to medicine all ills infallibly. A single drop, even less, is a dose, and it acts by paralysis.

I am curious to hear of this publication about Lord Byron and the Pisa circle.* I hope it will not annoy him, as to me I am supremely indifferent. If you have not shown the letter I sent you, don't, until Hunt's arrival, when we shall certainly meet. Your very sincere friend, P. B. SHELLEY.

Mary is better, though still excessively weak. [She had been unwell for some time; her afflictions mainly mental.]

Not long after, I followed in Byron's boat, the 'Bolivar' schooner. There was no fault to find with her, Roberts and the builder had fashioned her after their own fancy, and she was both fast and safe. I manned her with five able seamen, four Genoese and one Englishman. I put into the Gulf of Spezzia, and found Shelley in ecstasy with his boat, and Williams as touchy about her reputation as if she had been his wife. They were hardly ever out of her, and talked of the Mediterranean as a lake too confined and tranquil to exhibit her sea-going excellence. They longed to be on the broad Atlantic, scudding under bare poles in a heavy sou'wester, with plenty of sea room. I went out for a sail in Shelley's boat to see how they would manage her. It was great fun to witness Williams teaching the Poet how to

---

* John Watkins. *Memoirs of the Life and Writings of Lord Byron, with some of his Contemporaries.* 1822. The references to Shelley are particularly obnoxious.

68

steer, and other points of seamanship. As usual, Shelley had a book in hand, saying he could read and steer at the same time, as one was mental, the other mechanical.

'Luff!' said Williams.

Shelley put the helm the wrong way. Williams corrected him.

'Do you see those two white objects a-head? keep them in a line, the wind is heading us.' Then, turning to me, he said: 'Lend me a hand to haul in the main-sheet, and I will show you how close she can lay to the wind to work off a lee-shore.'

'No,' I answered; 'I am a passenger, and won't touch a rope.'

'Luff!' said Williams, as the boat was yawing about. 'Shelley, you can't steer, you have got her in the wind's eye; give me the tiller, and you attend the main-sheet. Ready about!' said Williams. 'Helms down—let go the fore-sheet—see how she spins round on her heel—is not she a beauty? Now, Shelley, let go the main-sheet, and boy, haul aft the jib-sheet!'

The main-sheet was jammed, and the boat unmanageable, or as sailors express it, in irons; when the two had cleared it, Shelley's hat was knocked overboard, and he would probably have followed, if I had not held him. He was so uncommonly awkward, that when they had things ship-shape, Williams, somewhat scandalised at the lubberly manœuvre, blew up the Poet for his neglect and inattention to orders. Shelley was, however, so happy and in such high glee, and the nautical terms so tickled his fancy, that he even put his beloved 'Plato' in his pocket, and gave his mind up to fun and frolic.

'You will do no good with Shelley,' I said, 'until you heave his books and papers overboard; shear the wisps of hair that hang over his eyes; and plunge his arms up to the elbows in a tar-bucket. And you, captain, will have no authority, until you dowse your frock coat and cavalry boots. You see I am stripped for a swim, so please, whilst I am on board, to keep within swimming distance of the land.'

The boy was quick and handy, and used to boats. Williams was not as deficient as I anticipated, but over-anxious and wanted practice, which alone makes a man prompt in emergency. Shelley was intent on catching images from the ever-changing sea and sky, he heeded not the boat. On my suggesting the addition to their crew of a Genoese sailor accustomed to the coast—such as I had on board the 'Bolivar',—Williams, thinking I undervalued his efficiency as a seaman, was scandalised—'as if we three seasoned salts were not enough to manage an open boat, when lubberly sloops and cutters of fifty or sixty tons were worked by as few men on the rough seas and iron-bound coast of Scotland!'

'Yes,' I answered, 'but what a difference between those sea-lions and you and our water-poet! A decked cutter besides, or even a frigate is easier handled in a gale or squall, and out-and-out safer to be on board of than an open boat. If we had been in a squall to-day with the main-sheet jammed, and the tiller put starboard instead of port, we should have had to swim for it.'

'Not I: I should have gone down with the rest of the pigs in the bottom of the boat,' said Shelley, meaning the iron pig-ballast.

When I took my departure for Leghorn on board the 'Bolivar', they accompanied me out of the bay, and then we parted. I arrived at Leghorn the same night. I found my Lord Inglese had at last mustered sufficient energy to move from Pisa to Monte Nero, near Leghorn; I condoled with him on the change, for his new flimsy-built villa—not unlike the suburban verandahed cockney boxes on the Thames—was ten times hotter than the old solid palace he had left, with its cool marble halls, and arched and lofty floors that defied the sun. He was satisfied with his boat, but by no means with its cost; he took little interest in her, and I could not induce him to take a cruise; he always had some excuse. The first time he came on board, he said in answer to something I pointed out in the rigging:

'People think I must be a bit of a sailor from my writings. All the sea-terms I use are from authority, and they cost me time, toil and trouble to look them out; but you will find me a land-lubber. I hardly know the stem from the stern, and don't know the name or use of a single rope or sail; I know the deep sea is blue, and not green, as that greenhorn Shakespeare always calls it.'

This was literally true; in regard to Byron, he neither knew nor cared to know, nor ever asked a question (excepting when writing) about sea-terms or sea-life.

On June 18, 1822, Shelley wrote to Gisborne: 'Hunt is not yet arrived, but I expect him every day. I shall see little of Lord Byron, nor shall I permit Hunt to form the intermediate link between him and me. I detest all society—almost all, at least—and Lord Byron is the nucleus of all that is hateful and tiresome in it. He will be half mad to hear of these memoirs.* As to me, you know my supreme indifference to such affairs, except that I must confess that I am sometimes amused by the ridiculous mistakes of these writers. Tell me a little of what they say of me besides my being an atheist. One thing I regret in it, I dread lest it should injure Hunt's prospects in the establishment of the journal, for Lord Byron is so mentally capricious that the least impulse drives him from his anchorage . . . The Williams's are now on a visit to us, and they are people who are very pleasing to me. But words are not the instruments of our intercourse. I like Jane more and more, and I find Williams the most amiable of companions. She has a taste for music, and an elegance of form and motions that compensate in some degree for the lack of literary refinement. You know my gross ideas of music, and will forgive me when I say that I listen the whole evening on our terrace to the simple melodies with excessive delight. I have a boat here. It cost me £80, and reduced me to some difficulty in point of money. However, it is swift and beautiful, and appears quite a vessel. Williams is captain, and we drive along this delightful bay in the evening wind under the summer moon until earth appears another world. Jane brings her guitar, and if the past and future could be obliterated, the present would content me so well that I could say with Faust to the passing moment "Remain thou, thou art so beautiful." Claire is with us, and the death of her child seems to have restored her to tranquillity. Her character is somewhat altered. She is vivacious and talkative; and though she teases me sometimes, I like her . . . Lord Byron, who is at Leghorn, has fitted up a splendid vessel, a small schooner on the American model, and Trelawny is to be captain. How long the fiery spirit of our pirate will accommodate itself to the caprice of the poet remains to be seen . . .'

Towards the end of June, 1822, the long expected family of the Hunts arrived by sea from England.

Byron observed, 'You will find Leigh Hunt a gentleman in dress and address.'

I found him that, and something more; and with a quaint

---

* See footnote p. 68.

fancy and cultivated mind. He was in high spirits, and disposed to be pleased with others. His anticipated literary projects in conjunction with Byron and Shelley were a source of great pleasure to him—so was the land of beauty and song. He had come to it as to a new home, in which as the immortal Robins* would have said: 'You will find no nuisance but the litter of the rose-leaves and the noise of the nightingales.' The pleasure that surpassed all the rest, was the anticipation of seeing speedily his friend Shelley. But, alas! all those things which seemed so certain:

> Those juggling fiends
> That keep the word of promise to our ear,
> And break it to our hope,†

so kept—and so broke—it with Leigh Hunt.

In his *Autobiography* Leigh Hunt, his mind turned querulous by remembered disappointment, painted a somewhat sinister picture of his first Italian meeting with Byron: 'In a day or two I went to see my noble acquaintance, who was in what the Italians call *villeggiatura* at Monte Nero; that is to say, enjoying a country house for the season. I there became witness to a singular adventure, which seemed to make me free of Italy and stilettos before I had well set foot in the country.

'The day was very hot; the road to Monte Nero was very hot, through dusty suburbs; and when I got there, I found the hottest-looking house I ever saw. It was salmon colour. Think of this, flaring over the country in a hot Italian sun!

'But the greatest of all the heats was within. Upon seeing Lord Byron, I hardly knew him, he was grown so fat; and he was longer in recognizing me, I had grown so thin. He took me into an inner room, and introduced me to Madame Guiccioli, then very young as well as handsome, who was in a state of great agitation. Her face was flushed, her eyes lit up, and her hair (which she wore hanging loose), streaming as if in disorder. The Conte Pietro, her brother, came in presently, also in a state of agitation, and having his arm in a sling. I then learned that a quarrel having taken place among the servants, the young Count had interfered, and been stabbed. He was

---

* Immortal, perhaps! But to the editor and to the compilers of reference books dead beyond resurrection, though possibly George Henry Robins (1778–1847), an auctioneer.

† Shakespeare. *Macbeth*, V. vii. 48.

very angry; Madame Guiccioli was more so, and could not admit the charitable comments of Lord Byron, who was for making light of the matter. They seemed to think the honour of their nation was at stake. Indeed, there was a look in the business not a little formidable; for though the stab was not much, the inflictor of it threatened more, and was at that minute keeping watch outside, with the avowed intention of assaulting the first person that issued forth. I looked out of the window, and met his eye glaring upwards like a tiger. He had a red cap on like a sansculotte, and a most sinister aspect, dreary and meagre—that of a proper caitiff.

'How long things had continued in this state I cannot say; but the hour was come when Lord Byron and his friend took their evening drive, and the thing was to be put an end to somehow. A servant had been despatched for the police, and was not returned.

'At length we set out, the lady earnestly entreating his lordship to keep back, and all of us uniting to keep in advance of Conte Pietro, who was exasperated.

'It was a curious moment for a stranger from England. I fancied myself pitched into one of the scenes in the *Mysteries of Udolpho*. Everything was new, foreign, and vehement. There was the lady, flushed and dishevelled, exclaiming against the "scelerato"; the young Count, wounded and threatening; and the assassin waiting for us with his knife. Nobody, however, could have put a better face on the matter than Lord Byron did,—composed, and endeavouring to compose: and as to myself, I was so occupied with the whole scene, that I had not time to be frightened. Forth we issue at the house door, all squeezing to have the honour of being first, when a termination is put to the tragedy by the man's throwing himself on a bench, extending his arms, and bursting into tears. His cap was half over his eyes; his face gaunt, ugly, and unshaved; his appearance altogether more squalid and miserable than an Englishman would conceive it possible to find in such an establishment. This blessed figure reclined weeping and wailing, and asking pardon for his offence; and to crown all, he requested Lord Byron to kiss him.

'The noble lord conceived such an excess of charity superfluous. He pardoned him, but said he must not think of remaining in his service; upon which the man renewed his weeping and wailing, and continued kissing his hand. I was then struck with the footing on which the gentry and their servants stand with each other in Italy, and the good-nature with which the strongest exhibitions of anger can be followed up. Conte Pietro, who was full of good qualities (for though he was here with his sister's lover, we must not judge of

73

Italian customs by English), accepted the man's hand, and even shook it heartily; and Madame Guiccioli, though unable to subside so quickly from her state of indignant exaltation, looked in relenting sort, and speedily accorded him her grace also, seeing my lord had forgiven him. The man was all penitence and wailing, but he was obliged to quit. The police would have forced him, if he had not been dismissed. He left the country, and called in his way on Shelley, who was shocked at his appearance, and gave him some money out of his very antipathy; for he thought nobody would help such an ill-looking fellow, if he did not.'

Byron wrote off to Moore: 'Leigh Hunt is here, after a voyage of eight months, during which he has, I presume, made the Periplus of Hanno the Carthaginian, and with much the same speed. He is setting up a Journal, to which I have promised to contribute; and in the first number the "Vision of Judgment, by Quevedo Redivivus", will probably appear, with other articles.

'Can you give us anything? He seems sanguine about the matter, but (entre nous) I am not. I do not, however, like to put him out of spirits by saying so; for he is bilious and unwell. . . . Do send Hunt anything in prose or verse of yours, to start him handsomely—any lyrical, *irical*, or what you please.'

Later in life the most able of the Hunt children, Thornton, recalled his impressions of the reunion between his father and Shelley, and how even as a small boy, he was moved 'by the shrill sound of his voice, as he rushed into my father's arms, which he did with an impetuousness and a fervour scarcely to be imagined by any who did not know the intensity of his feelings and the deep nature of his affection for that friend. I remember his crying out that he was "so *inexpressibly* delighted!—You cannot think how *inexpressibly* happy it makes me!" '

I I

SHELLEY, with his friend Williams, soon came in their boat, scudding into the harbour of Leghorn. They went with the Hunts to Pisa, and established them in Lord Byron's palace, Shelley having furnished a floor there for them. In a few days Shelley returned to Leghorn, and found Williams eager to be off. We had a sail outside the port in the two boats. Shelley was in a mournful mood; his mind depressed by a recent interview with Byron.

Byron, at first, had been more eager than Shelley for Leigh Hunt's arrival in Italy to edit and contribute to the proposed new Review [*The Liberal*], and so continued until his English correspondents had worked on his fears. They did not oppose, for they knew his temper too well, but artfully insinuated that he was jeopardising his fame and fortune, etc., etc., etc. Shelley found Byron so irritable, so shuffling and equivocating, whilst talking with him on the fulfilment of his promises with regard to Leigh Hunt,—that, but for imperilling Hunt's prospects, Shelley's intercourse with Byron would then have abruptly terminated; it was doomed to be their last meeting.

On Saturday, the 6th, Williams wrote the following letter to his wife at the Villa Magni.

'I have just left the quay, my dearest girl, and the wind blows right across to Spezzia, which adds to the vexation I feel at being unable to leave this place. For my own part, I should have been with you in all probability on Wednesday evening, but I have been kept day after day, waiting for Shelley's definitive arrangements with Lord B. relative to poor Hunt, whom, in my opinion, he has treated vilely. A letter from Mary, of the most gloomy kind, reached S. yesterday, and this mood of hers aggravated my uneasiness to see you; for I am proud, dear girl, beyond words to express, in the conviction, that *wherever* we may be together you could be cheerful and contented.

'Would I could take the present gale by the wings and reach you to-night; hard as it blows, I would venture across for *such* a reward. However, to-morrow something decisive shall take place; and if I am detained, I shall depart in a felúca, and leave

75

the boat to be brought round in company with Trelawny in the "Bolivar". He talks of visiting Spezzia again in a few days. I am tired to death of waiting—this is our longest separation, and seems a year to me. Absence alone is enough to make me anxious, and indeed, unhappy; but I think if I had left you in our own house in solitude, I should feel it less than I do now.— What can I do? Poor S. desires that I should return to you, but I know secretly wishes me not to leave him in the lurch. He too, by his manner, is as anxious to see you almost as I could be, but the interests of poor H. keep him here;—in fact, with Lord B. it appears they cannot do anything,—who actually said as much as that he did not wish(?) his name to be attached to the work, and of course to theirs.

'In Lord Byron's family all is confusion;—the cut-throats he is so desirous to have about him, have involved him in a second row; and although the present banishment of the Gambas from Tuscany is attributed to the first affair of the dragoon, the continued disturbances among his and their servants is, I am sure, the principal cause for its being carried into immediate effect. Four days (commencing from the day of our arrival at Leghorn) were only given them to find another retreat; and as Lord B. considers this a personal, though tacit attack upon himself, he chooses to follow their fortunes in another country. Genoa was first selected,—of that government they could have no hope;—Geneva was then proposed, and this proved as bad if not worse. Lucca is now the choice, and Trelawny was despatched last night to feel their way with the governor, to whom he carried letters. All this time Hunt is shuffled off from day to day, and now, heaven knows, when or how it will end.

'Lord B.'s reception of Mrs. H. was—as S. tells me—most shameful. She came into his house sick and exhausted, and he scarcely deigned to notice her; was silent, and scarcely bowed.* This conduct cut H. to the soul; but the way in which he

---

* Mrs. Hunt had a poor opinion of Byron; he none of her, and less than none of her children, 'dirtier and more mischievous than Yahoos'. Mrs. Hunt confided to her *Diary*: 'Can anything be more absurd than a peer of the realm and a *poet* making such a fuss about three or four children disfiguring the walls of a few rooms. The very children would blush for him— fye, Lord B.—fye!'

received our friend Roberts, at Dunn's* door, shall be described when we meet:—it must be acted. How I long to see you; I had written *when*, but I will make no promises, for I too well know how distressing it is to both of us to break them. Tuesday evening at furthest, unless kept by the weather, I *will* say, "Oh, Jane! how fervently I press you and our little ones to my heart."

'Adieu!—Take body and soul: for you are at once my heaven and earth;—that is all I ask of both. E. ELK. W—.

'S. is at Pisa, and will write to-night to me.'

The last entry in Williams's Journal is dated July 4, 1822, Leghorn.

'Processions of priests and religiosi have been for several days past praying for rain: but the gods are either angry, or nature too powerful.'

The affair of the dragoon alluded to in Williams's letter, as connected with the Gambas was this: As Byron and his companions were returning to Pisa on horseback, the road being blocked up by the party,—a sergeant-major on duty in their rear trotted his horse through the cavalcade. One of the awkward literary squad,—a resolute bore, but timid rider,—was nearly spilt, from his nag shying. To divert the jeers from his own bad riding, he appealed pathetically to Byron, saying:

'Shall we endure this man's insolence?'

Byron said: 'No, we will bring him to an account'; and instantly galloped after the dragoon into Pisa, his party following. The guard at the gate turned out with drawn swords, but could not stop them. Some of the servants of Byron and the Gambas were idling on the steps of his palace; getting a glimpse of the row, one of them armed himself with a stable-fork, rushed at the dragoon as he passed Byron's palace, and wounded him severely in the side.

An onlooker described the incident thus: 'I saw Masi [the serjeant-major] tottering in the saddle, ride as far as Don Beppe's cafe, where, no longer able to sit his horse, his helmet fell off; his hair was standing on end, his face was as white as a sheet and he fell down exclaiming "I am killed!" '

---

* Henry Dunn kept the English shop in Leghorn.

This scene was acted in broad daylight on the Lung' Arno, the most public place in the city, scores of people looking on! yet the police, with their host of spies and backed by the power of a despotic government, could never ascertain who struck the blow.

Not liking to meddle with the Poet, they imprisoned two of his servants, and exiled the family of Count Gamba. Byron chose to follow them. Such is the hatred of the Italians to their rulers and all who have authority over them, that the blind beggars at the corners of the streets,—no others are permitted to beg in Tuscany,—hearing that the English were without arms, sidled up to some of them, adroitly putting into their hands formidable stilettos, which they had concealed in the sleeves of their ragged gaberdines.

Against this that arch-spy, the Cavaliere Luigi Torelli, insisted 'that Lord Byron has mounted two small piece of field-artillery at the door of his room, and keeps a quantity of guns, pistols and daggers on the table', while, wherever they found their weapons, there can be no doubt that the English in Pisa went about armed. 'I saw', wrote Guerrazzi, 'all the Englishmen . . . whether they were friends of Byron's or not, going off with their arms to his palazzo, to defend their great national poet. And then I thought if he had been an Italian, the Italians would have united to stone him. And so I began to understand why the English are a great people.'

Shelley wrote me the following note about the dragoon.

MY DEAR T., Gamba is with me, and we are drawing up a paper demanded of us by the police. Mary tells me that you have an account from Lord Byron of the affair, and we wish to see it before ours is concluded. The man is severely wounded in the side, and his life is supposed to be in danger from the weapon having grazed the liver. It were as well if you could come here, as we shall decide on no statement without you. Ever yours truly, SHELLEY.

Mrs. Shelley, writing an account of the row, says:

'Madame G. and I happened to be in the carriage, ten paces behind, and saw the whole. Taaffe kept at a safe distance during the fray, but fearing the consequence, he wrote such a report that Lord Byron quarrelled with him; and what between insolence and abject humility he has kept himself in hot water when, in fact, he had nothing to fear.'

On Monday, July 8, 1822, I went with Shelley to his bankers, and then to a store. It was past one P.M. when we went on board our respective boats,—Shelley and Williams to return to their home in the Gulf of Spezzia; I in the 'Bolivar' to accompany them into the offing. When we were under weigh, the guard-boat boarded us to overhaul our papers. I had not got my port clearance, the captain of the port having refused to give it to the mate, as I had often gone out without. The officer of the Health Office consequently threatened me with forty days' quarantine. It was hopeless to think of detaining my friends. Williams had been for days fretting and fuming to be off; they had no time to spare, it was past two o'clock, and there was very little wind.

Sullenly and reluctantly I re-anchored, furled my sails, and with a ship's glass watched the progress of my friends' boat. My Genoese mate observed,—'They should have sailed this morning at three or four A.M., instead of three P.M. They are standing too much in shore; the current will set them there.'

I said, 'They will soon have the land-breeze.'

'May-be,' continued the mate, 'she will soon have too much breeze; that gaff top-sail is foolish in a boat with no deck and no sailor on board.' Then pointing to the S.W., 'Look at those black lines and the dirty rags hanging on them out of the sky—they are a warning; look at the smoke on the water; the devil is brewing mischief.'

There was a sea-fog, in which Shelley's boat was soon after enveloped, and we saw nothing more of her.

Although the sun was obscured by mists, it was oppressively sultry. There was not a breath of air in the harbour. The heaviness of the atmosphere and an unwonted stillness benumbed my senses. I went down into the cabin and sank into a slumber. I was roused up by a noise overhead and went on deck. The men were getting up a chain cable to let go another anchor. There was a general stir amongst the shipping; shifting berths, getting down yards and masts, veering out cables, hauling in of hawsers, letting go anchors, hailing from the ships and quays, boats sculling rapidly to and fro. It was almost dark, although only half-past six o'clock. The sea was of the colour, and looked as solid and smooth as a sheet of lead, and covered with an oily

G

scum. Gusts of wind swept over without ruffling it, and big drops of rain fell on its surface, rebounding, as if they could not penetrate it. There was a commotion in the air, made up of many threatening sounds, coming upon us from the sea. Fishing-craft and coasting-vessels under bare poles rushed by us in shoals, running foul of the ships in the harbour. As yet the din and hubbub was that made by men, but their shrill pipings were suddenly silenced by the crashing voice of a thunder squall that burst right over our heads. For some time no other sounds were to be heard than the thunder, wind, and rain. When the fury of the storm, which did not last for more than twenty minutes, had abated, and the horizon was in some degree cleared, I looked to seaward anxiously, in the hope of descrying Shelley's boat, amongst the many small craft scattered about. I watched every speck that loomed on the horizon, thinking that they would have borne up on their return to the port, as all the other boats that had gone out in the same direction had done.

I sent our Genoese mate on board some of the returning craft to make inquiries, but they all professed not to have seen the English boat. So remorselessly are the quarantine laws enforced in Italy, that, when at sea, if you render assistance to a vessel in distress, or rescue a drowning stranger, on returning to port you are condemned to a long and rigorous quarantine of fourteen or more days. The consequence is, should one vessel see another in peril, or even run it down by accident, she hastens on her course, and by general accord, not a word is said or reported on the subject. But to resume my tale. I did not leave the 'Bolivar' until dark. During the night it was gusty and showery, and the lightning flashed along the coast: at daylight I returned on board, and resumed my examinations of the crews of the various boats which had returned to the port during the night. They either knew nothing, or would say nothing. My Genoese, with the quick eye of a sailor, pointed out, on board a fishing-boat, an English-made oar, that he thought he had seen in Shelley's boat, but the entire crew swore by all the saints in the calendar that this was not so. Another day was passed in horrid suspense. On the morning of the third day I rode to Pisa. Byron had returned to the Lanfranchi Palace. I hoped to find a letter from the Villa Magni: there was none. I told my fears to Hunt, and then went upstairs to Byron. When I told him, his lip quivered, and his voice faltered as he questioned me. I sent a courier to Leghorn to despatch the 'Bolivar', to cruise along the coast, whilst I mounted my horse and rode in the same direction. I also despatched a courier along the coast to go as far as Nice.* On my arrival at Via Reggio I heard that a punt, a water-keg, and some bottles had been found on the beach. These things I recognised as having been in Shelley's boat when he left Leghorn. Nothing more was found for seven or eight days, during which time of painful suspense I patrolled the coast with the coast-guard, stimulating them to keep a good look-out by the promise of a reward. It was not until many days after this that my worst fears were confirmed. Two bodies were found on the shore,—one near Via Reggio, which I went and examined. The face and hands, and parts of the body not pro-tected by the dress, were fleshless. The tall slight figure, the jacket, the volume of Sophocles in one pocket, and Keats's poems in the other, doubled back, as if the reader, in the act of reading, had hastily thrust it away, were all too familiar to me to leave a doubt on my mind that this mutilated corpse was any other than Shelley's. The other body was washed on shore three miles distant from Shelley's, near the tower of Migliarino, at the Bocca Lericcio. I went there at once. This corpse was much more mutilated; it had no other covering than,—the shreds of a shirt, and that partly drawn over the head, as if the wearer had been in the act of taking it off,—a black silk handkerchief, tied sailor-fashion round the neck,—socks,—and one boot, indicat-ing also that he had attempted to strip. The flesh, sinews, and muscles hung about in rags, like the shirt, exposing the ribs and bones. I had brought with me from Shelley's house a boot of Williams's, and this exactly matched the one the corpse had on. That, and the handkerchief, satisfied me that it was the body of Shelley's comrade. Williams was the only one of the three who could swim, and it is probable he was the last survivor. It is likewise possible, as he had a watch and money, and was better

---

* Trelawny hoped that the crew had been picked up by some outward-bound vessel.

dressed than the others, that his body might have been plundered when found.

Trelawny's earlier account of Williams's body contains more details and less squeamishness: 'It was a humbling and loathsome sight deprived of hands, one leg, and the remaining leg deprived of the foot—the scalp was torn from the head and the flesh separated from the face, the eyes out, and all this mutilation not by time the destroyer—but fish-eaten—it was in the worst state of putrefaction —a livid mass of shapeless flesh. Lord B. looking at it said—"Are we all to resemble that?—why it might be the carcase of a sheep for all I can see"—and pointing to the black handkerchief said, "An old rag retains its form longer than a dead body—what a nauseous and disgusting sight." '

Shelley always declared that in case of wreck he would vanish instantly, and not imperil valuable lives by permitting others to aid in saving his, which he looked upon as valueless. It was not until three weeks after the wreck of the boat that a third body was found—four miles from the other two. This I concluded to be that of the sailor boy, Charles Vivian, although it was a mere skeleton, and impossible to be identified. It was buried in the sand, above the reach of the waves. I mounted my horse, and rode to the Gulf of Spezzia, put up my horse, and walked until I caught sight of the lone house on the sea-shore in which Shelley and Williams had dwelt, and where their widows still lived. Hitherto in my frequent visits—in the absence of direct evidence to the contrary—I had buoyed up their spirits by maintaining that it was not impossible but that the friends still lived; now I had to extinguish the last hope of these forlorn women. I had ridden fast, to prevent any ruder messenger from bursting in upon them. As I stood on the threshold of their house, the bearer, or rather confirmer, of news which would rack every fibre of their quivering frames to the utmost, I paused, and, looking at the sea, my memory reverted to our joyous parting only a few days before.

The two families, then, had all been in the verandah, overhanging a sea so clear and calm that every star was reflected on the water, as if it had been a mirror; the young mothers singing some merry tune, with the accompaniment of a guitar. Shelley's shrill laugh—I heard it still—rang in my ears, with

Williams's friendly hail, the general *buona notte* of all the joyous party, and the earnest entreaty to me to return as soon as possible, and not to forget the commissions they had severally given me. I was in a small boat beneath them, slowly rowing myself on board the 'Bolivar', at anchor in the bay, loath to part from what I verily believed to have been at that time the most united, and happiest, set of human beings in the whole world. And now by the blow of an idle puff of wind the scene was changed. Such is human happiness.

My reverie was broken by a shriek from the nurse Caterina, as, crossing the hall, she saw me in the doorway. After asking her a few questions, I went up the stairs, and, unannounced, entered the room. I neither spoke, nor did they question me. Mrs. Shelley's large grey eyes were fixed on my face. I turned away. Unable to bear this horrid silence, with a convulsive effort she exclaimed:

'Is there no hope?'

I did not answer, but left the room, and sent the servant with the children to them.

The following is Mary Shelley's account of the fatal voyage: 'The heats set in, in the middle of June; the days became excessively hot, but the sea breeze cooled the air at noon, and extreme heat always put Shelley in spirits: a long drought had preceded the heat, and prayers for rain were being put up in the churches, and processions of relics for the same effect took place in every town. At this time we received letters announcing the arrival of Leigh Hunt at Pisa. Shelley was very eager to see him. I was confined to my room by severe illness, and could not move; it was agreed that Shelley and Williams should go to Leghorn in the boat. Strange that no fear of danger crossed our minds! Living on the sea-shore, the ocean became as a plaything: as a child may sport with a lighted stick, till a spark inflames a forest and spreads destruction over all, so did we fearlessly and blindly tamper with danger, and make a game of the terrors of the ocean. Our Italian neighbours even trusted themselves as far as Massa in the skiff; and the running down the line of coast to Leghorn, gave no more notion of peril than a fair-weather island navigation would have done to those who had never seen the sea. Once, some months before, Trelawny had raised a warning voice as to the difference of our calm bay, and the open sea beyond; but Shelley and his friend, with their one sailor boy, thought themselves a match for the storms of the Mediterranean, in a boat which they looked upon as equal to all it was put to do.

'On the 1st of July they left us. If ever shadow of future ill darkened the present hour, such was over my mind when they went. During the whole of our stay at Lerici, an intense presentiment of coming evil brooded over my mind, and covered this beautiful place, and genial summer, with the shadow of coming misery—I had vainly struggled with these emotions—they seemed accounted for by my illness, but at this hour of separation they recurred with renewed violence. I did not anticipate danger for them, but a vague expectation of evil shook me to agony, and I could scarcely bring myself to let them go. The day was calm and clear, and a fine breeze rising at twelve they weighed for Leghorn; they made the run of about fifty miles in seven hours and a half: the "Bolivar" was in port, and the regulations of the health-office not permitting them to go on shore after sunset, they borrowed cushions from the larger vessel, and slept on board their boat.

'They spent a week at Pisa and Leghorn. The want of rain was severely felt in the country. The weather continued sultry and fine. I have heard that Shelley all this time was in brilliant spirits. Not long before, talking of presentiment, he had said the only one that he ever found infallible, was the certain advent of some evil fortune when he felt peculiarly joyous. Yet if ever fate whispered of coming disaster, such inaudible, but not unfelt, prognostics hovered around us. The beauty of the place seemed unearthly in its excess: the distance we were at from all signs of civilisation, the sea at our feet, its murmurs or its roaring for ever in our ears,—all these things led the mind to brood over strange thoughts, and, lifting it from everyday life, caused it to be familiar with the unreal. A sort of spell surrounded us, and each day, as the voyagers did not return, we grew restless and disquieted, and yet, strange to say, we were not fearful of the most apparent danger.

'The spell snapped, it was all over; an interval of agonising doubt —of days passed in miserable journeys to gain tidings, of hopes that took firmer root, even as they were more baseless—were changed to the certainty of the death that eclipsed all happiness for the survivors for evermore.'

The next day I prevailed on them to return with me to Pisa. The misery of that night and the journey of the next day, and of many days and nights that followed, I can neither describe nor forget. It was ultimately determined by those most interested, that Shelley's remains should be removed from where they lay, and conveyed to Rome, to be interred near the bodies of his child, and of his friend Keats, with a suitable monument, and that Williams's remains should be taken to England. To do this, in their then far advanced state of decomposition, and to obviate the obstacles offered by the quarantine laws, the ancient custom of burning and reducing the body to ashes was suggested. I wrote to our minister at Florence, Dawkins, on the subject, and solicited his friendly intercession with the Lucchese and Florentine governments, that I might be furnished with authority to accomplish our purpose.

The following was his answer:

DEAR SIR, An order was sent yesterday from hence to the Governor of Via Reggio, to deliver up the remains of Mr. Shelley to you, or any person empowered by you to receive them.

I said they were to be removed to Leghorn for interment, but that need not bind you. If they go by sea, the governor will give you the papers necessary to insure their admittance elsewhere. If they travel by land, they must be accompanied by a guard as far as the frontier,—a precaution always taken to prevent the possibility of infection. Quick-lime has been thrown into the graves, as is usual in similar cases.

With respect to the removal of the other corpse, I can tell you nothing till I hear from Florence. I applied for the order as soon as I received your letter, and I expect an answer to my letter by to-morrow's post.

I am very sensible of Lord Byron's kindness, and should have called upon him when I passed through Pisa, had he been anybody but Lord Byron. Do not mention trouble; I am here to take as much as my countrymen think proper to give me; and all I ask in return is fair play and good humour, which I am sure I shall always find in the S. S. S.* Believe me, dear sir, Yours very faithfully, W. DAWKINS.

Such were his subsequent influence and energy, that he ultimately overcame all the obstacles and repugnance of the Italians to sanction such an unprecedented proceeding in their territories.

---

* *Su Seguro Servidor.*

I 2

I GOT a furnace made at Leghorn, of iron-bars and strong sheet-iron, supported on a stand, and laid in a stock of fuel, and such things as were said to be used by Shelley's much loved Hellenes on their funeral pyres.

On August 13, 1822, I went on board the 'Bolivar', with an English acquaintance, having written to Byron and Hunt to say I would send them word when everything was ready, as they wished to be present. I had previously engaged two large feluccas, with drags and tackling, to go before, and endeavour to find the place where Shelley's boat had foundered; the captain of one of the feluccas having asserted that he was out in the fatal squall, and had seen Shelley's boat go down off Via Reggio, with all sail set. With light and fitful breezes we were eleven hours reaching our destination—the tower of Migliarino, at the Bocca Lericcio, in the Tuscan States. There was a village there, and about two miles from that place Williams was buried. So I anchored, landed, called on the officer in command, a major, and told him my object in coming, of which he was already apprised by his own government. He assured me I should have every aid from him. As it was too late in the day to commence operations, we went to the only inn in the place, and I wrote to Byron to be with us next day at noon. The major sent my letter to Pisa by a dragoon, and made arrangements for the next day. In the morning he was with us early, and gave me a note from Byron, to say he would join us as near noon as he could. At ten we went on board the commandant's boat, with a squad of soldiers in working dresses, armed with mattocks and spades, an officer of the quarantine service, and some of his crew. They had their peculiar tools, so fashioned as to do their work without coming into personal contact with things that might be infectious—long handled tongs, nippers, poles with iron hooks and spikes, and divers others that gave one a lively idea of the implements of torture devised by the holy inquisitors. Thus freighted, we started, my own boat following with the furnace, and the things I had brought from Leghorn. We pulled along the shore for some distance, and landed at a line of strong posts and railings which projected into the sea—forming the boundary dividing the Tuscan and Lucchese States. We walked along the shore to the grave, where Byron and Hunt soon joined us: they, too, had an officer and soldiers from the tower of Migliarino, an officer of the Health Office, and some dismounted dragoons, so we were surrounded by soldiers, but they kept the ground clear, and readily lent their aid. There was a considerable gathering of spectators from the neighbourhood, and many ladies richly dressed were amongst them. The spot where the body lay was marked by the gnarled root of a pine tree.

A rude hut, built of young pine-tree stems, and wattled with their branches, to keep the sun and rain out, and thatched with reeds, stood on the beach to shelter the look-out man on duty. A few yards from this was the grave, which we commenced opening—the Gulf of Spezzia and Leghorn at equal distances of twenty-two miles from us. As to fuel I might have saved myself the trouble of bringing any, for there was an ample supply of broken spars and planks cast on the shore from wrecks, besides the fallen and decaying timber in a stunted pine forest close at hand. The soldiers collected fuel whilst I erected the furnace, and then the men of the Health Office set to work, shovelling away the sand which covered the body, while we gathered round, watching anxiously. The first indication of their having found the body, was the appearance of the end of a black silk handkerchief—I grubbed this out with a stick, for we were not allowed to touch anything with our hands—then some shreds of linen were met with, and a boot with the bone of the leg and the foot in it. On the removal of a layer of brushwood, all that now remained of my lost friend was exposed—a shapeless mass of bones and flesh. The limbs separated from the trunk on being touched.

'Is that a human body?' exclaimed Byron; 'why it's more like the carcase of a sheep, or any other animal, than a man: this is a satire on our pride and folly.'

I pointed to the letters E. E. W. on the black silk handkerchief.

Byron looking on, muttered, 'The entrails of a worm hold together longer than the potter's clay, of which man is made.

87

Hold! let me see the jaw,' he added, as they were removing the skull, 'I can recognise any one by the teeth, with whom I have talked. I always watch the lips and mouth: they tell what the tongue and eyes try to conceal.'

I had a boot of Williams's with me; it exactly corresponded with the one found in the grave. The remains were removed piecemeal into the furnace.

'Don't repeat this with me,' said Byron; 'let my carcase rot where it falls.'

The funereal pyre was now ready; I applied the fire, and the materials being dry and resinous the pine-wood burnt furiously, and drove us back. It was hot enough before, there was no breath of air, and the loose sand scorched our feet. As soon as the flames became clear, and allowed us to approach, we threw frankincense and salt into the furnace, and poured a flask of wine and oil over the body. The Greek oration was omitted, for we had lost our Hellenic bard. It was now so insufferably hot that the officers and soldiers were all seeking shade.

'Let us try the strength of these waters that drowned our friends,' said Byron, with his usual audacity. 'How far out do you think they were when their boat sank?'

'If you don't wish to be put into the furnace, you had better not try; you are not in condition.'

He stripped, and went into the water, and so did I and my companion. Before we got a mile out, Byron was sick, and persuaded to return to the shore. My companion, too, was seized with cramp, and reached the land by my aid. At four o'clock the funereal pyre burnt low, and when we uncovered the furnace, nothing remained in it but dark-coloured ashes, with fragments of the larger bones. Poles were now put under the red-hot furnace, and it was gradually cooled in the sea. I gathered together the human ashes, and placed them in a small oak-box, bearing an inscription on a brass plate, screwed it down, and placed it in Byron's carriage. He returned with Hunt to Pisa, promising to be with us on the following day at Via Reggio. I returned with my party in the same way we came, and supped and slept at the inn. On the following morning we went on board the same boats, with the same things and party, and rowed down the little river near Via Reggio to the sea, pulled along the coast towards Massa, then landed, and began our preparations as before.

Three white wands had been stuck in the sand to mark the Poet's grave, but as they were at some distance from each other, we had to cut a trench thirty yards in length, in the line of the sticks, to ascertain the exact spot, and it was nearly an hour before we came upon the grave.

In the mean time Byron and Leigh Hunt arrived in the carriage, attended by soldiers, and the Health Officer, as before. The lonely and grand scenery that surrounded us so exactly harmonised with Shelley's genius, that I could imagine his spirit soaring over us. The sea, with the islands of Gorgona, Capraji, and Elba, was before us; old battlemented watch-towers stretched along the coast, backed by the marble-crested Apennines glistening in the sun, picturesque from their diversi-fied outlines, and not a human dwelling was in sight. As I thought of the delight Shelley felt in such scenes of loneliness and grandeur whilst living, I felt we were no better than a herd of wolves or a pack of wild dogs, in tearing out his battered and naked body from the pure yellow sand that lay so lightly over it, to drag him back to the light of day; but the dead have no voice, nor had I power to check the sacrilege—the work went on silently in the deep and unresisting sand, not a word was spoken, for the Italians have a touch of sentiment, and their feelings are easily excited into sympathy. Even Byron was silent and thoughtful. We were startled and drawn together by a dull hollow sound that followed the blow of a mattock; the iron had struck a skull, and the body was soon uncovered. Lime had been strewn on it; this, or decomposition, had the effect of staining it of a dark and ghastly indigo colour. Byron asked me to preserve the skull for him; but remembering that he had formerly used one as a drinking-cup, I was determined Shelley's should not be so profaned. The limbs did not separate from the trunk, as in the case of Williams's body, so that the corpse was removed entire into the furnace. I had taken the precaution of having more and larger pieces of timber, in consequence of my experi-ence of the day before of the difficulty of consuming a corpse in the open air with our apparatus. After the fire was well kindled we repeated the ceremony of the previous day; and more wine was poured over Shelley's dead body than he had consumed during his life. This with the oil and salt made the yellow flames glisten and quiver. The heat from the sun and fire was so intense that the atmosphere was tremulous and wavy. The corpse fell open and the heart was laid bare. The frontal bone of the skull, where it had been struck with the mattock, fell off; and, as the back of the head rested on the red-hot bottom bars of the furnace, the brains literally seethed, bubbled, and boiled as in a cauldron, for a very long time.

Byron could not face this scene, he withdrew to the beach and swam off to the 'Bolivar'. Leigh Hunt remained in the carriage. The fire was so fierce as to produce a white heat on the iron, and to reduce its contents to grey ashes. The only portions that were not consumed were some fragments of bones, the jaw, and the skull, but what surprised us all, was that the heart remained entire. In snatching this relic from the fiery furnace, my hand was severely burnt; and had any one seen me do the act I should have been put into quarantine.

After cooling the iron machine in the sea, I collected the human ashes and placed them in a box, which I took on board the 'Bolivar'. Byron and Hunt retraced their steps to their home, and the officers and soldiers returned to their quarters. I liberally rewarded the men for the admirable manner in which they behaved during the two days they had been with us.

As I undertook and executed this novel ceremony, I have been thus tediously minute in describing it.

Byron's idle talk during the exhumation of Williams's remains, did not proceed from want of feeling, but from his anxiety to conceal what he felt from others. When confined to his bed and racked by spasms, which threatened his life, I have heard him talk in a much more unorthodox fashion, the instant he could muster breath to banter. He had been taught during his town-life, that any exhibition of sympathy or feeling was maudlin and unmanly, and that the appearance of daring and indifference, denoted blood and high breeding.

In his *Autobiography* Hunt described the scene thus: 'The remains of Shelley and Mr. Williams were burnt after the good ancient fashion, and gathered into coffers. Those of Mr. Williams were subsequently taken to England. Shelley's were interred at Rome, in the

Protestant burial-ground, the place which he had so touchingly described in recording its reception of Keats. The ceremony of the burning was alike beautiful and distressing. Trelawny, who had been the chief person concerned in ascertaining the fate of his friends, completed his kindness by taking the most active part on this last mournful occasion. He and his friend Captain Shenley were first upon the ground, attended by proper assistants. Lord Byron and myself arrived shortly afterwards. His lordship got out of his carriage, but wandered away from the spectacle, and did not see it. I remained inside the carriage, now looking on, now drawing back with feelings that were not to be witnessed.

'None of the mourners, however, refused themselves the little comfort of supposing, that lovers of books and antiquity, like Shelley and his companion, Shelley in particular with his Greek enthusiasm, would not have been sorry to foresee this part of their fate. The mortal part of him, too, was saved from corruption; not the least extraordinary part of his history. Among the materials for burning, as many of the gracefuller and more classical articles as could be procured—frankincense, wine, etc.—were not forgotten; and to these Keats's volume was added. The beauty of the flame arising from the funeral pile was extraordinary. The weather was beautifully fine. The Mediterranean, now soft and lucid, kissed the shore as if to make peace with it. The yellow sand and blue sky were intensely contrasted with one another: marble mountains touched the air with coolness; and the flame of the fire bore away towards heaven in vigorous amplitude, waving and quivering with a brightness of inconceivable beauty. It seemed as though it contained the glassy essence of vitality. You might have expected a seraphic countenance to look out of it, turning once more before it departed, to thank the friends that had done their duty.

'Yet, see how extremes can appear to meet even on occasions the most overwhelming; nay, even by reason of them; for as cold can perform the effect of fire, and burn us, so can despair put on the monstrous aspect of mirth. On returning from one of our visits to the seashore, we dined and drank; I mean, Lord Byron and myself; dined little, and drank too much. Lord Byron had not shone that day, even in his cups, which usually brought out his best qualities. As to myself, I had bordered upon emotions which I have never suffered myself to indulge, and which, foolishly as well as impatiently, render calamity, as somebody termed it, "an affront, and not a misfortune". The barouche drove rapidly through the forest of Pisa. We sang, we laughed, we shouted. I even felt a gaiety the more shocking, because it was real and a relief. What the coachman thought of us, God knows; but he helped to make up a ghastly trio. He was a good-tempered fellow, and an affectionate husband and father; yet he had the reputation of having offered his master to kill a man. I wish to have no such waking dream again. It was worthy of a German ballad.'

In correspondence Byron himself said very little about the tragedy, though he always showed indignation about the injustice that had been done Shelley while he was still alive: 'You will have heard by this time that Shelley and another gentleman (Captain Williams) were drowned about a month ago (a *month* yesterday) in a squall of the Gulf of Spezia. There is thus another man gone about whom the world was ill-naturedly, and ignorantly, and brutally mistaken. It will, perhaps, do him justice *now*, when he can be no better for it.' (Letter to Moore, August 6, 1822.)

13

When I arrived at Leghorn, as I could not immediately go on to Rome, I consigned Shelley's ashes to our Consul at Rome, Mr. Freeborn, requesting him to keep them in his custody until my arrival. When I reached Rome, Freeborn told me that to quiet the authorities there, he had been obliged to inter the ashes with the usual ceremonies in the Protestant burying-place. When I came to examine the ground with the man who had the custody of it, I found Shelley's grave amidst a cluster of others. The old Roman wall partly inclosed the place, and there was a niche in the wall formed by two buttresses—immediately under an ancient pyramid, said to be the tomb of Caius Cestius. There were no graves near it at that time. This suited my taste, so I purchased the recess, and sufficient space for planting a row of the Italian upright cypresses. As the souls of heretics are foredoomed by the Roman priests, they do not affect to trouble themselves about their bodies. There was no 'faculty' to apply for, nor bishop's licence to exhume the body. The custode or guardian who dwelt within the inclosure and had the key of the gate, seemed to have uncontrolled power within his domain, and scudi impressed with the image of Saint Peter with the two keys, ruled him. Without more ado, masons were hired, and two tombs built in the recess. In one of these, when completed, I deposited the box, with Shelley's ashes, and covered it in with solid stone, inscribed with a Latin epitaph, written by Leigh Hunt. I received the following note at Leghorn previous to burning the body:

Pisa, 1st August, 1822

Dear Trelawny, You will of course call upon us in your way to your melancholy task; but I write to say, that you must not reckon upon passing through Pisa in a very great hurry, as the ladies particularly wish to have an evening, while you are here, for consulting further with us; and I myself mean, at all events, to accompany you on your journey, if you have no objection.

I subjoin the inscriptions—mere matter-of-fact memorandums—according to the wish of the ladies. It will be for the other inscriptions to say more. Yours sincerely, LEIGH HUNT.

PS.—Mrs. Shelley wishes very much that Capt. Roberts would be kind enough to write to his uncle about her desk, begging it to be forwarded as speedily as possible. If it is necessary to be opened, the best way will be to buy a key for that purpose; but if a key is not to be had, of course it must be broken open. As there is something in the secret drawers, it will be extremely desirable that as few persons meddle with it as possible.

PERCY BYSSHE SHELLEY, ANGLUS, ORAM ETRUSCAM LEGENS IN NAVIGIOLO INTER LIGURNUM PORTUM ET VIAM REGIAM, PROCELLÂ PERIIT VIII. NON. JUL. MDCCCXXII. ÆTAT. SUÆ XXX.

EDVARDUS ELLIKER WILLIAMS, ANGLICÂ STIRPE ORTUS, INDIÂ ORIENTALI NATUS, A LIGURNO PORTU IN VIAM REGIAM NAVIGIOLO PROFICISCENS, TEMPESTATE PERIIT VIII. NON. JUL. MDCCCXXII. ÆTAT. SUÆ XXX.

IO, SOTTOSCRITTA, PREGO LE AUTORITÀ DI VIA REGGIO O LIVORNO DI CONSEGNARE AL SIGNORE ODOARDO TRE-LAWNY, INGLESE, LA BARCA NOMINATA IL DON JUAN, E TUTTA LA SUA CARICA, APPARTENENTE AL MIO MARITO, PER ESSERE ALLA SUA DISPOZIZIONE.

MARIA SHELLEY

GENOVA, 16 SETT*bre*, 1822

To which I added two lines from Shelley's favourite play *The Tempest*.

> Nothing of him that doth fade,
> But doth suffer a sea change into something
> Rich and strange.

The other tomb built merely to fill up the recess, was likewise covered in in the same way—but blank without as within. I planted eight seedling cypresses. When I last saw them in 1844, the seven which remained, were about thirty-five feet in height. I added flowers as well. The ground I had purchased, I inclosed, and so ended my task.

Trelawny's original plans had been more elaborate, and, in his desire to find means of beautifying the grave, he had run foul of

JANE WILLIAMS

Keats's friend, Joseph Severn, who wrote to Browne: 'There is a mad chap come here whose name is Trelawny. I do not know what to make of him, further than his queer, and I was near saying, his shabby behaviour to me. He comes as the friend of Shelley, great, glowing and rich in romance. Of course I showed all my paint-pot politeness to him, to the very brim,—assisted him to remove the ashes of Shelley to a spot where he himself (when the world has done with his body) will lie. . . . I made the drawing which cost us some trouble, yet after expressing the greatest liking for it, the pair of Mustachios has shirked off from it, without giving us the yes or no —without even the why or wherefore. I am sorry at this most on Mr. Gott's* account, but I ought to have seen that this Lord Byron's jackal was rather weak in all the points that I could judge, though strong enough in stilettos.'

Shelley came of a long-lived race, and, barring accidents, there was no reason why he should not have emulated his forefathers in attaining a ripe age. He had no other complaint than occasional spasms, and these were probably caused by the excessive and almost unremitting strain on his mental powers, the solitude of his life, and his long fasts, which were not intentional, but proceeded from the abstraction and forgetfulness of himself and his wife. If food was near him, he ate it,—if not, he fasted, and it was after long fasts that he suffered from spasms. He was tall, slim, and bent from eternally poring over books; this habit had contracted his chest. His limbs were well proportioned, strong and bony—his head was very small—and his features were expressive of great sensibility, and decidedly feminine. There was nothing about him outwardly to attract notice, except his extraordinarily juvenile appearance. At twenty-nine, he still retained on his tanned and freckled cheeks, the fresh look of a boy—although his long wild locks were coming into blossom, as a polite hairdresser once said to me, whilst cutting mine.

It was not until he spoke that you could discern anything uncommon in him—but the first sentence he uttered, when excited by his subject, riveted your attention. The light from his very soul streamed from his eyes, and every mental emotion of which the human mind is susceptible, was expressed in his

---

* Joseph Gott (1785-1860), sculptor.

pliant and ever-changing features. He left the conviction on the minds of his audience, that however great he was as a Poet, he was greater as an orator. There was another and most rare peculiarity in Shelley,—his intellectual faculties completely mastered his material nature, and hence he unhesitatingly acted up to his own theories, if they only demanded sacrifices on his part,—it was where they implicated others that he forbore. Mrs. Shelley has observed, 'Many have suggested and advocated far greater innovations in our political and social system than Shelley; but he alone practised those he approved of as just.'

Godwin observed to me,—'that Byron must occasionally have said good things, though not capable, as Shelley was, of keeping up a long conversation or argument; and that Shelley must have been of great use to Byron, as from the commencement of their intimacy at Geneva, he could trace an entirely new vein of thought emanating from Shelley, which ran through Byron's subsequent works, and was so peculiar that it could not have arisen from any other source.' This was true. Byron was but superficial on points on which Shelley was most profound—and the latter's capacity for study, the depth of his thoughts as well as their boldness, and his superior scholarship, supplied the former with exactly what he wanted: and thus a portion of Shelley's aspirations were infused into Byron's mind. Ready as Shelley always was with his purse or person to assist others, his purse had a limit, but his mental wealth seemed to have none; for not only to Byron, but to any one disposed to try his hand at literature, Shelley was ever ready to give any amount of mental labour. Every detail of the life of a man of genius is interesting, and Shelley's was so pre-eminently, as his life harmonised with his spiritual theories. He fearlessly laid bare those mysterious feelings and impulses, of which few dare to speak, but in a form so purified from earthy matter that the most sensitive reader is never shocked. Shelley says of his own writings in the preface to the *Cenci*,—'they are little else than visions which impersonate my own apprehensions of the beautiful and the just,—they are dreams of what ought to be, or may be.' Whilst he lived, his works fell still-born from the press—he never complained of the world's neglect, or expressed any other feeling than surprise at the rancorous abuse wasted on an author who had no readers. 'But for them,' he said, laughing, 'I should be utterly unknown.' 'But for them,' I observed, 'Williams and I should never have crossed the Alps in chase of you. Our curiosity as sportsmen, was excited to see and have a shot at so strange a monster as they represented you to be.'

It must not be forgotten, that Shelley lived in the good old times, under the paternal government of the Tories, when liberal opinions were prohibited and adjudged as contraband of war. England was then very much like what Naples is now. Sidney Smith says:

'From the beginning of the century to the death of Lord Liverpool, was an awful period for any one who ventured to maintain liberal opinions. He was sure to be assailed with all the Billingsgate of the French Revolution; "Jacobin", "Leveller", "Atheist", "Incendiary", "Regicide", were the gentlest terms used, and any man who breathed a syllable against the senseless bigotry of the two Georges, was shunned as unfit for social life. To say a word against any abuse which a rich man inflicted, and a poor man suffered, was bitterly and steadily resented,' and he adds, 'that in one year, 12,000 persons were committed for offences against the Game Laws.'

Shelley's life was a proof that the times in which he lived were awful for those who dared to maintain liberal opinions. They caused his expulsion from Oxford, and for them his parents discarded him, every member of his family disowned him, and the savage Chancellor Eldon* deprived him of his children.

Sidney Smith says of this Chancellor, that he was 'the most heartless, bigoted, and mischievous of human beings, who passed a long life in perpetuating all sorts of abuses, and in making money of them.'

---

* John Scott, Earl of Eldon (1751–1838), Lord Chancellor 1801–1827. For forty years he opposed all religious and civil reform.

14

I⊤ is mentioned in my narrative, that when I left Leghorn, in the 'Bolivar', to burn the bodies, I despatched two large feluccas, with ground-tackling to drag for Shelley's foundered boat, having previously ascertained the spot in which she had been last seen afloat. This was done for five or six days, and they succeeded in finding her, but failed in getting her up. I then wrote the particulars to my friend Capt. Roberts, who was still at Genoa, asking him to complete the business. He did so, whilst I went on to Rome, and, as will be seen by the following letters, he not only found, but got her up, and brought her into the harbour of Leghorn.

Pisa, Sept. 1822

DEAR T., We have got fast hold of Shelley's boat, and she is now safe at anchor off Via Reggio. Every thing is in her, and clearly proves, that she was not capsized. I think she must have been swamped by a heavy sea; we found in her two trunks, that of Williams, containing money and clothes, and Shelley's, filled with books and clothes. Yours, very sincerely, DAN ROBERTS.

DEAR T., I consulted Ld. B., on the subject of paying the crews of the felucca employed in getting up the boat. He advised me to sell her by auction, and to give them half the proceeds of the sale. I rode your horse to Via Reggio. On Monday we had the sale, and only realised a trifle more than two hundred dollars.

The two masts were carried away just above board, the bowsprit broken off close to the bows, the gunwale stove in, and the hull half full of blue clay, out of which we fished clothes, books, spyglass, and other articles. A hamper of wine that Shelley bought at Leghorn, a present for the harbour-master of Lerici, was spoilt, the corks forced partly out of the bottles, and the wine mixed with the salt-water. You know, this is effected by the pressure of the cold sea-water.

We found in the boat two memorandum-books of Shelley's, quite perfect, and another damaged, a journal of Williams's, quite perfect, written up to the 4th of July. I washed the printed books, some of them were so glued together by the slimy mud that the leaves could not be separated, most of these things are now in Ld. B.'s custody. The letters, private papers, and Williams's journal, I left in charge of Hunt, as I saw there were many severe remarks on Ld. B.

Ld. B. has found out that you left at Genoa some of the ballast of the 'Bolivar', and he asked me to sell it for him. What a damned close calculating fellow he is. You are so bigoted in his favour that I will say no more, only God defend me from ever having anything more to do with him.

PS.—On a close examination of Shelley's boat, we find many of the timbers on the starboard quarter broken, which makes me think for certain, that she must have been run down by some of the feluccas in the squall. DAN ROBERTS.

An event so dramatic as the sudden death of Shelley was bound to breed a crop of legends. Of these the most persistent was the story that the boat had been sunk by pirates. It had its germ already in Trelawny's own evidence of his investigation among returning fishermen, where he tells (p. 80) how his Genoese mate thought that he had seen an English-made oar from Shelley's boat on board one of the vessels. It went the rounds of the Leghorn waterfront, where years later it was still current, and was picked up by Thornton Hunt: 'When Shelley's yacht was raised, a large hole was found stove in the stern. Shelley had on board a sum of money in dollars; and the supposition is, that the men on the other boat [an Italian boat which had been seen to follow the 'Don Juan' out of port] had tried to board Shelley's piratically, but had desisted because the collision caused the English boat to sink; and they abandoned it because the men saved would have become their accusers.'

In 1875 Trelawny's daughter, travelling in Italy, heard a rumour that in his dying confession, an old sailor had admitted that he was one of the crew of a ship which deliberately and with piratical intention rammed the 'Don Juan'. In this case the story was embroidered somewhat: the pirates were said to have thought Byron among the crew, and with him much gold. Trelawny, who could never resist a pirate-story, seized upon this legend and included it in his *Records*, but the evidence is against him.

Though Trelawny states (p. 80) that all other Livornese boats had returned safely to harbour, two craft had sighted the 'Don Juan' in difficulties. According to Taafe, the captain of the first of these had offered to take off Shelley and his party, and when they refused had

99

shouted, 'For God's sake reef your sails or you are lost.' One of the party, probably Williams, had tried to lower the sails, but had been prevented by another on board, probably Shelley. The crew of the second boat said very little, but as it seems likely that the 'Don Juan' sank finally as the result of a collision, it is more than probable that their silence was guilt-laden, caused rather by their consciousness of fatal error than by any remorse at their criminal intentions. At all events, as will be seen from Roberts's letters, neither money nor property had been stolen.*

Byron's spirit was always on the fret and fume to be doing something new and strange; he exhausted himself in speculating, plotting, and planning; but when it came to the point of execution, the inertness of his body and his halting gait held him fast, so that few men even amongst the poets did more in imagination and less in reality than he did. One of his pleas for hoarding money was, that he might buy a province in Chili or Peru, to which he once added archly, 'of course with a gold or silver mine to pay usance for my monies': at another time it was Mexico and copper; and when savage with the Britishers, he would threaten to go to the United States and be naturalised; he once asked me to apply to the American consul at Leghorn, and Commodore Jones of the American navy, then in the harbour, offered him a passage. Byron visited the ship, and was well pleased with his reception [see p. 59]; there was a beginning, but no middle or end to his enterprises. The under-current of his mind was always drifting towards the East; he envied the free and independent manner in which Lady Hester Stanhope lived in Syria, and often reverted to it. He said he would have gone there if she had not forestalled him.

Then his thoughts veered round to his early love, the Isles of Greece, and the revolution in that country—for before that time he never dreamt of donning the warrior's plume, though the peace-loving Shelley had suggested and I urged it. He asked me to get him any information I could amongst my friends at Leghorn of the state of Greece; but as it was a common practice of his to make such inquiries without any serious object, I took little heed of his request.

---

* For a detailed refutation of the piracy legend see the *Athenaeum*, December 25, 1875.

We were then at Pisa in the old palace, which he was about giving up, Mrs. Shelley having gone to Genoa, and taken for him the Casa Saluzzi at Albaro, near Genoa; the Hunts too were about moving to the same destination. I had determined to return to Rome, but stopped to convoy them in the 'Bolivar'.

When a lazy and passive master who has never learnt, or if he may have learnt has forgotten, how to put on his trousers, shave, or brush his hair, in a sudden ecstasy or impulse resolves to do everything for himself and everybody else, as Byron now attempted to do, the hubbub, din, and confusion that ensue are frightful. If the Casa Lanfranchi had been on fire at midnight it could not have been worse, nor I more pleased at escaping from it, as I did, under the plea of getting the flotilla ready at Leghorn.

In September we all left Tuscany, Byron by land, the Hunts in one felucca; and Byron's servants, and what the Yankee would have called a freight of notions, in another; for as Byron never sold or gave away anything he had acquired, there was all the rubbish accumulated in the many years he had lived in Italy, besides his men, women, dogs, and monkeys, and all that was theirs. In the 'Bolivar' I had only a few things, such as plate, books, and papers; we put into Lerici, and there all met again. I took Hunt to the Villa Magni where Shelley had lived. Byron came on board the 'Bolivar', we had a sail and a swim, after which he was seized with spasms and remained two days in bed. On my visiting him and questioning him as to his ailments, he said he was always 'bedevilled for a week after moving'.

'No wonder,' I answered, 'if you always make such a dire commotion before it.'

'Look in that book,' pointing to one on the table, *Thomas's Domestic Medicine*, 'look for a prescription.'

'For what? what is your complaint?' I said. 'How do you feel?'

'Feel! why just as that damned obstreperous fellow felt chained to a rock, the vultures gnawing my midriff, and vitals too, for I have no liver.' As the spasms returned, he roared out, 'I don't care for dying, but I cannot bear this! It's past joking, call Fletcher; give me something that will end it—or me! I can't stand it much longer.'

His valet brought some ether and laudanum, and we compounded a drench as prescribed in the book, with an outward application of hot towels, and other remedies. Luckily, the medico of Lerici was absent, so in two or three days our patient was well enough to resume his journey, and we all started for Genoa where we arrived without further accident.

All that were now left of our Pisan circle established themselves at Albaro—Byron, Leigh Hunt, and Mrs. Shelley. I took up my quarters in the city of palaces. The fine spirit that had animated and held us together was gone! Left to our own devices, we degenerated apace. Shelley's solidity had checked Byron's flippancy, and induced him occasionally to act justly, and talk seriously; now he seemed more sordid and selfish than ever. He behaved shabbily to Mrs. Shelley; I might use a harsher epithet. In all the transactions between Shelley and Byron in which expenses had occurred, and they were many, the former, as was his custom, had paid all, the latter promising to repay; but as no one ever repaid Shelley, Byron did not see the necessity of his setting the example; and now that Mrs. Shelley was left destitute by her husband's death, Byron did nothing for her. He regretted this when too late, for in our voyage to Greece he alluded to Shelley, saying, 'Tre, you did what I should have done, let us square accounts to-morrow; I must pay my debts.' I merely observed, 'Money is of no use at sea, and when you get on shore you will find you have none to spare'; he probably thought so too, for he said nothing more on the subject.

I was not surprised at Byron's niggardly ways, he had been taught them in boyhood by his mother. In early manhood he was a good fellow and did generous things; until bad company, called good society, spoilt and ruined him. To recover his fortune and sustain his pride, he relapsed into the penurious habits drilled into him in his youth.

At first, all had gone peacefully enough between Hunt and Byron at Albaro: 'Our manner of life was this. Lord Byron, who used to sit up at night writing *Don Juan* (which he did under the influence of gin and water), rose late in the morning. He breakfasted; read; lounged about, singing an air, generally out of Rossini; then took a bath, and was dressed; and coming downstairs, was heard, still singing, in the courtyard, out of which the garden ascended, by a few steps, at the back of the house. The servants, at the same time, brought out two or three chairs. My study, a little room in a corner, with an orange tree at the window, looked upon this courtyard. I was generally at my writing when he came down, and either acknowledged his presence by getting up and saying something from the window, or he called out "Leontius!" (a name into which Shelley had pleasantly converted that of "Leigh Hunt") and came up to the window with some jest or other challenge to conversation. His dress, as at Monte Nero, was a nankin jacket, with white waistcoat and trousers, and a cap, either velvet or linen, with a shade to it. In his hand was a tobacco box, from which he helped himself occasionally to what he thought a preservative from getting too fat. Perhaps, also, he supposed it good for the teeth. We then lounged about, or sat and talked, Madame Guiccioli, with her sleek tresses, descending after her toilet to join us. The garden was small and square, but plentifully stocked with oranges and other shrubs; and, being well watered, it looked very green and refreshing under the Italian sky. The lady generally attracted us up into it, if we had not been there before.' (Hunt. *Autobiography*.) But not for long. Too many differences of temperament, of upbringing and of manners, stood between the two; and there was always Mrs. Hunt (and the Hunt children) to exacerbate the distaste Byron felt for his guests.

The relationship between the two men set their mutual acquaintances to fierce partisanship which lasted throughout the lifetime of those who remembered both of them—and has not yet died down. Teresa Guiccioli was inevitably a supporter of Byron: 'If Lord Byron appeared to be in good spirits, Hunt called him heartless; if he took a bath, a sybarite. If he tried to make a joke with him, he was guilty of the insufferable liberties that a great nobleman will allow himself with a poor man. If he presented Hunt with numerous copyrights, with the sole intention of helping him, it could only be because he lacked an editor. If he was charitable, it was out of ostentation. If he was adored by the lady who regarded him as superior to the rest of humanity, it was because he had the soul of a slave and a mediocre intelligence. And finally, when he sacrificed all that he cared for, to serve the Greek cause, it was because he was tired of the sentimentality of Mme Guiccioli.' (*Vie de Lord Byron en Italie.*)

At about this time Byron wrote a letter defending himself against charges of treating Hunt in a niggardly fashion. The letter also gives some indication of his attitude to Hunt, as an acquaintance, to Shelley—and to friendship generally: 'I presume that you, at least, know enough of me to be sure that I could have no intention to insult

Hunt's poverty. On the contrary, I honour him for it; for I know what it is, having been as much embarrassed as ever he was, without perceiving aught in it to diminish an honourable man's self-respect. If you mean to say that, had he been a wealthy man, I would have joined in his Journal, I answer in the negative. . . . I engaged in the Journal* from good-will towards him, added to respect for his character, literary and personal; and no less for his political courage, as well as regret for his present circumstances: I did this in the hope that he might, with the same aid from literary friends of literary contributions (which is requisite for all journals of a mixed nature), render himself independent.

'I have always treated him, in our personal intercourse, with such scrupulous delicacy, that I have forborne intruding advice which I thought might be disagreeable, lest he should impute it to what is called "taking advantage of a man's situation".

'As to friendship, it is a propensity in which my genius is very limited. I do not know the *male* human being, except Lord Clare, the friend of my infancy, for whom I feel anything that deserves the name. All my others are men-of-the-world friendships. I did not even feel it for Shelley, however much I admired and esteemed him; so that you see, not even vanity could bribe me into it, for, of all men, Shelley thought highest of my talents,—and, perhaps, of my disposition.

'I will do my duty to my intimates, upon the principle of doing as you would be done by. I have done so, I trust, in most instances. I may be pleased with their conversation—rejoice in their success— be glad to do them service, or to receive their counsel and assistance in return. But as for friends and friendship, I have (as I already said) named the only remaining male for whom I feel anything of the kind, excepting, perhaps, Thomas Moore. I have had, and may have still, a thousand friends, as they are called, in *life*, who are like one's partners in the waltz of this world—not much remembered when the ball is over, though very pleasant for the time. Habit, business, and companionship in pleasure or in pain, are links of a similar kind, and the same faith in politics is another.'

The death of Shelley, and Byron's estrangement from Leigh Hunt, gave to Trelawny a new position with regard to Byron; a position which, according to Lady Blessington, Byron accepted: 'He said that since the death of Shelley, he had become greatly attached to Mr. Trelawny . . . for the devotion to the dead and such kindness to the

---

* See p. 107.

living as he had shown on that occasion. The distinguished bravery of this gentleman has created a lively admiration in the mind of Byron: who reverts with complacency to many instances of it witnessed by him since the commencement of their acquaintance. It sounded strangely enough in my ears to hear one Englishman praise another for bravery: a quality so indigenous in our countrymen as rarely to be made a subject of encomium: yet, Byron's being a life of contemplation and literary labour may account for the importance he attaches to more active pursuits.'

15

BYRON, in common with actors and other public characters, considered it indispensable to the preservation of his popularity that he should keep continually before the public; and that an alliance with an able and friendly newspaper would be an easy way of doing so. Not that he would or could submit to the methodical drudgery of continually writing for one, but that he might occasionally use it for criticising and attacking those who offended him, as a vent for his splenetic humours. Shelley, knowing Byron could not reason, and that his criticism degenerated into rancorous personality, opposed the scheme; still, Byron had a hankering to try his powers in those hand-to-hand conflicts then in vogue, even in the great Reviews. When he consented to join Leigh Hunt and others in writing for the *Liberal*, I think his principal inducement was in the belief that John and Leigh Hunt were proprietors of the *Examiner*; so when Leigh Hunt at Pisa told him he was no longer connected with that paper, Byron was taken aback, finding that Hunt would be entirely dependent on the success of their hazardous project, while he would himself be deprived of that on which he had set his heart,—the use of a weekly paper in great circulation.

In my Introduction to Leigh Hunt's *Autobiography* (Cresset Press, 1949) I attempted to outline the relationship between Byron and Leigh Hunt with particular reference to the publication and failure of the *Liberal*. Because the passage is so apposite I reprint it here: 'He [Hunt] lived for three-quarters of a century; he was born in 1784, the year that Dr. Johnson died, and when he himself died, in 1859, Bernard Shaw was already three years old; but despite his longevity and the variety of his acquaintance, he has suffered from being shown to posterity principally through the spectacles of the biographers of the more petulant contemporaries. He had many friends and surprisingly few enemies, but his disagreements still prejudice the judgment of readers because his two outstanding antagonists, Byron and Dickens, were of a quality that makes them the easy clay of biography. Byron has a school of devotees with temples in Albemarle Street and Athens; Dickens chalked his glorious caricatures on the walls of national memory and made them the symbols of an established religion.

'Towards Hunt, Byron behaved in his usual irritating and auto-cratic manner—and it must be admitted that his offensiveness had, in this case, more than usual justification. But his biographers cannot hide his weakness and, in consequence, they are almost reasonable in their counter-blows against the hard-hitting author of *Lord Byron and Some of His Contemporaries*. They do not deny the power of Hunt, but instead, they fling around their twentieth-century shoulders the lordly cloak of their hero—they praise, they patronise and then they gibe; but only the gibes cling.

'It was Byron who had first suggested the triple editorship of a periodical to be called the "Hesperides", and Shelley in his greatness of heart had called it a "generous proposal" that Hunt should be brought from England to Italy to take up his duties in the partner-ship. But Byron's suggestions were vain idylls; he liked the notion of playing patron to an unfortunate advocate of liberty, he savoured the grandiose quality of the gesture—Hunt, his wife, six children and a goat to be transported to Italy at his bidding—with more honesty, he relished the possibility of being able to print some of his most vituperative writing that could never find a public through his usual medium, his Tory publisher, John Murray. But, if the suggestion was Byron's, it was Shelley who insisted on its fruition; without Shelley's zestful urging Byron might well have left the idea unful-filled, as an *idea* as excellent and as warming as the gin and water by which it had first been inspired but as a *plan* less satisfactory and more inconvenient than another case of spirits.

'There was no obvious reason for the failure of their periodical once the editors had softened its precious name into the more human and more saleable *The Liberal*. They were all three skilled, and at times superlative writers, though only one, and that the least—Leigh Hunt—could be called a skilled editor. They also had powerful collaboration at home: Hazlitt (*My First Acquaintance with Poets* ap-peared in the third number), Hogg and Horace Smith as contribu-tors, and Hunt's experienced brother, John, as publisher. But there was no editorial direction; how could there be with three editors, so various in their views and yet all equally unbusinesslike? Mutual re-criminations about the position, liabilities and responsibilities of John Hunt wracked the tottering union, and the offences that the editors, each in his own genius, had cast in the teeth of London opinion, united the most desperate confederates in opposition to their endeavours. "The Tories were shocked that Lord Byron should grace the popular side by his direct countenance and assistance; the Whigs were shocked that he should share his confidence and coun-sels with anyone who did not unite the double recommendation of birth and genius—but themselves." The first reviews were slashing; the reviewers exclaimed with fine self-righteousness "that it was only to be expected": "The *Liberal* is the joint production of Lord Byron, the late Mr. Shelley, and Mr. Leigh Hunt, and some other translated cockneys; they [the readers] are, therefore, prepared for blasphemy and impurity of every kind to a certain extent, but we doubt that they can anticipate all the atrocity of the *Liberal*."

'In fact, despite the reviewers, the *Liberal* need not have collapsed (the first number made a profit of almost four hundred pounds), but Shelley was dead, and without Shelley's unifying enthusiasm the insidious differences of temperament between the surviving editors grew, sharpened and became cataclysmic. Byron wanted immediate and striking profits; the *Liberal* teetered between the black and the red. Hunt wanted collaboration and needed also security.

'Above all Byron wanted to be rid of the Hunts. Though he had vowed magnanimously on Shelley's death that he would stand to Hunt "in Mr. Shelley's place, and said that I should find the same friend that the other had been", he did not hide his dissatisfaction from the public, and Theodore Hook was able to write in *John Bull*: "[Byron] is weary and sick to death of the Hunts; he repents that he ever went into partnership with them in the money-making speculation of the magazine. He writes word that 'Hunt is a bore: he is', says his lordship, 'a proser; Mrs. Hunt is no great things; and the six children perfectly untractable'."

'Hunt would have left Italy but could not; Byron went his way to Greece.

'Venom spattered between the two and splashed into biography. But in the end it was the living Hunt and not the dead Byron who suffered most from their meeting and their parting.'

The death of Shelley, and the failure of the *Liberal*, irritated Byron; the cuckoo note, 'I told you so', sung by his friends, and the loud crowing of enemies, by no means allayed his ill-humour. In this frame of mind he was continually planning and plotting how to extricate himself. His plea for hoarding was that he might have a good round tangible sum of current coin to aid him in any emergency, as 'money,' he observed, 'is the only true and constant friend a wise man puts his trust in. I can now raise nine or ten thousand, and with that I can buy an island in the Greek Archipelago, or a principality of auriferous soil in Chili or Peru. Lady Hester Stanhope's way of life in

Syria would just suit my humour.' I urged him on, for I was bent on travel and willing to go anywhere. He exhausted himself in planning, projecting, beginning, wishing, intending, postponing, regretting, and doing nothing; the unready are fertile in excuses, and his were inexhaustible; so I determined to be off.

Here it may be useful to sketch in the background to events in Greece. The country had been under Turkish rule since 1460, but some traditions of national greatness survived, and Turkish methods of delegating authority provided the machinery for a nationalist administration.

The Ionian Islands, which come much into Trelawny's story, had been seized by the French in 1797. Two years later a combined Russian and Turkish force evicted the French, and in 1800 an independent republic was formed under the suzerainty of Turkey and under the protection of Russia. By the Treaty of Tilsit this arrangement was abrogated and in 1807 French troops returned; thereby constituting a direct menace to British power in the Mediterranean, and indirectly bringing Britain, long affected in national sentiment by the cause of Hellenism, into the sphere of Greek affairs. In 1809, 1810 and 1811 British troops captured all the Ionian Islands except Corfu and Paxos, and in 1814 the French surrendered the islands, which, by the Treaty of Paris, became a British Protectorate.

Meanwhile a developing sense of international justice, the widening influence of theories springing from the American and the French Revolutions, and the growing strength of British Liberalism had their effect both in Greece itself and on the imaginations and sentiments of people the world over.

Time and time again in his poetry Byron returned to the dream 'that Greece might still be free' and Byron's words in *Childe Harold*, written as early as 1810:

> Hereditary bondsmen! know ye not
> Who would be free themselves must strike the blow?
> By their right aims the conquest must be wrought?
> Will Gaul or Muscovite redress ye? no!
> True, they may lay your proud despoilers low,
> But not for you will Freedom's altars flame.
> Shades of the Helots! triumph o'er your foe!
> Greece! change thy lords, thy state is still the same;
> Thy glorious day is o'er, but not thy years of shame.

though they may have had little effect in Greece itself, roused strong emotions, and some activity, in the English-speaking world.

Nor had Shelley been without interest in the plight of Greece. In fact their mutual Philhellenism had been one of the strongest bonds between two poets who were otherwise so often incompatible. When, finally, the Greeks rebelled on April 22, 1821; when the Turks responded with savage vigour, hanging the Patriarch Gregorios in Constantinople, as the responsible head of all Christians under the Sultan, and massacring the inhabitants of the island of Chios, Shelley showed his indignation in the lyrical drama *Hellas*, 'a mere improvise'.

'The apathy of the rulers of the civilised world,' he wrote in his Preface to *Hellas*, 'is something perfectly inexplicable to a mere spectator of this mortal scene. We are all Greeks. Our laws, our literature, our religion, our arts have their root in Greece. . . .' And it is more than probable that, had Shelley lived, he too would have taken up arms for Greece.

This first Greek rebellion was ill-timed and organised by men who counted wrongly on Russian support, but nevertheless the insurgents met with considerable success in the Morea and the islands, and by the end of 1821 those areas were almost entirely cleared of Turks.

However, internal dissensions had set in, dissensions which were to delay tragically the eventual victory of the Greek independence movement. Local leaders mistrusted centralised organisation, some sought personal aggrandisement or wealth, others, like Mavro-cordato (who controlled Western Greece), dreamt of a new Hellas but lacked the military power and ability to bring their dreams into actuality. Fighters intrigued against politicians; the politicians were divided by differences of opinion about the possibility, worth and right of Russian intervention.

In the face of new Turkish threats, all these differences could be temporarily composed, as they were at the Assembly of Epidaurus in January 1822, and, with some show of unity, the Greeks could defeat Turkish efforts to subdue the revolt. But harmony never lasted for long. At the time when Trelawny 'determined to be off', faction was violent in Greece.

At this time a committee was formed in London to aid the Greeks in their war of independence, * and shortly after I wrote

---

* From 1821 there had been various attempts to raise, in England, money for the Greeks, and these efforts were intensified by news of the massacre of Chios (April 1822). But it was not until 3 March, 1823, that London had a

LEIGH HUNT

to one of the most active movers in it, Lieut. Blaquiere, to ask information as to their objects and intentions, and mentioned Byron as being very much interested on the subject of Greece; the Lieutenant wrote, as from the committee, direct to Byron, in the grandiloquent style which all authorities, especially self-constituted ones, delight in. In the early part of 1823 Blaquiere on his way to the Ionian Islands, stopped at Genoa, and saw Byron, whom he informed of his intention to visit Greece, in order to see how matters were progressing. He said that his lordship had been unanimously elected a member of the Greek Committee, and that his name was a tower of strength; he brought Byron's credentials, and a mass of papers. The propositions of the committee came at the right moment; the Pilgrim was dissatisfied with himself and his position. Greece and its memories warmed him, a new career opened before him. His first impulses were always ardent, but if not acted on instantly, they cooled. He was a prompt penman, often answering in hot haste letters that excited his feelings, and following his first replies up by others to allay their fervour, or as the Persians have it, 'eating his words'. But the Greek Committee were not to be fobbed off; they resolved to have him on any terms, so they assented to all he suggested. The official style of the documents sent by the committee, the great seal and the prodigality of wax and diplomatic phrases, as well as the importance attached to his name, and the great events predicted from his personal exertions, tickled the Poet's fancy,—and moreover they lauded and my-lorded him to his heart's content.

> With as little a web as this, will I ensnare as great a fly as
> Cassio. *

The negotiation with the committee occupied some months before Byron, perplexed in the extreme, finally committed himself. He might well hesitate. It would have been difficult to find a man more unfit for such an enterprise; but he had a

---

Committee equivalent to the many on the Continent. On that day twenty-five friends of Greece met at the Crown and Anchor in the Strand; among them was Byron's friend, Hobhouse. In the next years the numbers of the London Greek Committee rose to almost a hundred.

* Shakespeare. *Othello*, II. i. 169.

great name, and that was all the committee required. The marvel was that he lent it. Moore, Byron's biographer, suggests that he embarked in this crusade to rekindle his mental light and failing popularity, whereas the chronology of his works proves that his mental powers waxed stronger as he grew older, and that his last poems were his best. That envy, malice, and hatred be-dogged his steps, snarling and snapping, is true, but neither his power nor popularity had declined, nor did he think so. In after years, on my talking with the late Mr. Murray, his publisher, on this subject, he said, 'I observed no falling off in his Lordship's powers or popularity during the latter period of his life, quite the reverse; but I heard such general censures on him from literary and other people who frequented my shop, and they spoke in such a depreciating tone of his later writings, that I became greatly alarmed as his publisher; and as I entertained a warm personal regard for his Lordship, I lightly touched on the subject in my letters to him. I was a great fool for so doing, for Mr. Giffard, the ablest scholar of them all, and one who did not throw his words away, as well as a few men of the same stamp, occasionally dropped remarks which satisfied me I had done wrong in alluding to the subject, for it was after reading the latter cantos of *Don Juan* that Mr. Giffard said:

' "Upon my soul, I do not know where to place Byron. I think we can't find a niche for him unless we go back and place him after Shakspeare and Milton"—after a pause—"there is no other place for him." '

I observed to Murray that Moore had only seen Byron in society; his Life of his brother Bard was a mystification; his comments might be considered very eloquent as a rhapsody, if they had been spoken over the Poet's grave, but they give no idea of the individuality of the man.

'The most valuable parts of Moore's Life are the letters addressed to you,' I continued; 'and as they were designed for publication, you should have printed them with his prose works.'

Murray replied, 'You are quite right. If ever a statute of lunacy is taken out against me, it must be on the plea of my mad agreement with Moore for Byron's Life, by which I lost credit, and a great deal of money; but it is not too late to redeem my error so far as the public is concerned; rather than leave it as it is I will get Lockhart, or somebody else, to do the thing as it should be done.'

I have been seduced into this digression to show from what a small squad of malignants came the cry of Byron's failing powers and popularity.

Trelawny has little that is good to say about Byron, except when criticism of his Lordship would seem to ally him with Moore. However, in this case Trelawny would seem to be right. Byron's powers were not failing, he was merely growing middle-aged, and was making desperate attempts to hide the fact from himself. Teresa Guiccioli was physically demanding, Pisa was becoming monotonous. Byron wanted to write further cantos of *Don Juan*, but John Murray, 'the most nervous of God's booksellers' who 'prints for too many Bishops', was against the project.

Above all, Byron wanted to prove himself in action, an ageing man's obvious effort to reclaim an activity of youth. Hence his eagerness to respond to the calls from Greece, and, for the moment, the satisfaction of planning change: a move to Genoa out of the reach of Teresa.

In December, 1822, I laid up the Poet's pleasure-boat, paid off the crew, retaining the first mate in my service as a groom, and early in the following year, 1823, started on horseback— with the aforesaid sailor, mounted, to act as tender,—to take a cruise inland. So during Byron's negotiation with the Greek Committee, and Blaquiere's visit to Albaro, I was absent, but being apprised of what was going on I was not surprised when in Rome at receiving the following note:

June 15, 1823

My DEAR T., You must have heard that I am going to Greece. Why do you not come to me? I want your aid, and am exceedingly anxious to see you. Pray come, for I am at last determined to go to Greece; it is the only place I was ever contented in. I am serious, and did not write before, as I might have given you a journey for nothing; they all say I can be of use in Greece. I do not know how, nor do they; but at all events let us go. Yours, etc., truly, N. BYRON.

To show Byron's vacillating state of mind, I quote some passages from letters I received at that time.

Captain Roberts, in a letter dated May 26, 1823, Genoa, says, 'Between you and me, I think, there is small chance of Byron's going to Greece; so I think from the wavering manner in which he speaks of it; he said the other day, "Well, Captain, if we do not go to Greece, I am determined to go somewhere, and hope we shall all be at sea together by next month, as I am tired of this place, the shore, and all the people on it." '

Ten days after, in a letter dated the 5th June, Roberts writes me:

'Byron has sold the "Bolivar" to Lord Blessington for four hundred guineas, and is determined to go to Greece: he says, whilst he was in doubt, fearing it might prove a reality, he did not like to bring you here; now, he wishes much to see you to have your opinion as to what steps it will be most necessary to take. I have been on board several vessels with him; as yet he has not decided on any of them. I think he would find it answer, now he has sold the schooner, to buy the three-masted clipper we saw at Leghorn, to refit and arm her, as I am much of your way of thinking, for a big gun or two, and legs to run and wings to pursue, as the case may be, for the Greek waters are pestered with pirates. I have written by his desire to Dunn about her; if you come here by way of Leghorn, pray overhaul her, and then you will be able to give him your opinion. I think she will do excellently well, except the accommodation—the cabin is small. He has asked me to be of the party.'

Four days after I had received the above, Mrs. Shelley having just seen Byron, wrote me from Genoa, June 9th:

'Lord Byron says, that as he has not heard from Greece, his going there is uncertain; but if he does go, he is extremely desirous that you should join him, and if you will continue to let him know where you may be found, he will inform you as soon as he comes to any decision.'

This was not the last of Byron's counter-messages to me, besides commissions which I was urged instantly to execute; knowing him, I took no heed nor made any preparations until he wrote me that he had chartered a vessel. On the 22nd I received this note from him:

DEAR T., I have engaged a vessel (now on her way to Leghorn to unload), and on her return to Genoa we embark. She is called the 'Hercules'; you can come back in her, if you like, it will save you a land journey. I need not say I shall like your company of all things. I want a surgeon, native or foreign, to take charge of medical stores, and be in personal attendance. Salary, a hundred pounds a year, and his treatment at our table, as a companion and a gentleman. He must have recommendations, of course. Could you look out for me? Perhaps you can consult Vacca, to whom I have written on the same subject; we are, however, pressed for time a little. I expect you with impatience, and am ever yours, N. B.

Byron's letters to his literary allies were written carefully, expressly to be shown about. He said, on seeing the word *private* on a letter, 'That will insure its becoming public. If I really wish mine to be private, I say things that my correspondents don't wish divulged.' When he wrote on the spur of the moment his letters were often obscure and peevish; if he gave them to me to read, and I told him they would offend, he would rewrite them still more offensively. Omitting his more lengthy scrawls, as they would require tedious notes to explain them, I give two or three short samples of his ordinary natural style.

On his hearing that a naval officer of the 'Despatch' sloop of war had boarded his boat at Leghorn, and taken away her pennant, he wrote to me:

Pisa, August 10, 1822

DEAR T., I always foresaw and told you that they would take every opportunity of annoying me in every respect. If you get American papers and permission to sail under their flag, I shall be very glad, and should much prefer it, but I doubt that it will be very difficult. Yours, N. B.

Byron had a dispute with Captain Roberts on a very frivolous subject; he sent me a letter to forward to the Captain; I refused to forward it, saying it would not do, on which he wrote me the following.

Genoa, 9*m.* 28*d.* 1822

MY DEAR T., I enclose you a letter from, and another to, Captain R., which may be more to your taste, but at any rate it contains all that I have to say on the subject; you will, I presume, write and inclose it or not, according to your own opinion [it was one of his long-winded offensive epistles, so I did not send it]. I repeat that I have no wish for a quarrel, but if it comes unlooked for, it must be received accordingly. I recognise no right in any man to interfere between me and men in my pay, of whose conduct I have the best right to judge. Yours, ever and afterwards, N. B.

9th Month, 21d. [?] 1822

MY DEAR T., Thank you, I was just going to send you down some books, and the compass of the 'Don Juan', which I believe belongs to Captain Roberts; if there is anything of yours on board the 'Bolivar', let me know, that I may send it or keep it for you. I don't know how our account stands; you will let me know if there is any balance due to you that I may pay it. I am willing to make any agreement with a proper person in the arsenal to look after her, and also to have the rigging deposited in a safe place. I have given the boy and one of the men their clothes, and if Mr. Beeze had been civil, and Frost honest, I should not have been obliged to go so near the wind with them. But I hate bothering you with these things. I agree with you in your parting sentence, and hope we shall have better luck another time. There is one satisfaction, however, which is, that the displeasures have been rather occasioned by untoward circumstances, and not by the disposition of any party concerned. But such are human things even in little; we would hardly have had more plague with a first-rate. No news of any kind from England, which don't look well. Yours, ever and truly, N. B.

This referred to a threatened prosecution of his 'Vision of Judgment', which had been published in Hunt's *Liberal*.

'Towards the end of September [wrote Leigh Hunt] Lord Byron and myself, in different parties, left Pisa for Genoa. Tuscany had been rendered uncomfortable to him by the misadventures both there and at Leghorn; and at Genoa he would hover on the borders of his inclination for Greece. Perhaps he had already made arrangements for going thither.

'On our way to Genoa we met at Lerici. He had an illness at that place; and all my melancholy was put to its height by seeing the spot which my departed friend had lived in, and his solitary mansion on the seashore. Lerici is wild and retired, with a bay and rocky eminences; the people suited to it, something between inhabitants of sea and land. In the summer time they will be up all night dabbling in the water and making wild noises. Here Trelawny joined us. He took me to the Villa Magni (the house just alluded to); and we paced over its empty rooms and neglected garden. The sea fawned upon the shore, as though it could do no harm.

'At Lerici we had an earthquake. The shock was the smartest we experienced in Italy. At Pisa there had been a dull intimation of one, such as happens in that city about once in three years. In the neighbourhood of Florence we had another, less dull, but lasting only for an instant. It was exactly as if somebody with a strong hand had jerked a pole up against the ceiling of the lower room right under one's feet. This was at Maiano, among the Fiesolan hills. People came out of their rooms, and inquired of one another what was the matter. At Lerici I awoke at dawn with an extraordinary sensation, and directly afterwards the earthquake took place. It was strong enough to shake the pictures on the wall; and it lasted a sufficient time to resemble the rolling of a waggon under an archway, which it did both in noise and movement. I got up and went to the window. The people were already collecting in the open place beneath it; and I heard, in the clear morning air, the word *Terremoto* (earthquake) repeated from one to another. The sensation for the next ten minutes or so was very distressing. You expected the shock to come again, and to be worse. However, we had no more of it. We congratulated ourselves the more, because there was a tower on a rock just above our heads, which would have stood upon no ceremony with our inn. They told us, if I remember, that they had an earthquake on this part of the coast of Italy about once every five years. Italy is a land of volcanoes, more or less subdued. It is a great grapery, built over a flue. If the earthquake did not come, it was thought the crops were not so good.

'From Lerici we proceeded part of our way by water, as far as Sestri. Lord Byron went in a private boat; Trelawny in another; myself and family in a felucca. It was pretty to see the boats with their white sails, gliding by the rocks over that blue sea. A little breeze coming on, our seamen were afraid, and put into Porto Venere, a deserted town a short distance from Lerici.

'After resting a few hours, we put forth again, and had a lazy, sunny passage to Sestri, where a crowd of people assailed us, like savages at an island, for our patronage and portmanteaux. They were robust, clamorous, fishy fellows, like so many children of the Tritons in Raphael's pictures: as if those plebeian gods of the sea

117

had been making love to Italian chambermaids. Italian goddesses have shown a taste not unsimilar, and more condescending; and English ones, too, in Italy, if scandal is to be believed. But Naples is the headquarters of this overgrowth of wild luxury. Marino, a Neapolitan, may have had it in his eye when he wrote that fine sonnet of his, full of gusto, brawny and bearded, about Triton pursuing Cymothoe. (See *Parnaso Italiano*, tom. 41, p. 10.)

'From Sestri we proceeded over the maritime part of the Apennines to Genoa. Their character is of the least interesting sort of any mountains, being neither distinct nor wooded; but undulating, barren, and coarse; without any grandeur but what arises from an excess of that appearance. They lie in a succession of great doughy billows, like so much enormous pudding, or petrified mud.

'Genoa again! With what different feelings we beheld it from those which enchanted us the first time! Mrs. Shelley, who preceded us, had found houses both for Lord Byron's family and my own at Albaro, a neighbouring village on a hill. We were to live in the same house with her; and in the Casa Negrotto we accordingly found an English welcome. There were forty rooms in it, some of them such as would be considered splendid in England, and all neat and new, with borders and arabesques. The balcony and staircase were of marble; and there was a little flower garden. The rent of this house was twenty pounds a year. Lord Byron paid four-and-twenty for his, which was older and more imposing, and a good piece of ground. It was called the Casa Saluzzi. Mr. Landor and his family had occupied a house in the same village—the Casa Pallavicini.'

It was in Genoa that Byron met Lady Blessington, and for the moment his boredom evaporated. The meeting took place on April Fool's Day, 1823. Next day Byron wrote to Moore: 'Your other allies, whom I have found very agreeable personages, are Milor Blessington and *épouse*, travelling with a very handsome companion, in the shape of a "French Count"* who has all the air of a *Cupidon déchaîné*, and is one of the few specimens I have seen of our ideal of a Frenchman *before* the Revolution—an old friend with a new face, upon whose like I never thought that we should look again.'

The whole party delighted Byron, above all the beautiful and

---

* Count Alfred d'Orsay (1801–1852). Marguerite Blessington's *cavaliere serviente*. Son of one of Napoleon's generals, he was handsome and gloriously dandified. Blessington later married him to his only daughter, but the marriage was a failure, and after Blessington's death in 1829, the Count returned to Lady Blessington and was faithful to her for the remaining twenty years of her life.

intelligent Marguerite. 'Miladi,' he writes in the same letter, 'seems highly literary . . . She is also very pretty even in a morning.'

And, after a few moments of doubt, Lady Blessington liked Byron. It is of this meeting and of the Byron of April and May, 1823, that she writes: 'The impression of the first few minutes disappointed me, as I had, both from the portraits and descriptions given, conceived a different idea of him. I had fancied him taller, with a more dignified and commanding air; and I looked in vain for the hero-looking sort of person with whom I had so long identified him in imagination. His appearance is, however, highly prepossessing; his head is finely shaped, and the forehead open, high, and noble; his eyes are grey and full of expression, but one is visibly larger than the other; the nose is large and well shaped, but, from being a little *too thick*, it looks better in profile than in front-face; his mouth is the most remarkable feature in his face: the upper lip of Grecian shortness, and the corners descending; the lips full and finely cut. In speaking, he shows his teeth very much, and they are white and even; but I observed that even in his smile—and he smiles frequently—there is something of a scornful expression in his mouth that is evidently natural, and not, as many suppose, affected. This particularly struck me. His chin is large and well shaped, and finishes well the oval of his face. He is extremely thin, indeed so much so that his figure has almost a boyish air; his face is peculiarly pale, but not the paleness of ill-health, as its character is that of fairness—the fairness of a dark-haired person—and his hair (which is getting rapidly grey) is of a very dark brown, and curls naturally; he uses a good deal of oil in it, which makes it look still darker. His countenance is full of expression, and changes with the subject of conversation; it gains on the beholder the more it is seen, and leaves an agreeable impression. I should say that melancholy was its prevailing character, as I noticed that when any observation elicited a smile—and there were many, as the conversation was gay and playful—it appeared to linger but for a moment on his lip, which instantly resumed its former expression of seriousness. His whole appearance is remarkably gentlemanlike, and he owes nothing of this to his toilet, as his coat appears to have been many years made, is much too large, and all his garments convey the idea of having been purchased ready-made, so ill do they fit him. There is a *gaucherie* in his movements, which evidently proceeds from the perpetual consciousness of his lameness, that appears to haunt him; for he tries to conceal his foot when seated, and when walking, has a nervous rapidity in his manner. He is very slightly lame, and the deformity of his foot is so little remarkable that I am not now aware which foot it is. His voice and accent are peculiarly agreeable, but effeminate—clear, harmonious, and so distinct, that though his general tone in speaking is rather low than high, not a word is lost. His manners are as unlike my preconceived notions of them as is his appearance. I had expected to find him a dignified, cold, reserved and haughty person, resembling those mysterious personages he so loves to paint in his works, and with whom he has been so often identified by the good-natured world; but nothing can be more different; for were I to point out the prominent defect of Lord Byron, I should say it was flippancy, and a total want of that natural self-possession and dignity which ought to characterize a man of birth and education.' (*Conversations of Lord Byron with the Countess of Blessington.*)

For Byron the relationship that grew up between them was both restful and invigorating. He did not have to pretend that he was in love with her, but instead could talk freely to her about everything —particularly himself. There is an almost idyllic air in this description: 'When I looked on the calm and beautiful blue sea spread out to-day as we rode along, and the fair and fertile country through which we were passing, with the brilliant sky above us, and the musical voice of Byron sounding in my ears, my spirits felt relieved from the gloom that has clouded them of late, and I enjoyed the charms of this sunny land. Byron, too, admitted that the air and scenery produced an exhilarating effect on his spirits; but added smiling, "it is merely an affair of nerves, to which we are all more or less subject".

'He has a passion for flowers, and purchases bouquets from the venders on the road, who have tables piled with them. He bestows charity on every mendicant who asks it; and his manner in giving is gentle and kind. The people seem all to know his face, and to like him; and many recount their affairs, as if they were sure of his sympathy. Though now but in his thirty-sixth year, Byron talks of himself as if he were at least fifty, nay, likes to be considered old. It surprises me to witness the tenacity with which his memory retains every trivial occurrence connected with his sojourn in England, and his London life. Persons and circumstances, that I should have supposed could never have made any impression on his mind, are remembered as freshly as if recently seen. For example, speaking of a mutual acquaintance, Byron said "— was the first man I saw wear pale lemon-coloured gloves, and devilish well they looked".

'Strange that such a mind should retain such puerilities!

'Byron is neither a bold nor a good rider, although it is evident that he has pretensions to horsemanship; and the mode in which his horse is caparisoned would go far to prove this ambition.'

This new-found peace may have had some effect on Byron's negotiations with the London Greek Committee. He was no longer quite so anxious to be leaving for Greece, though the project was still uppermost in his mind. On May 10, Lady Blessington wrote: 'Rode out, and met Byron near Nervi. He talks of going to Greece, and made many jests on his intention of turning soldier. The excitement of this new mode of life seems to have peculiar attractions for him; and perhaps the latent desire of rendering his name as celebrated in feats of arms as it already is in poetry, influences him in this undertaking.'

And there were more valid reasons for delay than the presence of a charming woman. Byron wanted to help Greece, but how and where? No one seemed able to tell him, least of all the London Greek Committee which could sort out neither its own intentions nor the reports from the chaos in Greece.

Byron waited for instructions, but not idly. He was even prepared to say what those instructions should be, and in his sensible letter of May 12, 1823, he outlines his views on Greece and his ideas for the future activity of the Committee: 'I have great pleasure in acknowledging your letter, and the honour which the Committee have done me. My first wish is to go up into the Levant in person, where I might be enabled to advance, if not the cause, at least the means of obtaining information which the Committee might be desirous of acting upon. . . . The principal material wanted by the Greeks appears to be, first, a park of field artillery—light and fit for mountain service; secondly, gunpowder; thirdly, hospital or medical stores. . . . I am in correspondence with Signor Nicolas Karellas who is now at Pisa; but his latest advice merely stated that the Greeks are at present employed in organising their *internal* government. . . . The Turks are an obstinate race, and will return to the charge for years to come. . . . With regard to the formation of a brigade, I would presume to suggest that the attention of the Committee had better, perhaps, be directed to the employment of *officers* of experience, than the enrolment of *raw British* soldiers. . . .'

So Byron pours out his practical advice, together with sound military and political opinion. He wants engineers, he wants officers who can speak Italian, he wants all volunteers warned that they are due for hardships in Greece; he even suggests that Greece and the islands might be brought to the attention of the British public as suitable areas for speculation and emigration.

This is not the letter of a haverer, but the letter of a man who knows what he wants to do, if only others would make up their minds.

16

FORWARDING my traps to Leghorn, I was soon on the road to Genoa. My sailor groom had returned to his family, and I engaged an American born negro to fill his place. In Italy, I invariably travelled on horseback. The distances from one town to another are short, the scenery is varied, and the climate beautiful; besides, Italy is peculiarly adapted to this slow, yet only way of thoroughly seeing a country. Most travellers fly through in a string, like a flock of wild geese, merely alighting at the great cities. As the weather was hot and the days long, we started every morning at four or five o'clock, and jogged along until ten or eleven, then pulled up at town, village, or solitary locanda, or in default of these, looked out for a wood, dell, ruin, or other place that promised shade and water. Then dismounting we fed our horses from nose-bags, made up a fire, boiled coffee, breakfasted off such things as we had brought with us, smoked our pipes and fell asleep. Our provender was carried by the black, in old fashioned saddle-bags. In that fine climate our wants were so few, that they provided ample stowage room. I had two excellent Hungarian cavalry horses, bought from an Austrian colonel. Our usual day's travel was from thirty-five to forty-five miles; the best half of the distance, we always accomplished before breakfast, so that our day's journey was completed at four or five in the evening, and every day both horses and men improved in condition. If there is any healthier or pleasanter way of life than this, I can only say, I have never enjoyed it.

However long the journey, it was never tedious, and I always regretted its termination. I stopped two days at Florence, and then shaped my course for the sea-board, through Massa and Rapallo, Sarzana, Lerici and Spezzia, on which coast everything was familiar to me, and associated with the memories of my lost friends Shelley and Williams. My horses stopped at their accustomed locandas, and many familiar faces came out to welcome me.

I arrived early at Lerici, and determined to sleep there, and finish my journey to Genoa on the following day. In the evening, I walked to the Villa Magni, where the Shelleys had last lived, and the ground-floor having neither door nor window, I walked in. Shelley's shattered skiff in which he used to go adventuring, as he termed it, in rivers and canals, was still there: in that little flat-bottomed boat he had written many beautiful things:

> Our boat is asleep on Serchio's stream,
> The sails are furled like thoughts in a dream,
> The helm sways idly, hither and thither;
> Dominic, the boatman, has brought the mast,
> And the oars and the sail: but 'tis sleeping fast. *

And here it was, sleeping still on the mud floor, with its mast and oars broken. I mounted the stairs or rather ladder into the dining-room they had lived in, for this and four small bed-rooms was all the space they had. As I surveyed its splatchy walls, broken floor, cracked ceiling, and poverty-struck appearance, while I noted the loneliness of the situation, and remembered the fury of the waves that in blowing weather lashed its walls, I did not marvel at Mrs. Shelley's and Mrs. Williams's groans on first entering it; nor that it had required all Ned Williams's persuasive powers to induce them to stop there. We men had only looked at the sea and scenery, and would have been satisfied with a tent. But women look to a house as their empire. Ladies without a drawing-room are like pictures without frames, or birds without feathers; knowing this, they set to work with a will, and transformed it into a very pleasant abode.

One of the customs of the natives of this bay reminded me of the South Sea Islanders. At sunset the whole population of men, women, and children, took to the water, sporting in it for hours like wild ducks; we occasionally did the same, Shelley especially delighting in the sport. His wife looked grave, and said 'it was improper'. Shelley protested vehemently against the arbitrary power of the word, saying, 'Hush Mary, that insidious word has never been echoed by these woods and rocks: don't teach it them. It was one of the words my fellow serpent whispered into Eve's ear, and when I hear it, I wish I was far

---

* Shelley. *The Boat on the Serchio.*

away on some lone island, with no other inhabitants than seals, sea-birds and water-rats.' Then turning to his friend, he continued, 'At Pisa, Mary said a jacket was not proper, because others did not wear them, and here it's not proper to bathe, because everybody does. Oh! what shall we do.'

The next day I started at daylight for Genoa, and when I came near Albaro, I sent my horses to the city, and walked to the Casa Saluzzi; of which all the doors and windows were open, as is usual, in Italian country houses during summer evenings. I walked in, and as I did not see any of Byron's people, I looked into five or six of the fifty or sixty rooms, which the palace contained, before I found the Pilgrim's penetralia; he was so deeply absorbed that he did not hear my steps. There he sat with a pen in his hand and papers before him, with a painfully perplexed expression and heated brow, such as an inspired Pythoness might have had on her tripod.* I thought it a sacrilege to profane his sanctuary, and was hesitating whether I should retreat or advance, when his bull-dog Moretto came in from the hall: so I spoke to the dog.

Byron recognising my voice, sprang up with his usual alacrity and shook my hand with unusual warmth. After a hasty chat, he hallooed out lustily for his servants, for there were no bells: he was going out of the room, saying, 'You must be hungry, we will see what there is in the house.'

I assured him I was not, and that I could not stop, as I wished to see Mrs. Shelley† and the Leigh Hunts.

'Aye, aye,' he observed, 'they are flesh-eaters—you scorn my lenten fare, but come back soon, I will dispatch my salad and sardines, and then we will discuss a bottle of hock, and talk over matters; I have a great deal to tell you, but I must first balance these cursed bills; I have been an hour poring over this one you found me at, and my *tottle* don't square with Lega‡; in the time thus lost I might have written half a canto of *Don Juan*— and the amount of the bill is only one hundred and forty-three lire, which is not six pounds. In cases of lunacy, the old demon

---

* The priestess of Apollo at Delphi, who prophesied seated on a tripod.
† Mary Shelley soon returned to England—to 'this sunless country'—to sorrow and bitterness.
‡ Lega Zambelli, Byron's steward.

124

Eldon decided men's sanity by figures; if I had been had up before him (I was very near being so), and he had given me the simplest sum in arithmetic, I should have been consigned to durance vile:

> 'For the rule of three it puzzles me,
> And practice drives me mad.' *

In about an hour and a half, I returned to the Casa Saluzzi, and found the Poet, still hard at work on his weekly bills: he observed archly, 'I have found out in another account of the steward's, that he has cheated himself; that is his affair, not mine.' This put him in good humour, so he gathered up the scattered accounts and put them away. He then read me his correspondence with the Greek Committee, or rather the last portion of it, and a letter from Blaquiere, from Greece, and told me what he thought of doing. Promising to see Byron the following day, I left him and walked to my locanda at Genoa. It was plain enough from what I had just seen, that with regard to money, his mind had undergone no change. He thought he was in honour bound to go to Zante to meet Blaquiere—the rest seemed to depend on blind chance. The Committee suggested no definite plan, nor could he form one.

Mental as well as physical diseases are hereditary. Byron's arrogant temper he inherited, his penurious habits were instilled into him by his mother; he was reared in poverty and obscurity and unexpectedly became a Lord, with a good estate: this was enough to unsettle the equanimity of such a temperament as his. But fortune as well as misfortune comes with both hands full, and when, as he himself said, he awoke one morning and found himself famous, his brain grew dizzy, and he foolishly entered the great donkey sweepstakes, and ran in the ruck with his long-eared compeers—galled in the race, he bolted off the course, and rushed into the ranks of that great sect that worships golden images. If you come too near the improvident or the reckless, there is danger of being engulfed in the vortex

---

* Multiplication is vexation,
Division is as bad;
The Rule of Three doth puzzle me
And Practice drives me mad.
Nursery Rhyme.

they create, whereas with the thrifty, you may do well enough. Thus ruminating, I reached my inn, the Croce di Malta.

The next day Byron called, he wished me to go on board the brig he had chartered—'the Hercules', Capt. Scott,—to see her equipments and accommodations, and report thereon. I did so, and was very much dissatisfied. She was a collier-built tub of 120 tons, round-bottomed, and bluff-bowed, and of course, a dull sailer, with the bulkheads, the horse-boxes, and other fittings newly put up, ill-contrived, and scamped by the contractor. The captain, one of the rough old John Bull stamp, was well enough—the mate better, and no fault to be found with the crew, but that they were too few in number. For such an expedition we should have had a well-manned and fast-sailing clipper-built craft, adapted to the light winds and summer seas prevailing in the Greek Archipelago, so that after calling at the Ionian Islands, we could have used her as a yacht, run over to the Morea, touching at several ports not blockaded by the Turks, and ascertained the exact state of the war, its wants, capabilities, and more especially, the characters of those who conducted it. We might then have exacted conditions before committing ourselves to any specific line of action. Under the English flag, this and much more might have been done. On saying this to Byron, he answered:

'There was no other vessel than the "Hercules" to be had at Genoa.'

'Leghorn is the place for shipping,' said I.

'Why, then, did you not come here sooner? I had no one to help me.'

'You had Captain Roberts, the very man for the occasion; we might as well have built a raft and so chanced it.'

Then smiling, he replied, 'They say I have got her on very easy terms.'

'Aye, but the time she will be on her voyage, will make her a bad bargain; she will take a week to drift to Leghorn, and it should be done in twenty hours.'

'We must make the best of it. I will pay her off at the Ionian Islands, and stop there until I see my way, for here we can learn nothing. Blaquiere is to meet me at Zante by appointment, and he is now in the Morea.'

126

On the 13th of July, 1823, we shipped the horses, four of Byron's, and one of mine, and in the evening, Byron, Gamba, and an unfledged medical student with five or six servants embarked. I and my negro completed the complement. On my observing to Byron the Doctor would be of no use, as he had seen no practice, he answered, 'If he knows little I pay little, and we will find him plenty of work.' The next day it was a dead calm, so we re-landed; on the 15th we weighed anchor at daylight, several American ships in compliment to Byron, sending their boats to tow us out of the bay, but made very little progress; we lay in the offing all day like a log upon the main under a broiling sun,—the Italians skipping about, gesticulating, and chattering like wild monkeys in a wood. The Pilgrim sat apart, solemn and sad,—he took no notice of anything nor spoke a word. At midnight the sea breeze set in and quickly freshened, so we shortened sail and hauled our wind. As soon as the old tub began to play at pitch and toss, the noisy Italians, with the exception of the Venetian gondolier, Baptista, crept into holes and corners in consternation. The horses kicked down their flimsy partitions, and my black groom and I had to secure them, while the sea got up and the wind increased. I told Byron that we must bear up for port, or we should lose our cattle—'Do as you like,' he said. So we bore up, and after a rough night, re-anchored in our former berth; as the sun rose the wind died away, and one by one the land-lubbers crawled on deck. Byron having remained all night on deck, laughed at the miserable figure they cut; they all went on shore, and I set to work with two or three English carpenters to repair damages.

In the evening we took a fresh departure, and the weather continuing fine, we had no other delay than that which arose from the bad sailing qualities of our vessel. We were five days on our passage to Leghorn, not averaging more than twenty miles a day. We all messed and most of us slept, on deck. Byron unusually silent and serious, was generally during the day reading Scott's *Life of Swift*, Col. Hippesley's *Expedition to*

South America, Grimm's *Correspondence*, or *Rochefoucault*. This was his usual style of reading on shore. We were two days at Leghorn completing our sea stores. A Mr. Hamilton Brown[e] and two Greeks, who had previously applied to Byron for a passage, came on board. One of the Greeks called himself Prince Shilizzi,* the other, Vitaili, assumed no higher rank than Captain. The friends who accompanied them on board, whispered me to be wary of them, asserting that the Prince was a Russian spy, and the Captain in the interests of the Turks. This was our first sample of the morality of the modern Greeks. On my telling this to Byron, he merely said, 'And a fair sample too of the ancient as well as modern, if Mitford is to be believed.'†

Our Scotch passenger, with no other handle to his name than plain Mr. Hamilton Brown, was an acquisition; he had been in office in the Ionian Islands, spoke Italian and Romaic, and knew a good deal of the Greeks, as well as the characters of the English residents in command of the Islands. From what we learnt from him we altered our plan, and instead of Zante decided on going to Cephalonia, as Sir C. J. Napier was in command there, and the only man in office favourably disposed to the Greeks and their cause. We remained two days at Leghorn completing our stores. I don't remember that Byron went on shore more than once, and then only to settle his accounts with his agent Webb. As we were getting under weigh, my friend Grant‡ came on board, and gave Byron the latest English papers, Reviews, and the first volume of Las Cases' *Memoirs of Napoleon*, just out. On July 23, 1823, we put to sea in the finest possible weather; drifting leisurely along the Italian coast, we sighted Piombino, a town in the midst of the pestilential lagoons of the Maremma famous for its wild fowl and fevers; a dark line of jungle fringed the shore for many leagues; we crossed the mouth of the muddy Tiber; saw the Alban Mount, and Mount Soracte, the landmarks which point out the site of Rome. On coming near Lonza, a small

---

* A relative of Alexander Mavrocordato.
† William Mitford (1784–1878). *History of Greece.*
‡ An old friend of Trelawny, possibly from Eastern days.

islet, converted into one of their many dungeons by the Neapolitan government, I said to Byron:

'There is a sight that would curdle the milky blood of a poet-laureate.'

'If Southey was here,' he answered, 'he would sing hosannas to the Bourbons. Here kings and governors are only the jailors and hangmen of the detestable Austrian barbarians. What dolts and drivellers the people are to submit to such universal despotism. I should like to see, from this our ark, the world submerged, and all the rascals on it drowning like rats.'

I put a pencil and paper in his hand, saying:

'Perpetuate your curses on tyranny, for poets like ladies generally side with the despots.'

He readily took the paper and set to work. I walked the deck and prevented his being disturbed. He looked as crest-fallen as a riotous boy, suddenly pounced upon by a master and given an impossible task, scrawling and scratching out, sadly perplexed. After a long spell, he said:

'You think it is as easy to write poetry as smoke a segar,—look, it's only doggerel. Extemporising verses is nonsense; poetry is a distinct faculty,—it won't come when called,—you may as well whistle for a wind; a Pythoness was primed when put upon her tripod. I must chew the cud before I write. I have thought over most of my subjects for years before writing a line.'

He did not, however, give up the task, and sat pondering over the paper for nearly an hour; then gnashing his teeth, he tore up what he had written, and threw the fragments overboard.

Seeing I looked disappointed:

'You might as well ask me to describe an earthquake, whilst the ground was trembling under my feet. Give me time,—I can't forget the theme: but for this Greek business I should have been at Naples writing a Fifth canto of *Childe Harold*, expressly to give vent to my detestation of the Austrian tyranny in Italy.'

Sometime after, I suggested he should write a war song for the Greeks; he did so afterwards. I saw the original amongst his papers at Missolonghi, and made a copy of it which I have lost.

Proceeding on our voyage, it was not until we had been some days fairly at sea, with no land to look back upon, that the Pilgrim regained something of his self-command,—he may have felt the truth of the old song:

> Now we're in for it, dam'ee what folly, boys,
> To be downhearted, yo ho.

His sadness intermitted, and his cold fits alternated with hot ones. Hitherto he had taken very little notice of anything, and when he talked it was with an effort. The lonely and grim-looking island of Stromboli was the first object that riveted his attention; it was shrouded in the smoke from its eternal volcanic fires, and the waves rolling into the deep caverns at its base, boomed dismally. A poet might have compared it to the bellowings of imprisoned demons.

Our Captain told us a story at night. It was an old tale told by all Levant sailors, and they are not particular as to names and dates.

'That a ship from the port of London was lying off this island loading with sulphur, when her Captain, who was on shore superintending the men, distinctly saw Alderman Curtis,—'*

'Not Alderman Curtis,' shouted Byron, 'but cut-throat Castlereagh!'

'Whoever it was, my Lord,' continued the Skipper, 'he was walking round and round the edge of the burning crater; his mate and crew were witnesses of the same: and when the vessel returned to England they heard that the person they had seen was dead; and the time of his death tallied exactly with the above event, as entered in the ship's log-book.'

Byron, taking up the yarn-spinning, said:

'Monk Lewis† told me, that he took lodgings at Weimar in Germany, and that every morning he was awakened by a

---

* Sir William Curtis (1752–1829). Lord Mayor of London 1795. Leader of the City Tories and their M.P. from 1798–1818, he was the butt of much Whig ridicule.

† Matthew Gregory Lewis (1775–1818). At the age of twenty wrote *Ambrosio, or the Monk*, a novel full of horror, which brought him fame as a Gothic novelist—and his nickname.

rustling noise, as of quantities of papers being torn open and eagerly handled; the noise came from a closet joining his room; he several times got out of bed and looked into it, but there was no one there. At length he told the servant of the house: the man said, "Don't you know the house is haunted? It belonged formerly to a lady; she had an only son, he left her and went to sea, and the ship was never heard of,—but the mother still believed he would return, and passed all her time in reading foreign newspapers, of which the closet was full; and when she died, at the same hour every morning, in that closet, her spirit is heard frantically tearing open papers."

'Monk Lewis,' added Byron, 'though so fond of a ghost story, was not superstitious, he believed nothing. Once at a dinner party he said to me, across the table, "Byron, what did you mean by calling me Apollo's sexton* in your English Bards?" I was so taken aback I could not answer him, nor could I now. Now, Tre,' he said, 'it's your turn to spin a yarn.'

'I will tell you one of presentiment,' I said, 'for you believe in that.'

'Certainly, I do,' he rejoined.

'The Captain of Lord Keith's† ship, when she was lying at Leghorn, was on a visit to Signor Felleichi, at Pisa; the Captain was of a very gay and talkative turn; suddenly he became silent and sad; his host asked if he was ill? he said "No, I wish I was on board my ship; I feel as if I was going to be hanged." At last he was persuaded to go to bed; but, before he got to his room, an express arrived with the news that his ship was on fire. He instantly posted to Leghorn, went on board, worked his ship out of the harbour to avoid perilling the other vessels lying there, but in spite of great exertion the fire reached the magazine, and every soul perished. A little middy on shore at Leghorn, with a heart as great as his Captain's, gave a boatman

---

* Oh! wonder-working LEWIS! Monk, or Bard
  Who fain would make Parnassus a church-yard!
  Lo! wreaths of yew, not laurel, bind thy brow,
  Thy Muse a Sprite, Apollo's sexton thou!

† George Elphinstone, Lord Keith (1746–1823). Commanded the fleet which took Cape Town, 1795–97, and landed Abercromby's army in Aboukir Bay, 1801.

a draft on Signor Felleichi for sixty pounds, to put him alongside his ship.'

The Poet had an antipathy to everything scientific; maps and charts offended him; he would not look through a spy-glass, and only knew the cardinal points of the compass; buildings the most ancient or modern he was as indifferent to as he was to painting, sculpture, and music. But all natural objects, and changes in the elements, he was generally the first to point out and the last to lose sight of. We lay-to all night off Stromboli; Byron sat up watching it. As he went down to his cabin at day-light, he said:

'If I live another year, you will see this scene in a fifth canto of *Childe Harold.*'

In the morning we entered the narrow strait of Messina, passed close by the precipitous promontory of Scylla, and at the distance of a mile on the opposite shore, Charybdis; the waters were boiling and lashed into foam and whirlpools by the conflicting currents and set of the sea; in bad weather it is dangerous to approach too near in small craft. The Poet had returned to his usual post by the taffrail; and soon after Messina was spread out before us, with its magnificent harbour, quays, and palaces; it was a gorgeous sight, and the surrounding scenery was so diversified and magnificent, that I exclaimed:

'Nature must have intended this for Paradise.'

'But the devil,' observed the Poet, 'has converted it into Hell.'

After some deliberation, the wind blowing fresh and fair, we reluctantly passed the city, and scudded through the Straits along the grim and rugged shores of Calabria; at 2 P.M. we got into the vortex of another whirlpool, and the conflicting winds, currents, and waves contending for mastery, held us captive. Our vessel was unmanageable, and there we lay oscillating like a pendulum for two hours close to the rocks, seeing vessels half-a-mile from us scudding by under double reefed topsails. The spell broken, we resumed our course. On passing a fortress called the Pharo, in the narrowest part of the Strait, we had a good view of Mount Etna, with its base wreathed in mists, while the summit stood out in bold relief against the sky. To the east we had the savage shores of Calabria, with its grey and jagged rocks; to the west the sunny and fertile coast of Sicily,— gliding close by its smooth hills and sheltered coves, Byron would point to some serene nook, and exclaim, 'There I could be happy!'

18

It was now the 30th of July, twelve days since our departure from Genoa, our ship would do anything but go a-head, she was built on the lines of a baby's cradle, and the least touch of Neptune's foot set her rocking. I was glad of this, for it kept all the land-lubbers in their cribs. Byron was not at all affected by the motion, he improved amazingly in health and spirits, and said, 'On shore when I awake in the morning, I am always inclined to hang myself, as the day advances, I get better, and at midnight I am all cock-a-whoop. I am better now than I have been for years.' You never know a man's temper until you have been imprisoned in a ship with him, or a woman's until you have married her. Few friendships can stand the ordeal by water; when a yacht from England with a pair of these thus tried friends touches,—say at Malta or Gibraltar,— you may be sure that she will depart with one only. I never was on ship-board with a better companion than Byron, he was generally cheerful, gave no trouble, assumed no authority, uttered no complaints, and did not interfere with the working of the ship; when appealed to, he always answered, 'Do as you like.' Everyday at noon, he and I jumped overboard in defiance of sharks or weather; it was the only exercise he had, for he could not walk the deck. His favourite toys—pistols, were not forgotten; empty bottles and live poultry served as targets; a fowl, duck or goose, was put into a basket, the head and neck only visible, hoisted to the main yard-arm: and we rarely had two shots at the same bird. No boy cornet enjoyed a practical joke more than Byron. On great occasions when our Captain wished to be grand, he wore a bright scarlet waistcoat; as he was very corpulent, Byron wished to see if this vest would not button round us both. The captain was taking his siesta one day, when he persuaded the boy to bring up the waistcoat. In the mean time as it was nearly calm and very hot, I opened the coops of the geese and ducks, who instinctively took to the water. Neptune, the Newfoundland dog, jumped after them, and Moretto the bull-dog, followed him.

'Now,' said Byron, standing on the gangway, with one arm

in the red waistcoat, 'put your arm in, Tre, we will jump overboard, and take the shine out of it.'

So we did.

The captain hearing the row on deck, came up, and when he
saw the gorgeous garment he was so proud of, defiled by sea
water, he roared out, 'My Lord, you should know better than
to make a mutiny on board ship [the crew were laughing at the
fun], I won't heave to, or lower a boat, I hope you will both
be drowned.'

'Then you will lose your *frite*' (for so the Captain always
pronounced the word freight), shouted Byron.

As I saw the dogs worrying the ducks and geese, I returned
on board with the waistcoat, pacified the skipper, lowered a
boat, and with the aid of a boy, sculled after the birds and
beasts; the Newfoundlander brought them to us unharmed,
but Moretto the bull-dog did not mouth them so tenderly.
After the glare and oppressive heat of the day, the evenings
and nights were delightful: balmy air, no dew, and light enough
to distinguish everything near.

Fletcher, Byron's 'yeoman bold', as was his custom in the
afternoon, was squatted under the lee of the caboose, eating his
supper, and drinking bottled porter which he dearly loved. I
said, 'You are enjoying yourself, Fletcher.'

'Yes,' he answered, 'and you had better do so whilst you can:
my master can't be right in his mind.'

'Why?' I asked.

'If he was, he would not have left Italy, where we had everything, and go to a country of savages; there is nothing to eat in
Greece, but tough Billy Goats, or to drink, but spirits of turpen-
tine. Why, sir, there is nothing there but rocks, robbers, and
vermin.'—Seeing his master coming up the companion ladder,
he raised his voice —'I defy my Lord to deny it—you may ask
him.'

'I don't deny it,' said Byron; 'what he says is quite true to
those who take a hog's eye view of things. But this I know, I
have never been so happy as I was there; how it will be with me,
now that my head is as grey, and my heart as hard, as the rocks,
I can't say.'

I followed Fletcher's advice and example in regard to the

supper, and the Poet, saying he could not resist temptation, joined me. We discussed the pleasures and independence of sea-life as contrasted with the eternal restraint and botheration on shore. Here, I observed, we have only the elements to contend with, and a safe port under our lee, whereas on shore we never know what mischief is brewing; a letter, or the idle gossip of a good-natured friend, stops our digestion—how smoothly the time glides on, now we are out of the reach of men and mischief-makers.

'Women, you should say,' exclaimed Byron; 'if we had a womankind on board, she would set us all at loggerheads, and make a mutiny, would she not, Captain?'

'I wish my old woman was here,' replied the skipper, 'she would make you as comfortable in my cabin at sea, as your own wife could in her parlour on shore.'

Byron started and looked savage—the Captain went on, as unconscious of offending as a carthorse would be, after crushing your toes with his hoof. 'My wife,' he continued, 'on my last voyage from Rio, saved my ship. We had touched there for water, homeward bound: she waked me up at night,—her weather eye was always open,—the men were *desarting* in a crimp's shore-boat. In the morning it came on to blow like blazes.'

'If we are to have a yarn, Captain, we must have strong waters.'

'I have no objection to a glass of grog,' said the Captain; 'I am not a temperance man, but I can't *abide* drunkenness at sea. I like to have my allowance.'

'How much is that?' asked Byron.

'No more than will do me good.'

'How much is that?'

'Why, a bottle of good old Jamaica rum sarves me from 11 A.M. till 10 P.M., and I know that can't hurt any man.'

Byron read a critique on O'Meara's *Napoleon at St. Helena*, in the *Quarterly*. He remarked, 'If all they assert is true, it only affects the character of the author. They do not disprove a single statement in the book: this is their way! If they crush an author, it must be in the shell, as they tried to do with me: if the book has life enough to out-live the year, it defies their malice—for who reads a last year's review? Whilst our literature is domineered over by a knot of virulent bigots and rancorous partisans, we shall have no great or original works. When did parsons patronise genius? If one of their black band dares to think for himself, he is drummed out, or cast aside, like Sterne and Swift. Where are the great poets and writers the Reviewers predicted were to be the leviathans of our literature? Extinct: their bones hereafter may be grubbed up in a fossil state with those of the reptiles that puffed them into life. If this age has produced anything good or great, which I doubt, it has been under every possible discouragement.

'People say that I have told my own story in my writings: I defy them to point out a single act of my life by my poems, or of my thoughts, for I seldom write what I think. All that has been published about me is sheer nonsense, as will be seen at my death, when my real life is published: everything in that is true. When I first left England I was gloomy. I said so in my first canto of *Childe Harold*. I was then really in love with a cousin' (Thirza, he was very chary of her name) 'and she was in a decline. On my last leaving England I was savage; there was enough to make me so. There is some truth as to detail in the *Dream*, and in some of my shorter poems. As to my marriage, which people made such ridiculous stories about, it was managed by Lady Jersey and others. I was perfectly indifferent on the subject; thought I could not do better, and so did they. I wanted money. It was an experiment, and proved a failure. Everything is told in my memoirs exactly as it happened. I told Murray Lady Byron was to read the MS. if she wished it, and requested she would add, omit, or make any comments she pleased, now, or when it was going through the press.'

It is strange that Byron, though professing to distrust everybody, should have had no misgiving as to the fate of his memoirs; he was glad Moore sold them to Murray, as he thought that ensured publication. He considered it indispensable to his honour that the truths he could not divulge during his life should be known at his death. He knew Moore prided himself on his intimacy with lords and ladies, for he was always talking of them, and that the chief aim and object of that Poet's whole life was pleasure at any price. Had he fulfilled his trust by giving Byron's memoirs to the world, he would have compromised himself with society, as they contained many a reminiscence which would have cast a shadow on the fashionable circles which Tom Moore delighted to honour. When the question was raised after Byron's death, of the publication or suppression of his memoirs, his friend Tom Moore acted as if he was quite indifferent on the subject; so he must have been, for although he permitted others to read them, he never found time to do so himself. He consulted the most fashionable man he knew on the subject, Lutterell, who, as Rogers says, 'cared nothing about the matter, and readily voted they should be put in the fire.' Byron said, 'some few scenes and names in his memoirs it might be necessary to omit, as he had written the whole truth. Moore and Murray were to exercise their own discretion on that subject.' He added, 'that the truth would be known and believed when he was dead, and the lies forgotten.' So there is nothing to extenuate the great wrong done to Byron by Tom Moore.

Byron's autobiography contained a narrative of the principal events of his life; with running comments on those he came in contact with, or who crossed his path. It was written in a straightforward, manly manner, and in a vigorous, fearless style, and was apparently truthful as regarded himself;—if it was not the whole truth, it contained much more of that commodity than other writers have generally left us in their memoirs. Autobiography was the kind of reading he preferred to all others.

19

Byron formed his opinion of the inhabitants of this planet from books; personally he knew as little about them as if he belonged to some other. From reading Rochefoucauld, Machiavelli, and other soured cynics, he learnt to distrust people in general; so, as he could do nothing without them and did not know how to manage them, he was always complaining of being over-reached, and never getting what he wanted. I don't think he ever knew what he did want: few there are that do.

To resume my log on board the good ship 'Hercules'. On the 2nd of August, the islands of Cephalonia and Zante were in sight, and shortly after Byron pointing out the Morea said, 'I don't know why it is, but I feel as if the eleven long years of bitterness I have passed through since I was here, were taken off my shoulders, and I was scudding through the Greek Archipelago with old Bathurst, in his frigate [the 'Salsette'].' That night we anchored in the roadstead; the next morning we worked into Argostoli, the harbour of Cephalonia, and anchored near the town. An officer from the Health Office having examined our papers and log, gave us pratique. The secretary of the Resident, Captain Kennedy, came on board; he told us Colonel Napier was absent, but that we might depend on the Colonel's readiness to aid us in anything that his orders to observe strict neutrality permitted. The captain gave us the latest news from the seat of war, and said Blaquiere had gone to England, at which Byron was sorely vexed. The truth flashed across his mind, that he had been merely used as a decoy by the committee. 'Now they have got me thus far they think I must go on, and they care nothing as to the result. They are deceived, I won't budge a foot farther until I see my way; we will stay here; if that is objected to, I will buy an island from the Greeks or Turks; there must be plenty of them in the market.' The instinct that enables the vulture to detect carrion afar off, is surpassed by the marvellous acuteness of the Greeks in scenting money. The morning after our arrival a flock of ravenous Zuliote* refugees alighted on our decks, attracted by Byron's dollars. Lega, the steward, a thorough miser, coiled himself on the money-chest like a viper. Our sturdy skipper was for driving them overboard with hand-spikes. Byron came on deck in exuberant spirits, pleased with their savage aspect and wild attire, and, as was his wont, promised a great deal more than he should have done; day and night they clung to his heels like a pack of jackals, till he stood at bay like a hunted lion, and was glad to buy them off, by shipping them to the Morea. On Colonel Napier's return to the island, he warmly urged Byron, and indeed all of us, to take up our quarters at his house; from first to last, all the English on the island, the military as well as the civilians, vied with each other in friendly and hospitable acts. Byron preferred staying on board; every afternoon he and I crossed the harbour in a boat, and landed on a rock to bathe; on one of these occasions he held out his right leg to me, saying:

'I hope this accursed limb will be knocked off in the war.'

'It won't improve your swimming,' I answered; 'I will exchange legs if you will give me a portion of your brains.'

'You would repent your bargain,' he said; 'at times I feel my brains boiling, as Shelley's did whilst you were grilling him.'

Browne records another swimming incident: 'Trelawny offered to wager that he could swim from Ithaca across to the nearest point of Cephalonia (a distance of about six miles) but the high land on the other side made it seem much nearer. On our embarking, he persisted in swimming after the boat a very long way, when, as it began to wax late, he was compelled to come in:—Byron rather unfairly badgering him on what he termed his failure. But Trelawny was a capital swimmer, fully equal to contend with Byron himself.' (*A Narrative of a visit to the Seat of War in Greece.*)

After bathing, we landed in an olive grove, eating our frugal supper under the trees. Our Greek passengers during the voyage said, that the Greeks generally were in favour of a monarchical government; the Greeks on the island confirmed this, saying it

---

* The Souliotes, a Christian Albanian tribe, had allied themselves with the anti-Turkish but Moslem Albanian leader, Ali Pasha, but had been defeated in a series of hard-fought battles, and virtually driven from the mainland.

was the only way of getting rid of the robber chiefs who now tyrannised and kept the country in a state of anarchy; and as they must have a foreigner for a king, they could not do better than elect Byron. The Poet treated this suggestion lightly, saying, 'If they make me the offer, I may not refuse it. I shall take care of my own "sma peculiar"; for if it don't suit my humour, I shall, like Sancho, * abdicate.' Byron several times alluded to this, in a bantering vein; it left an impression on his mind. Had he lived to reach the congress of Salona as commissioner of the loan, the dispenser of a million silver crowns would have been offered a golden one.†

Our party made an excursion to the neighbouring island of Ithaca; contrasted with the arid wastes and barren red hills of Cephalonia, the verdant valleys, sparkling streams, and high land, clothed in evergreen shrubs, were strikingly beautiful. After landing, it was proposed to Byron to visit some of the localities that antiquaries have dubbed with the titles of Homer's school,—Ulysses' stronghold, etc.: he turned peevishly away, saying to me, 'Do I look like one of those emasculated fogies? Let's have a swim. I detest antiquarian twaddle. Do people think I have no lucid intervals, that I came to Greece to scribble more nonsense? I will show them I can do something better: I wish I had never written a line, to have it cast in my teeth at every turn.' Brown and Gamba went to look for some place where he might pass the night, as we could not get mules to go on until the next day.

After a long swim, Byron clambered up the rocks, and, exhausted by his day's work, fell asleep under the shade of a wild fig-tree at the mouth of a cavern. Gamba, having nothing to do, hunted him out, and awakened him from a pleasant dream, for which the Poet cursed him. We fed off figs and olives, and passed our night at a goatherd's cottage.‡

In the morning we rode through the pleasant little island to

---

* *Don Quixote* II ch. LIII.

† At the time when Trelawny was preparing his *Recollections* the question of a King for Greece was very much a matter for public debate; Leopold of Saxe-Coburg being the favourite candidate.

‡ This is a somewhat romanticised description for the cottage of a Triestino merchant who had lost his money.

Vathy, the capital. The Resident, Captain Knox, his lady, and everyone else who had a house, opened their doors to welcome us, and the Pilgrim was received as if he had been a prince.

After this reception it seems incredible that the whole party should be packed off to a monastery for the night, and in fact Trelawny's memory is not dependable; the events which he now describes took place, not during the visit to Vathy, but on the first night after the return to Cephalonia.

On the summit of a high mountain in the island, there is an ancient monastery, from which there is a magnificent view of the Ionian Sea, Greece, and many islands. The day after our arrival we ascended it, our party amounting to ten or twelve, including servants and muleteers. As usual, it was late when we started; there was not a breath of air, and the heat was intense. Following a narrow zig-zag path between rocks and precipices in single file, as our mules crept upwards our difficulty increased, until the path became merely stone steps, worn by time and travel in the solid limestone. We all dismounted but Byron; he was jaded and irritable, as he generally was when deprived of his accustomed midday siesta: it was dusk before we reached the summit of the mountain. The Abbot had been apprised by the Resident of our visit; and when we neared the monastery, files of men stood on each side of our path, bearing pine torches. On coming up to the walls we saw the monks in their grey gowns, ranged along the terrace; they chaunted a hymn of glorification and welcome to the great lord, saying, 'Christ has risen to elevate the cross and trample on the crescent in our beloved Greece.' The Abbot, clad in his sacerdotal robes, received Byron in the porch, and conducted him into the great hall, illuminated for the occasion; the monks and others clustered round the honoured guest; boys swung censers with frankincense under the Poet's nose. The Abbot, after performing a variety of ceremonies in a very dignified manner, took from the folds of his ample garments a roll of paper, and commenced intoning through his nasal organs a turgid and interminable eulogium on my 'Lord Inglese', in a polyglot of divers tongues; while the eyes of the silent monks, anxious to observe the effect of the holy father's eloquence, glanced from the Abbot to the Lord.

Byron had not spoken a word from the time we entered the monkery; I thought he was resolved to set us an example of proper behaviour. No one was more surprised than I was, when suddenly he burst into a paroxysm of rage, and vented his ire in a torrent of Italian execrations on the holy Abbot and all his brotherhood. Then turning to us with flashing eyes, he vehemently exclaimed:

'Will no one release me from the presence of these pestilential idiots? they drive me mad!' Seizing a lamp, he left the room.

The consternation of the monks at this explosion of wrath may be imagined. The amazed Abbot remained for some time motionless, his eyes and mouth wide open; holding the paper he had been reading in the same position, he looked at the vacant place left by Byron, and then at the door through which he had disappeared. At last he thought he had solved the mystery, and in a low tremulous voice said,—significantly putting his finger to his forehead:

'Eccolo, è matto poveretto!' (Poor fellow, he is mad.)

Leaving Hamilton Brown to pacify the monks, I followed Byron. He was still fretting and fuming, cursing the 'whining dotard', as he called the Abbot, who had tormented him. Byron's servant brought him bread, wine, and olives. I left him and joined the mess of the monks in their refectory. We had the best of everything the island produced for supper. Our host broached several flasks of his choicest vintages: but although he partook largely of these good things, they failed to cheer him. We were all glad to retire early to our cells.

More happened during the night, of great significance in view of later events: 'Lord Byron retired almost immediately from the "sala". Shortly afterwards we were astonished and alarmed by the entry of Dr. Bruno, wringing his hands and tearing his hair—a practice much too frequent with him—and ejaculating: "O Maria, santissima Maria, se non e gia morte—cielo, perche non son morto io!" It appeared that Lord Byron was seized with violent spasms in the stomach and liver, and his brain was excited to dangerous excess, so that he would not tolerate the presence of any person in his room. He refused all medicine, and stamped and tore all his clothes and bedding like a maniac. We could hear him rattling and ejaculating. Poor Dr. Bruno stood lamenting in agony of mind, in anticipation of the most dire results if immediate relief were not obtained by powerful cathartics, but Lord Byron had expelled him from the room by main force. He now implored one or more of the company to go to his lordship and induce him, if possible, to save his life by taking the necessary medicine. Trelawny at once proceeded to the room, but soon returned, saying that it would require ten such as he to hold his lordship for a minute, adding that Lord Byron would not leave an unbroken article in the room. The doctor again essayed an entrance, but without success. The monks were becoming alarmed, and so, in truth, were all present. The doctor asked me to try to bring his lordship to reason: "He will thank you when he is well," he said, "but get him to take this one pill, and he will be safe." It seemed a very easy undertaking, and I went. There being no lock on the door, entry was obtained in spite of a barricade of chairs and a table within. His lordship was half undressed, standing in a far corner like a hunted animal at bay. As I looked determined to advance in spite of his imprecations of "Back! Out of my sight! Fiends, can I have no peace, no relief from this hell? Leave me, I say!" he lifted the chair nearest to him, and hurled it direct at my head. I escaped as I best could, and returned to the "sala". The matter was obviously serious, and we all counselled force and such coercive measures as might be necessary to make him swallow the curative medicine. Mr. Hamilton Browne, one of our party, now volunteered an attempt, and the silence that succeeded his entrance augured well for his success. He returned much sooner than expected, telling the doctor that he might go to sleep; Lord Byron had taken both the pills, and had lain down on my mattress and bedding, prepared for him by my servant—the only regular bed in the company, the others being trunks and portable tressels, with such softening as might be procured for the occasion. Lord Byron's beautiful and most commodious patent portmanteau bed, with every appliance that profusion of money could provide, was mine for the night.' (Mackay. *Medora Leigh*, quoting a Mr. S— who was an eyewitness.)

In the morning, Byron came forth refreshed, and acted as if he had forgotten the occurrences of the evening. The Abbot had not, and he took care not to remind him of them. A handsome donation was deposited in the alms-box, and we mounted our mules and departed, without any other ceremony than a hasty benediction from the Holy Father and his monks.

However we might have doubted the sincerity of their ovation on receiving us, we did not question the relief they felt and expressed by their looks on our departure.

The next day we retraced our steps through the flowery ravines and tranquil glades of this lovely islet, our road winding along the foot of the mountains. The grey olive-trees, bright green fig, and rampant vine, that grew above our heads, screened us from the sun; the fresh breeze from the sea, with the springs of purest water gushing out of the rocks, soothed the Poet's temper. He turned out of the path to look at a natural grotto, in a grove of forest trees, and said, 'You will find nothing in Greece or its islands so pleasant as this. If this isle were mine, —"I would break my staff and bury my book."—What fools we all are!'

On reaching our former landing-place, we had to wait a long time for a boat to ferry us across the strait to Cephalonia. As usual, he and I took to the water; in the evening we crossed, and it was night when we regained our old quarters on board the 'Hercules'.

It was near noon of the next day, when I had occasion to speak to Byron on pressing business. I descended to his cabin,— he was fast asleep. I repeatedly called him by name; at first in a low voice,—then louder and louder; at last he started up in terror, staring at me wildly. With a convulsive sigh he said, 'I have had such a dream! I am trembling with fear. I am not fit to go to Greece. If you had come to strangle me I could have done nothing.'

I said, 'Who could against a nightmare? the hag don't mind your pistols or your bible' (he always had these on a chair close to the side of his bed). I then talked on other subjects until he was tolerably composed, and so left him.

The conflicting accounts that came day by day from the Morea distracted us; to ascertain the real state of things, I proposed to go there. Byron urged me to stay until he went, so I remained for some time; but when he talked of leaving the ship and taking a house, I determined to be off.

Byron had hoped that, before long, Blaquiere would arrive with specific reports on events in Greece, with detailed directions for his own role, and with a definite commission from the London Greek

145

Committee. But instead he heard that Blaquiere was back in England, and from Greece the news was oppressive with evidence of faction; and such was the reputation of the great 'Veeron' that he looked like being pulled apart by the various elements which competed for his favour. The Souliotes wanted Byron's money. Metaxas, the Governor of Missolonghi, wanted his presence. Mavrocordato thought that the one real hope for the Greek cause lay in the island interests, and wanted Byron to join them. Kolokotrones was in camp at Salamis and would have welcomed Byron as his friend, if only Byron could be persuaded to give up all other causes. Petro Bey, according to one group President of the Greek Executive, merely wanted £1000 from Byron so that he could start out on some private expedition he had dreamed up.

Broadly speaking, there were two major conflicting interests in Greece and these two had brought the country to the verge of civil war—even in the face of the national enemy. On the one hand stood the primates and chieftains of the Morea, on the other hand the merchants and the sea-faring classes, and as corollary to these two principal groups there were two governments, one under Petro Bey, with Kolokotrones as his vice-President, and the other under Koundouriottes. But neither government had any real executive power, nor any funds save those derived from the whims of individuals, and the situation was further complicated by a geographical division of loyalties: Eastern Greece was controlled by Odysseus, at present working more or less amiably with Kolokotrones; Western Greece still looked to Mavrocordato for leadership, though he was for the moment a refugee on Hydra.

And all the time the Turks blockaded the Greek coast and the Greek fleet, starved for money, lay idle in the islands.

Byron's political sagacity, in the face of this situation, was considerable. He was not going to be rushed into taking sides; even after the arrival of his commission from the London Committee (a commission which was less whole-hearted than he had hoped, and which made him little more than an agent for receiving stores and money) he was prepared to wait until the Greeks decided not to fight among themselves before he decided to help them fight the Turks. No coward, he was tempted to go over to the Morea in the third week of August, but Captain Scott of the 'Hercules' was not inclined to risk his ship through the Turkish blockade, and Byron's intelligence got the better of his natural impatience. Nor had he Trelawny's naïve enthusiasm for action.

In his *Journal* he wrote: 'I did not come here to join a faction, but a nation, and to deal with honest men, and not with speculators or peculators (charges bandied about daily by the Greeks of each other), it will require much circumspection to avoid the character of a partisan, and I perceive it to be the more difficult as I have received invitations from more than one of the contending parties, always under the pretext that *they* are the "real Simon Pure".'

20

I WELL knew that once on shore Byron would fall back on his old routine of dawdling habits, plotting—planning—shilly-shallying—and doing nothing. It was a maxim of his, 'If I am stopped for six days at any place, I cannot be made to move for six months.'

Hamilton Brown agreed to go with me; he was a most valuable ally. In my hasty preparations for going, I was tearing up and throwing overboard papers and letters. Byron stopped me, saying, 'Some day you will be sorry for this; they are parts of your life. I have every scrap of paper that was ever written to me,—letters, notes,—even cards of invitation to parties. There are chests-full at Hanson's, Douglas Kinnaird's, and Barry's, at Genoa.* They will edify my executors.'

'Is this quite fair to your correspondents?' I asked.

'Yes; for they have mine and might use them against me. Whilst I live they dare not,—I can keep them all in order; when I die and my memoirs are published,—my executors can verify them by my letters if their truth is questioned.'

I told Byron that two Frenchmen, just landed, wished to see him; I thought they were officers. He said, 'Ask Hamilton Brown to see what they want. I can't express myself like a gentleman in French. I never could learn it,—or anything else according to rule.' He even read translations of French books in preference to the originals. His ignorance of the language was the reason that he avoided Frenchmen and was never in France. †

In our voyage from Italy, Byron persuaded me to let him have my black servant, as, in the East, it is a mark of dignity to have a negro in your establishment. He likewise coveted a green embroidered military jacket of mine; which, as it was too small for me, I gave him; so I added considerably to his

---

* J. Hanson, Banker, was Byron's executor. Douglas Kinnaird, brother of the eighth Lord Kinnaird and Byron's close friend, was Hanson's partner; Barry his agent in Genoa.

† But see p. 28 where Trelawny gives a different reason for Byron's avoiding France.

dignity. I engaged one of the refugee Zuliotes (or Zodiacs, as old Scott, our captain, called them) to go with me. He was a vain, lazy, swaggering braggart,—sullen and stupid as are most of his tribe.

Byron gave us letters addressed to the Greek government, if we could find any such constituted authorities,—expressing his readiness to serve them when they had satisfied him how he could do so, etc., etc., etc. As I took leave of him, his last words were, 'Let me hear from you often,—come back soon? If things are farcical, they will do for *Don Juan*; if heroical, you shall have another canto of *Childe Harold*.'

'From the moment Lord Byron embarked in the Greek cause, his mind seemed so completely absorbed by the subject, that it rendered him deaf to the calls of the muse; at least he repeatedly assured us, that, since his departure from Genoa, he had not written a single line: and though it appeared from his conversation, that he was arranging in his head the materials of a future canto of *Don Juan*, he did not feel his poetical vein sufficiently strong to induce him to venture on the undertaking.' (Julius Millingen. *Memoirs of the Affairs of Greece.*)

Hamilton Brown and I went on board a light boat of the country, called a caique, crossed over with a fair wind in the night, and landed early the next morning on a sandy beach, at a solitary ruined tower near Pyrgos. A dirty squad of Moorish mercenaries,* quartered at the tower, received us; some of them accompanied us to the village of Pyrgos; where, as we could not procure horses or mules, we slept.

In the morning we commenced our journey to Tripolitza, the capital of the Peloponnesus, visiting the military stations on our way. We slept at the ruined villages, and were generally well received when our mission was known. The country is so poor and barren, that but for its genial climate it would be barely habitable. In the best of times there would not be plenty; but now that war had passed over the land with fire and slaughter there was scarcely a vestige of habitation or cultivation.

The only people we met besides soldiers, looked like tribes of

---

* Possibly Albanian Moslems.

half-starved gipsies; over our heads, on some towering rock, occasionally we saw a shepherd with his long gun, watching us, and keeping guard over small flocks of goats and sheep, whilst they fed off the scanty shrubs that grew in the crevices under them; they were attended, too, by packs of the most savage dogs I ever saw. Except in considerable force, the Greek soldiers dared not meddle with these warlike shepherds and their flocks. Many of the most distinguished leaders in the war, and the bravest of their followers, had been shepherds.

To compensate for the hard fare and bodily privations to be endured, there was ample food for the minds of any who love the haunts of genius. Every object we saw was associated with some great name, or deed of arts or arms, that still live in the memory of all mankind. We stopped two or three days at Tripolitza, and then passed on to Argos and Napoli di Romania; every step of our way was marked by the ravages of the war. On our way to Corinth, we passed through the defiles of Dervenakia; our road was a mere mule-path for about two leagues, winding along in the bed of a brook, flanked by rugged precipices. In this gorge, and a more rugged path above it, a large Ottoman force, principally cavalry, had been stopped, in the previous autumn, by barricades of rocks and trees, and slaughtered like droves of cattle by the wild and exasperated Greeks. It was a perfect picture of the war, and told its own story; the sagacity of the nimble-footed Greeks, and the hopeless stupidity of the Turkish commanders, were palpable: detached from the heaps of dead, we saw the skeletons of some bold riders who had attempted to scale the acclivities, still astride the skeletons of their horses, and in the rear, as if in the attempt to back out of the fray, the bleached bones of the negroes' hands still holding the hair ropes attached to the skulls of their camels—death, like sleep, is a strange posture-master. There were grouped in a narrow space five thousand or more skeletons of men, horses, camels, and mules; vultures had eaten their flesh, and the sun had bleached their bones. In this picture the Turks looked like a herd of bisons trapped and butchered in the gorges of the rocky mountains. The rest of their battles, amidst scenery generally of the same rugged character, only differed in their magnitude. The Asiatic Turks are lazy, brave, and stupid. The Greeks, too crafty to fight if they could run, were only formidable in their fastnesses. It is a marvel that Greece and Greeks should be again resuscitated after so many ages of death-like slavery. No people, if they retain their name and language, need despair; 'There is nothing constant but mutability!'

We arrived at Corinth a short time after the Acrocorinthus had, for the second time, fallen into the hands of the insurgents; and there saw Colocotroni and other predatory chiefs. Thence we crossed to the Isle of Salamis, and found the legislative and executive bodies of the provisional government accusing each other of embezzling the public money. Here, too, we saw the most potent leaders of the chief Greek military factions,— Primates, Hydriotes, Mainotes, Mareotes, Ipsareotes, Caudeotes, and many others, each and all intent on their own immediate interests. There, too, I saw the first specimens of the super-subtle Phanariotes, pre-eminent in all evil, reared at Constantinople, and trained in the arts of deception by the most adroit professors in the world. These pliant and dexterous intriguers glided stealthily from tent to tent and from chief to chief, impregnating their brains with wily suggestions, thus envenoming their feuds and causing universal anarchy. Confounded at this exhibition of rank selfishness, we backed out of these civil broils, and sailed for Hydra; one of our commissions being to send deputies from that island to England to negotiate a loan. We speedily accomplished this, and Hamilton Brown went to London with the deputies. I re-landed in Greece and went to Athens.* Odysseus held undisputed sway there and in Eastern Greece, the frontiers of the war, and had played an important part in the insurrection. Descended from the most renowned race of Klephtes, he was a master of the art of mountain warfare, and a thorough Greek in cunning; strong-bodied, nimble-footed, and nimble-witted. I bought horses, hired soldiers, and accompanied him on an expedition to Euboea, then in the hands of the Turks; and under his auspices became familiar with many of the most interesting localities,—Attica, Marathon, Thebes, Thermopylae, Cheronea, Livadia, Talanta,

---

* Where (according to a somewhat doubtful story) Trelawny excelled himself by purchasing a harem; twelve to fifteen strong, including a negress.

Mount Parnes, Pindus and Cythæron. Our headquarters were on Parnassus. Our ambuscades, onslaughts, rock-fighting, forays, stalking Turkish cavalry, successes and failures, intermingled with conferences, treaties, squabbles, intrigues, and constant change, were exciting at the time: so is deer-stalking; so was the Caffre [Kaffir] war to those engaged in it; but as they are neither edifying nor amusing to write nor to read about, I shall not record them.

In the three months since Trelawny had left Byron had not been idle. On September 6, 1823, he had taken a house at Metaxata. There he received the envoys of the various Greek factions, and tried to organise the Philhellenes into something approaching unity. His situation was complicated somewhat by the fact that under the Foreign Enlistment Act of 1819, British subjects were not allowed to serve as soldiers under a foreign government, and although Byron's offence was still in intention rather than fact, he could not risk the whole cause by some petty infringement of the law. In this, however, he was much helped by the activities of the Resident, Charles Napier, who was himself anxious to obtain a command in Greece, and most anxious to persuade the distinguished transient that he was suitably equipped for such a task. Therefore, though Napier was quick to urge other Philhellenes, Finlay, Von Quass and Millingen among them, not to tarry in Cephalonia, he showed every courtesy to Byron.

His efforts were rewarded. Byron became convinced that he was the right man for the job. In a letter written to the Committee on October 10, 1823, he wrote: 'Colonel Napier will present to you this letter. Of his military character it were superfluous to speak: of his personal, I can say . . . that it is as excellent as his military: in short, a better or a braver men is not easily to be found. *He* is our man to lead a regular force, or to organise a national one for the Greeks. Ask the army—ask any one. He is besides a personal friend of both Prince Mavrocordato, Colonel Stanhope, and myself, and in such concord with all three that we should all pull together—an indispensable, as well as a rare point, especially in Greece at present . . .'

In the same letter Byron dealt with the subject that was most often in his thoughts—the raising of a loan in London; and showed remarkable sanity: '. . . To enable a regular force to be properly organised, it will be requisite for the loan-holders to set apart at least £500,000 sterling for that particular purpose—perhaps more; but by so doing they will guarantee their own monies, "and make assurance doubly sure". They can appoint commissioners to see that part properly expended—and I recommend a similar precaution for the whole.'

Meanwhile Byron was spending a great deal of his own money on Greek affairs. He paid out four thousand pounds or more to the Greek Government for the naval squadron at Hydra—and still the fleet did not sail to the relief of Missolonghi. He organised a personal bodyguard of forty Souliotes, only to find that their chiefs were keeping all the moneys he spent on their pay. He financed Trelawny and Browne on their trip to the mainland, even although he did not much care for its purpose. And he had money troubles of his own: 'I must not omit the conduct of the Ionian bankers towards Lord Byron, which grieved him much. He had sent his letters of credit from one of the first houses of the Mediterranean [Webb and Co.], directed to Messrs. Caridi and Corgialegno, two of the richest proprietors and merchants in the island. The former, either from fear of political consequences, or from incapability, replied, and perhaps truly, that he could not answer his bills. But the uncourteous manner was what offended Lord Byron. He neither came in person, nor sent an answer in writing, but a clerk with a refusal. . . . M. Corgialegno was more courteous, but still betrayed a little of the Jew.' (Gamba.)

There were numerous minor details to be dealt with—the question of Millingen's salary for example—and letters to be written to Greece, to London, to sympathisers all over the world. The Greek deputies who were to go to London to arrange the Loan were almost as obdurate as the Greek fleet. And Byron had to receive, and receive tactfully, all the visitors, Greek and English, who came to Metaxata.

At the time there was a certain feeling in London that Byron had made his gesture by coming towards Greece, and that he was not going to do much more, but on the whole his activities were respected and, for the first time for many years, even the English Press looked upon him favourably. Those who knew the circumstances were not inclined to accuse him of unnecessary dilatoriness or malingering: 'Much credit is certainly due to Lord Byron for the prudence which characterised his conduct.' (Millingen.)

The events of early October seemed to remove some of the reasons for Byron's remaining at Metaxata. He himself describes them in a letter to the Committee written on October 13, 1823: '. . . The long desired squadron has arrived in the waters of Missolonghi and intercepted two Turkish corvettes—ditto transports—destroying or taking all four. . . . The Greeks had fourteen sail, the Turks *four*—but the odds don't matter—the victory will make a very good *puff*, and be of some advantage besides. . . . The mathematical, medical, and

153

musical preparations of the Committee have arrived. . . . they are excellent of their kind, but till we have an engineer and a trumpeter (we have chirurgeons already) mere "pearls to swine", as the Greeks are quite ignorant of mathematics, and have a bad ear for our music.'

At about the same time the London-bound emissaries of the Greek Government passed through Metaxata. But still Byron was not eager to move. The differences among the Greeks were not yet resolved and therefore the main reason for his inactivity remained. Undoubtedly, however, he remained partly because he was enjoying himself. 'I like this place,' he said to Dr. James Kennedy, who later set the statement down in his *Conversations on Religion with Lord Byron and Others*, 'I do not know why—and dislike to move. There are not to be sure, many allurements here, neither from the commodiousness of the house nor the bleak view of the black mountain; there is no learned society, nor the presence of beautiful women; and yet, for all that, I would wish to remain, as I have found myself more comfortable, and my time passes more cheerfully than it has for a long time.'

This same Dr. Kennedy served in lieu of 'learned society', and made a bold if unsuccessful attempt to convert Lord Byron. ' "Has your lordship," said Kennedy, "read any of the books I took the liberty of sending." "I have begun," replied Byron, "very fairly: I have given some of your tracts to Fletcher, who is a good sort of man, but still wants, like myself, some reformation, and I hope he will spread them among the other servants, who require it still more. . . . You have sent me an account of the death of Lord Rochester, as a tract, *par excellence*, having a particular reference to me. . . . But I am not quite satisfied with Lord Rochester's conversion; there will always remain this uncertainty about it, that perhaps had he recovered, and been placed among his former companions, he would have relapsed. . . ." I admitted that this was true; yet I added, "We shall be perfectly satisfied if we find that your lordship, who follows him in some points, should also preserve a resemblance of him at his departure".'

Late in October, Byron received a pressing invitation from the Greek Executive that he should cross to the Morea about the middle of November. Although the differences between the main parties were not yet resolved, and although desultory fighting had broken out between them, Byron was almost persuaded to go and had his preparations well advanced when Hamilton Browne returned and advised that he should instead throw in his lot with Mavrocordato and proceed to Missolonghi.

154

A reason, perhaps an excuse, for further delay was now available, but on November 22 another arrival at Metaxata urged Byron to decisive action. Colonel Stanhope, a veteran of the Napoleonic and Mahratta Wars, was something of a crank. 'He came up,' wrote Byron, '(as they all do who have not been in this country before) with some high-flown notions of the sixth form at Harrow or Eton, but Colonel Napier and I soon set him right . . .'

But he did at least persuade Byron to write a strong letter to the Morea Government on November 30, 1823: '. . . We have heard some rumours of new dissensions, nay, of the existence of a civil war. With all my heart I pray that these reports may be false or exaggerated, for I can imagine no calamity more serious than this; and I must frankly confess that unless union and order are established, all hopes of a Loan will be vain; and all the assistance which the Greeks could expect from abroad . . . will be suspended or destroyed; and, what is worse, the great powers of Europe . . . will be persuaded that the Greeks are unable to govern themselves, and will, perhaps, themselves undertake to settle your disorders in such a way as to blast the brightest hopes, of yourselves and of your friends. . . .'

Stanhope went on to Missolonghi. Mavrocordato had raised the Turkish blockade and there was now little in the way of Byron if he chose to go over. But still he delayed. In a letter written actually the day after Byron sailed, but before the news reached him, Stanhope described, for the benefit of the London Committee, the eagerness with which those in Missolonghi awaited Lord Byron: '. . . All are looking forward to Byron's arrival as they would to the coming of the Messiah. Three ships have been successively despatched for him, and he promises he is on the eve of departure, but two of these ships have, one after the other, been obliged to quit the harbour of Cephalonia without him. The third ship has not returned.'

And Byron was not on the third ship. He had chosen to make the crossing with his retinue in two small Ionian vessels. As luck would have it on the night of December 30 nine of the fourteen vessels in Mavrocordato's fleet were off chasing a Turkish brig, and so the Turks had put out from Patras. Byron himself was allowed to pass, the Turks imagining that the ship was some small coasting-vessel. Gamba, with Byron's baggage on board the other vessel, was captured, but was released through the intervention of a Turkish captain who recognised the skipper of the Ionian ship as a man who had once saved his life in the Black Sea. Byron's baggage was also recovered not long after.

Byron's adventures were not yet over, for he was almost shipwrecked twice, but, at last, he landed at Missolonghi on January 5,

155

1824. The moment is described by Gamba: 'Lord Byron's arrival was welcomed with salvos of artillery, firing of muskets, and wild music. Crowds of soldiery, and citizens of every rank, sex, and age, were assembled on the shore to testify their delight. Hope and content were pictured in every countenance.' (*A Narrative of Lord Byron's Last Journey to Greece.*)

Millingen takes up the tale: 'When Lord Byron landed, he wore a military uniform. By appearing in that dress for the first time, and on so solemn an occasion, he no doubt wished it to be understood, that his intention, on coming out to Greece, was, to devote himself especially to military operations.

'His house was filled with soldiers; his receiving room resembled an arsenal of war, rather than the habitation of a poet. Its walls were decorated with swords, pistols, Turkish sabres, dirks, rifles, guns, blunderbusses, bayonets, helmets, and trumpets, fantastically suspended, so as to form various figures; and attacks, surprises, charges, ambuscades, battles, sieges, were almost the only topics of his conversation with the different captains.'

And Trelawny heard the news:

In January, 1824, I heard that Byron was at Missolonghi; that a loan was about being negotiated in London, and that Colonel Stanhope and other English had arrived in Athens. I pressed upon Odysseus the necessity of our instantly returning thither, which we did. Shortly after, Stanhope proposed, and Odysseus agreed, to hold a congress at Salona, and that I should go to Missolonghi to invite Byron and the chiefs of Western Greece to attend it. I started on my mission with a band of followers; and we had been two days winding through the mountain passes,—for nothing can induce the Greeks to cross level ground, if there are Turks or the rumour of enemies near,—when a messenger from Missolonghi on his way to Salona, conveying the startling news of Byron's death, crossed our path, as we were fording the river Evvenus.

It is unfortunate both to history and to sentiment that Trelawny was not with Byron at Missolonghi, but other colleagues in the Greek adventure have filled in the gaps.

From the moment of his landing Lord Byron threw himself wholeheartedly into the role of general. 'He is soldier-mad,' wrote Stanhope, and others bore out this opinion. 'Each day we have offers of service from some foreigner or other . . . Lord Byron admitted almost all of them, either into the artillery corps, or a sort of chosen guard; thinking it of utmost importance to engage as many officers as possible, in order to be prepared for the disciplining of the soldiery, when we should be able to augment the number of our regular forces.' (Gamba.)

They were a difficult group, these foreign adventurers: 'What a queer set! What an assemblage of romantic, adventurous, restless, crack-brained young men from the four corners of the world! How much courage and talent to be found among them; but how much more of pompous vanity, of weak intellect, of mean selfishness, of utter depravity!' (Howe. *Journal*.)

Byron was still dipping into his own pocket to pay for Greek Independence: £300 for the artillery, a contribution towards the cost of a new force—2000 troops for an attack on Lepanto—a force with Byron as *archistrategos*, some more money to keep the naval squadron at sea.

Despite his financial and military exertions, the Turks slipped out of Patras on January 18, drove off the Greek brigs and appeared once more off Missolonghi. The Lepanto expedition had to be cancelled, and worse still, William Parry, the artillery commander, could not get his field-pieces across from Ithaca.

Byron wanted to attempt a cutting-out expedition, but was forced to abandon the project, and to reconcile himself to the incessant rain, the indiscipline and the bickering of Missolonghi.

For there was trouble within the garrison. Stanhope, a man full of magnificent schemes but weak in achievement, was getting on Byron's nerves. 'It is odd enough,' said Byron on one occasion, 'that Stanhope, the soldier is all for writing down the Turks, and I, the writer am all for shooting them down.' Mavrocordato was always scheming to separate Byron from Stanhope and the absent Trelawny. There was still no sign of real aid from the London Committee and the rival Government in Morea was succeeding in undermining the loyalty of some of his Greek troops.

Parry arrived with his guns at the end of January. Byron seems to have taken a fancy to this rowdy adventurer, and wrote in his *Journal*: 'Parry seems a fine rough subject, but will hardly be ready for the field these three weeks; he and I will (I think) be able to draw together.'

And Parry, who got on none too well with any of the other Philhellenes either in London or Missolonghi, appears to have encouraged in Byron a feeling of disillusionment and disappointment. His account of Byron at this time is symptomatic: 'I soon perceived not only that Lord Byron had no friend in Greece, but that he was surrounded by persons whom he neither loved nor trusted. Beyond the walls of his own apartment . . . he had neither security nor repose. He had the ungovernable Souliotes both to appease and control. Against the intrigues of the very persons he came to help and benefit he was obliged to be constantly on guard. . . . His confidence even in Prince Mavrocordato was not always unshaken. His youthful friend Count Gamba was destitute of experience . . . the foreign officers and English adventurers were all dissatisfied. . . . Whether he had actually received promises of greater succour from England than had ever been sent . . . I know not; but it was evident to me . . . that he felt himself deceived and abandoned, I had almost said betrayed. . . .' (*The Last Days of Lord Byron.*)

Parry's opinion is not always reliable, but his general impressions of Byron early in February 1824 are probably accurate enough.

And now it was Byron who wanted action; action to make him forget treachery and chicanery, action to make him capable of ignoring the incessant rain. To him action meant reviving the Lepanto project; and, despite difficulties with the artillery and disaffection among the volunteers, his plans went forward. But Kólokotrones had also heard of the plans and rather than let Byron, and therefore Mavrocordato, win a major victory, he sent agents to inspire the Souliotes to mutiny.

These efforts were successful. Just as the advance guard was due to leave on February 14, the Souliotes refused to march. Such was Byron's anger and disappointment that he had what was probably an epileptic fit. 'There was a flush in his countenance, which seemed to indicate great nervous agitation; and as I thought his Lordship had been much harassed for several days past, I recommended him, at least, to qualify his cider with some brandy . . . he complained of a very strange sensation. . . . He rose from his seat, but could not walk, staggered a step or two, and fell into my arms . . . In another minute his teeth were closed, his speech and senses gone, and he was in strong convulsions.'

Byron recovered, but the shock to his system was great, and was not softened by the fact that the Souliotes continued to act in a thoroughly mutinous manner, and actually murdered one of the German Adventurers. Eventually Byron was forced to threaten to leave Missolonghi with all the foreign adventurers unless the Souliotes left, and had to reinforce his threat with a large bribe—out of his own pocket. 'All this harassed him very much, and though he made a fine display when his energies were roused into action, his general health suffered from this excessive mental stimulus and exertion. Greater and increasing debility was the consequence . . . he gradually decayed.' (Parry.)

158

Still, he had not given up the idea of winning a second Battle of Lepanto. Only six days after his fit Byron wrote to Douglas Kinnaird: 'We shall have work this year, for the Turks are coming down in force; and, as for me, I must stand by the cause. I shall shortly march . . . against Lepanto with two thousand men. . . . So far I have succeeded in supporting the Government of Western Greece, which would otherwise have been dissolved. If you have received the eleven thousand and odd pounds, these with what I have in hand, and my income for the current year, to say nothing of contingencies will, or might, enable me to keep the "sinews of war" properly strung . . . let the Greeks only succeed, and I don't care for myself.

'I have been very seriously unwell, but am getting better, and can ride about again; so pray quiet our friends on that score.'

At this time he was freed from at least one worry: Stanhope went off to the mainland, but once there his personality obtruded in another way—Stanhope, like Trelawny, was completely taken in by the dashing brigand Odysseus, and began pressing Byron to desert his connection with Mavrocordato and to take up instead the support of Odysseus. 'He has a very strong mind,' wrote Stanhope on March 6, 'a good heart, and is brave as his sword; he is a doing man; he governs with a strong arm, and is the only man in Greece that can preserve order. . . .'

In Missolonghi itself, money rather than war was Byron's main worry. The citizens asked for financial aid so that they could repair the fortifications; Mavrocordato reported categorically that 'the till is not only empty, but in debt as well'; Gamba came into disfavour for using some of Byron's private funds to pay the artillery. All this, with his weakness, disappointment and the continual rain, reduced Byron's mental and physical resistance. 'At this moment', writes Parry, 'there was a combination of circumstances, all tending to irritate the naturally sensitive disposition of Lord Byron and to weaken his hopes of a great and glorious result. He was more a mental being, if I may use this phrase, than any man I ever saw. He lived on thought more than on food. As his hopes of the cause of Greece failed . . . he became peevish; and, if I may so speak, little-minded.'

In this state he even quarrelled with his servant, Fletcher, but the discovery, on April 6, of yet another treacherous plot within Missolonghi brought him out for one last grand occasion to lead a show of military might in an effort to impress the citizens.

But his disillusionment was now complete, and disillusionment finally broke his health in April 1824.

'My master', said his servant Fletcher, 'continued his usual custom of riding daily when the weather would permit, until the 9th of

April. But on that ill-fated day he got very wet; and on his return home his Lordship changed the whole of his dress; but he had been too long in his wet clothes, and the cold, of which he had complained more or less ever since we left Cephalonia, made this attack be more severely felt. Though rather feverish during the night, his Lordship slept pretty well, but complained in the morning of a pain in his bones and a head-ache: this did not, however, prevent him from taking a ride in the afternoon, which I grieve to say was his last. On his return, my master said that the saddle was not perfectly dry, from being so wet the day before, and observed that he thought it had made him worse. His Lordship was again visited by the same slow fever, and I was sorry to perceive, on the next morning, that his illness appeared to be increasing. He was very low, and complained of not having had any sleep during the night. His Lordship's appetite was also quite gone. I prepared a little arrow-root, of which he took three or four spoonfuls, saying it was very good, but could take no more. It was not till the third day, the 12th, that I began to be alarmed for my master. In all his former colds he always slept well, and was never affected by this slow fever. I therefore went to Dr. Bruno and Mr. Millingen, the two medical attendants, and inquired minutely into every circumstance connected with my master's present illness: both replied that there was no danger, and I might make myself perfectly easy on the subject, for all would be well in a few days.—This was on the 13th. On the following day I found my master in such a state, that I could not feel happy without supplicating that he would send to Zante for Dr. Thomas. After expressing my fears lest his Lordship should get worse, he desired me to consult the doctors; which I did, and was told there was no occasion for calling in any person, as they hoped all would be well in a few days. —Here I should remark, that his Lordship repeatedly said, in the course of the day, he was sure the doctors did not understand his disease; to which I answered, "Then, my Lord, have other advice by all means."—"They tell me," said his Lordship, "that it is only a common cold, which, you know, I have had a thousand times."—"I am sure, my Lord," said I, "that you never had one of so serious a nature."—"I think I never had," was his Lordship's answer. I repeated my supplications that Dr. Thomas should be sent for, on the 15th, and was again assured that my master would be better in two or three days. After these confident assurances, I did not renew my entreaties until it was too late. With respect to the medicines that were given to my master, I could not persuade myself that those of a strong purgative nature were the best adapted for his complaint, concluding that, as he had nothing on his stomach, the only effect would be to create pain: indeed this must have been the case with a person in perfect health. The whole nourishment taken by my master, for the last eight days, consisted of a small quantity of broth at two or three different times, and two spoonfuls of arrow-root on the 18th, the day before his death.'

'During the last days of Lord Byron's illness', writes Dr. Millingen, 'he was remarkably taciturn; but his mind was occupied by anxious thoughts. . . . I was not a little surprised to hear him ask me on the 15th, whether I could not do him the favour of inquiring in the town for any very old and ugly witch? As I turned his question in derision, he repeated to me with a serious air: "Never mind whether I am superstitious or not; but I again entreat of you to bring me the most celebrated one there is, in order that she may examine whether this sudden loss of my health does not depend on the evil eye. She may devise some means to dissolve the spell." '

But the same authority stands as evidence for the fact that Byron's superstition did not encourage him to accept a death-bed conversion. 'Although I seldom left Lord Byron's pillow during the latter part of his illness, I did not hear him make any, even the smallest, mention of religion. At one moment I heard him say: "Shall I sue for mercy?" After a long pause he added: "Come, come, no weakness! Let's be a man to the last." ' (Millingen.)

This self-imposed manliness did not allow Byron to overcome his horror of bleeding. 'It was not possible to convince him. He even burst into a fit of irritation, saying that he well knew that the lancet had killed more people than the lance. He agreed to take one of his usual pills, and to swallow some blackcurrant tea.' (Bruno.) But the doctors insisted and Byron was subjected to constant bleeding by his doctors, that 'damned set of butchers'. This drastic remedy could not save him.

On the 18th he addressed Millingen,* saying: 'Your efforts to

---

* Julius Millingen, who is clear and straight enough in his accounts of Byron's last days, later disgraced himself twice. First he sent in a bill for £200 to Byron's executors, and then he went over to the Turks. A fellow doctor, the American Samuel Gridley Howe, indicated exactly what he thought of Millingen in one short but biting phrase, 'Thank God he is not an American', and Trelawny describes the man's actions and character, with anger but justice, in a letter he wrote to the *London Literary Gazette* in 1831 on reading a review of Millingen's book: 'Out of three thousand adventurers, of all sorts and conditions, all serving for pay and plunder, one man alone was mercenary and base enough to abandon the cause . . . to be a deserter to the enemy . . . His name, and deservedly, was never mentioned in Greece after his treachery without being accompanied by universal execrations . . .

preserve my life will be vain. Die I must: I feel it. Its loss I do not lament; for to terminate my wearisome existence I came to Greece . . . One request let me make to you. Let not my body be hacked, or be sent to England. Here let my bones moulder—Lay me in the first corner without pomp or nonsense.'

'It was Easter day, on which holiday, after twelve o'clock, the Greeks are accustomed to discharge their fire-arms and artillery. Fearing that the noise might be injurious to my Lord, we thought of marching our artillery brigade out of the city, and by exercising our guns, to attract the crowd from the vicinity of his house. At the same time, the town guard patroled the streets, and informing the people of the danger of their benefactor, invited them to make as little noise as possible near the place where he lay. Our scheme succeeded perfectly; but, nevertheless, we should not have been induced to quit the house if we had been aware of the real state of our friend. I do not think that he suspected it himself, even so late as three in the afternoon. . . .

'It was about six o'clock in the evening when he said, "I want to go to sleep now"; and immediately turning round, he fell into that slumber, from which, alas! he never awoke. From that moment he seemed incapable of sense or motion: but there were occasional symptoms of suffocation, and a rattling in the throat, which induced his servants now and then to raise his head. Means were taken to rouse him from his lethargy, but in vain. He continued in this state for four-and-twenty hours; and it was just a quarter past six o'clock on the next day, the 19th, that he was seen to open his eyes, and immediately shut them again. The physicians felt his pulse—he was gone!' (Gamba.)

The Provisional Government of Western Greece issued a proclamation.

'The present day of festivity and rejoicing has become one of sorrow and of mourning. The Lord Noel Byron departed this life at six o'clock in the afternoon, after an illness of ten days; his death being caused by an inflammatory fever. Such was the effect of his Lordship's illness on the public mind, that all classes had forgotten their usual recreations of Easter, even before the afflicting event was apprehended.

'The loss of this illustrious individual is undoubtedly to be deplored by all Greece; but it must be more especially a subject of lamentation at Missolonghi, where his generosity has been so conspicuously displayed, and of which he had even become a citizen, with the further determination of participating in all the dangers of war.

'Every body is acquainted with the beneficent acts of his Lordship, and none can cease to hail his name as that of a real benefactor.

'Until, therefore, the final determination of the national government be known, and by virtue of the powers with which it has been pleased to invest me, I hereby decree,

'1st. To-morrow morning, at daylight, thirty-seven minute guns will be fired from the Grand Battery, being the number which corresponds with the age of the illustrious deceased.

'2d. All the public offices, even the tribunals, are to remain closed for three successive days.

'3d. All the shops, except those in which provisions or medicines are sold, will also be shut; and it is strictly enjoined that every species of public amusement, and other demonstrations of festivity at Easter, shall be suspended.

'4th. A general mourning will be observed for twenty-one days.

'5th. Prayers and a funeral service are to be offered up in all the churches.

'Given at Missolonghi,   (Signed) A. Mavrocordato.
this 19th day of April, 1824.   George Praidis, Secretary.'

Thus, by a stroke of fate, my hopes of being of use in Greece were extinguished: Byron and Stanhope, as commissioners of the loan, would have expended it on the war; and the sordid and selfish Primates, Machiavellian Phanariotes, and lawless Captanria would have been held in check. Byron thought all men rogues, and put no trust in any. As applied to Greeks, his scepticism was perfect wisdom. Stanhope was of a frank and hopeful nature; he had carefully examined the state of things, and would have been an able coadjutor, for he possessed those inestimable qualities,—energy, temper, and order—which Byron lacked. The first thing Stanhope did, was to establish a free press: many opposed this as premature, if not dangerous, but it was of eminent service, and the only institution founded at that time which struck root deep into the soil.

Colonel Stanhope gave me the following note to Byron, but the Colonel's prophetic warning was too late:

Salona, 17 April, 1824

MY DEAR LORD BYRON, We are all assembled here with the exception of your Lordship and Monsieur Mavrocordato. I hope you will both join us; indeed, after the strong pledges given, the President ought to attend. As for you, you are a sort of Wilberforce, a saint whom all parties are endeavouring to seduce; it's a pity that you are not divisible, that every prefecture might have a fraction of your person. For my own part, I wish to see you fairly out of Missolonghi, because your health will not stand the climate and the constant anxiety to which you are there subjected..

I shall remain here till we receive your and the President's answer; I mean then to go to Egina, Zante, and England. If I can be of any service, you may command my zealous services.

Once more, I implore you to quit Missolonghi, and not to sacrifice your health and, perhaps, your life in that Bog. I am ever your most devoted, LEICESTER STANHOPE.

21

WITH desponding thoughts I entered Missolonghi on the third day from my leaving Salona. Any spot on the surface of the earth, or in its bowels, that holds out a prospect of gain, you will find inhabited; a morass that will produce rice, the crust of a volcano in which the vine will grow; lagunes, in which fish abound, are temptations which overcome the terror of pestilence or death. So I was not surprised at seeing Missolonghi, situated as it is on the verge of the most dismal swamp I had ever seen. The marvel was that Byron, prone to fevers, should have been induced to land on this mudbank, and stick there for three months shut in by a circle of stagnant pools which might be called the belt of death. Although it was now the early spring, I found most of the strangers suffering from gastric fevers. It was the 24th or 25th of April when I arrived; Byron had died on the 19th. I waded through the streets, between wind and water, to the house he had lived in; it was detached, and on the margin of the shallow slimy sea-waters. For three months this house had been besieged, day and night, like a bank that has a run upon it. Now that death had closed the door, it was as silent as a cemetery. No one was within the house but Fletcher, of which I was glad. As if he knew my wishes, he led me up a narrow stair into a small room, with nothing in it but a coffin standing on trestles. No word was spoken by either of us; he withdrew the black pall and the white shroud, and there lay the embalmed body of the Pilgrim—more beautiful in death than in life. The contraction of the muscles and skin had effaced every line that time or passion had ever traced on it; few marble busts could have matched its stainless white, the harmony of its proportions, and perfect finish; yet he had been dissatisfied with that body, and longed to cast its slough. How often I had heard him curse it! He was jealous of the genius of Shakspeare—that might well be—but where had he seen the face or form worthy to excite his envy? I asked Fletcher to bring me a glass of water. On his leaving the room, to confirm or remove my doubts as to the cause of his lameness, I uncovered the Pilgrim's feet, and was answered—the great mystery was solved. Both his feet were clubbed, and his legs withered to the knee—the form and features of an Apollo, with the feet and legs of a sylvan satyr. This was a curse, chaining a proud and soaring spirit like his to the dull earth. In the drama of *The Deformed Transformed*, I knew that he had expressed all he could express of what a man of highly-wrought mind might feel when brooding over a deformity of body: but when he said:

> I have done the best which spirit may to make
> Its way with all deformity, dull deadly,
> Discouraging weight upon me,

I thought it exaggerated as applied to himself; now I saw it was not so. His deformity was always uppermost in his thoughts, and influenced every act of his life, spurred him on to poetry, as that was one of the few paths to fame open to him,—and as if to be revenged on Nature for sending him into the world 'scarce half made up', he scoffed at her works and traditions with the pride of Lucifer; this morbid feeling ultimately goaded him on to his last Quixotic crusade in Greece.

No other man, afflicted as he was, could have been better justified than Byron in saying:

> I ask not
> For valour, since deformity is daring;
> It is its essence to o'ertake mankind
> By heart and soul, and make itself the equal—
> Ay, the superior of the rest. There is
> A spur in its halt movements, to become
> All that the others cannot, in such things
> As still are free to both, to compensate
> For step-dame Nature's niggardness at first;
> They war with fearless deeds, the smiles of fortune,
> And oft, like Timour the lame Tartar, win them.

Knowing and sympathising with Byron's sensitiveness, his associates avoided prying into the cause of his lameness; so did strangers, from good breeding or common humanity. It was generally thought his halting gait originated in some defect of the right foot or ankle—the right foot was the most distorted, and it had been made worse in his boyhood by vain efforts to set it right. He told me that for several years he wore steel splints, which so wrenched the sinews and tendons of his leg, that they increased his lameness; the foot was twisted inwards, only the edge touched the ground, and that leg was shorter than the other. His shoes were peculiar—very high heeled, with the soles uncommonly thick on the inside and pared thin on the outside—the toes were stuffed with cotton-wool, and his trousers were very large below the knee and strapped down so as to cover his feet. The peculiarity of his gait was now accounted for; he entered a room with a sort of run, as if he could not stop, then planted his best leg well forward, throwing back his body to keep his balance. In early life whilst his frame was light and elastic, with the aid of a stick he might have tottered along for a mile or two; but after he had waxed heavier, he seldom attempted to walk more than a few hundred yards, without squatting down or leaning against the first wall, bank, rock, or tree at hand, never sitting on the ground, as it would have been difficult for him to get up again. In the company of strangers, occasionally, he would make desperate efforts to conceal his infirmity, but the hectic flush on his face, his swelling veins, and quivering nerves betrayed him, and he suffered for many days after such exertions. Disposed to fatten, incapable of taking exercise to check the tendency, what could he do? If he added to his weight, his feet would not have supported him; in this dilemma he was compelled to exist in a state of semi-starvation; he was less than eleven stone when at Genoa, and said he had been fourteen at Venice. The pangs of hunger which travellers and shipwrecked mariners have described were nothing to what he suffered; their privations were temporary, his were for life, and more unendurable, as he was in the midst of abundance. I was exclaiming, 'Poor fellow, if your errors were greater than those of ordinary men, so were your temptations and provocations,' when Fletcher returned with a bottle and glass, saying, 'There is nothing but slimy salt water in this horrid place, so I have been half over the town to beg this bottle of porter,' and, answering my ejaculation of 'Poor fellow!' he said:

'You may well say so, sir, these savages are worse than any highwaymen; they have robbed my Lord of all his money and his life too.'

Whilst saying this, Fletcher, without making any remark, drew the shroud and pall carefully over the feet of his master's corpse—he was very nervous and trembled as he did it; so strongly had his weak and superstitious nature been acted upon by the injunctions and threats of his master, that, alive or dead, no one was to see his feet, for if they did, he would haunt him, etc., etc.

Fletcher gave me a sheet of paper, and from his dictation I wrote on Byron's coffin the particulars of his last illness and death. This account differs in many particulars from the one already published; in the same way that the fresh rough notes of an eye-witness, taken on the spot, differ on passing through the hands of the editor of a review to be served out to the public as an article to serve a cause or strengthen a faction—so let it be, I shall not question it.

A letter from his half-sister, Augusta Leigh, was on his writing-table. This lady was the only relation Byron had, or at least acknowledged; and he always spoke of her in the most affectionate terms. He was in the act of writing to her when he was taken ill. This unfinished letter I copied,—as the original would run many risks of being lost before it reached its destination. It is interesting as the last of Byron's writings—as an index, too, of his real and inward feelings; those letters that have been published were written, as I have already observed, under an assumed character and for effect.

His sister's letter contained a long transcript of one from Lady Byron; with a minute mental and physical account of their child, Ada. Lady Byron's letter mentioned a profile of the child. I found it, with other tokens that the Pilgrim had most treasured, scattered on the floor,—as rubbish of no marketable value, and trampled on. I rescued from destruction a cambric handkerchief stained with his blood, and marked with a lady's name in hair; a ringlet; a ribbon; and a small glove. These relics I folded up with some of his own hair that I had shorn from his head.

168

This unfinished letter was the last of Byron's writings; it is to his half-sister, Augusta Leigh.

Missolonghi, Feb. 23, 1824

MY DEAREST AUGUSTA, I received a few days ago, your and Lady B.'s report of Ada's health, with other letters from England; for which I ought to be, and am (I hope) sufficiently thankful, as they are of great comfort and I wanted some, having been recently unwell—but am now much better, so that you must not be alarmed.

You will have heard of our journeys and escapes, and so forth,—perhaps with some exaggeration; but it is all very well now, and I have been some time in Greece, which is in as good a state as could be expected considering circumstances. But I will not plague you with politics—wars—or earthquakes, though we have had a rather smart one three nights ago, which produced a scene ridiculous enough, as no damage was done, except to those who stuck fast in the scuffle to get first out of the doors or windows; amongst whom, some recent importations from England, who had been used to quieter elements, were rather squeezed in the press for precedence.

I have been obtaining the release of about nine-and-twenty Turkish prisoners,—men, women, and children, and have sent them, at my own expense, home to their friends; but one pretty little girl of nine years of age, named Hato or Hatagée, has expressed a strong wish to remain with me or under my care;—and I have nearly determined to adopt her, if I thought that Lady B. would let her come to England as a companion to Ada (they are about the same age), and we could easily provide for her,—if not, I can send her to Italy for education. She is very lively and quick, and with great black Oriental eyes and Asiatic features. All her brothers were killed in the revolution. Her mother wishes to return to her husband, who is at Previsa; but says that she would rather entrust the child to me in the present state of the country. Her extreme youth and sex have hitherto saved her life, but there is no saying what might happen in the course of the war (and of such a war). I shall probably commit her to the care of some English lady in the islands for the present. The child herself has the same wish, and seems to have a decided character for her age. You can mention this matter, if you think it worth while. I merely wish her to be respectably educated and treated; and if my years and all things be considered,—I presume it would be difficult to conceive me to have any other views.

With regard to Ada's health, I am glad to hear that she is so much better; but I think it right that Lady B. should be informed and guard against it accordingly; that her description of much of her disposition and tendencies very nearly resemble that of my own at a similar age,—except that I was much more impetuous. Her preference of *prose* (strange as it may now seem) *was*, and indeed *is*, mine (for I hate reading verse—and always did); and I never invented anything but 'boats,— ships,' and generally something relative to the ocean. I showed the report to Colonel Stanhope, who was struck with the resemblance of parts of it to the paternal line,—even now.

But it is also fit, though unpleasant, that I should mention,— that my recent attack, and a very severe one,—had a strong appearance of epilepsy;—why, I know not—for it is late in life. Its first appearance at thirty-six, and, so far as I *know*, it is *not* hereditary;—and it is that it may not *become* so, that you should tell Lady B. to take some precautions in the case of Ada.

My attack has not returned,—and I am fighting it off with abstinence and exercise, and thus far with success;—if merely casual, it is all very well——

Gordon, in his *History of the Greek Revolution*, speaking of Byron just before his death, says: 'His health declined, and we cannot be surprised, considering what he had suffered, and was daily suffering, from the deceptions practised upon him, and importunate solicitations for money. Parry talked a great deal and did little; Mavrocordato promised everything, and performed nothing, and the Primates, who engaged to furnish 1500 dollars towards the expenses of the fortifications, could not produce a farthing, and in lieu thereof presented him with the freedom of the town. The streets and country were a bed of mire, so he could not take any exercise out of doors.'

To return to what passed in Byron's house. On hearing a noise below, I went down into the public room, and found

170

Parry with a comrade carousing. This man (Parry) had been a clerk in the civil department of the Ordnance at Woolwich, and was sent out by the committee with the munitions of war, as head fire-master. In revolutions, however severely the body may suffer for want of pay and rations, your vanity is pampered to satiety by the assumption of whatever rank or title you may have a fancy for. Mavrocordato dubbed himself Prince; Byron, Commander-in-Chief; Parry the ordnance clerk, Major.

I said, 'Well, major, what do you think was the cause of Lord Byron's death?'

'Think? I don't think anything about it; I am a practical man, not a humbugging thinker; he would have been alive now if he had followed my advice. He lived too low: I told him so a thousand times. Two or three days before he slipped his wind, he said: "Parry, what do you think is the matter with me, the doctors don't know my complaint?" No, I said, nor nothing else, my lord; let me throw them out of the window. "What will do me good, Parry?" Brandy, my lord; nothing but brandy will save you; you have only got a chill on an empty stomach; let me mix you a stiff glass of grog, and you will be all right to-morrow, but he shook his head, so I gave him up as a lost man. My father,' he continued, 'lived to a great age on brandy, and then he would not have died, but the doctor stopped his drink, and the death-rattle choked his scuppers.'

'What did the doctors do, Parry, with Lord Byron?'

'Do! why they physicked and bled him to death. My lord called them assassins to their faces, and so they are. A pair of more conceited ignorant scamps I never saw; they are only fit to stand at the corners of alleys to distribute Doctor Eady's hand-bills.'

The fire-master was a rough burly fellow, never quite sober, but he was no fool, and had a fund of pot-house stories which he told in appropriately slang language; he was a mimic, and amused Byron by burlesquing Jeremy Bentham and other members of the Greek committee. Besides these accomplishments, he professed a thorough knowledge of the art of fortification, and said he was the inventor of shells and fire-balls that would destroy the Ottoman fleet and the garrison of Lepanto. All he did, however, was to talk and drink. He was three months in Greece,

171

returned to England, talked the committee out of 400*l.* for his services, and drank himself into a madhouse. When he could get no more brandy to keep down the death-rattle, he died as he said his father had done. Six artificers whom he brought to Greece with him, staid there only a fortnight, and cost the committee 340*l.*

Out of the first loan of 800,000*l.*, negotiated in England, the Greeks got 240,000*l.* The money Byron advanced by way of loan was repaid by the Greeks; but I believe it was invested in the Greek loan, and so lost.

As so much of the history of British intervention in Greece is concerned with financial affairs, and as Trelawny even drags them in at this solemn moment in his story, it is necessary to give a little more information on 'the Greek Loan'.

After its inception the London Greek Committee had tried to raise money by public appeal, but though the results were not negligible the sums received were hardly enough to keep Revolution alive. Something in the nature of £10,000 was collected by the middle of 1824, to which can be added another £10,000 collected by the Society of Friends. (The American Philhellenic Committees collected about £20,000, and the total contribution from foreign friends of Greece was not more than £100,000.)

The Greeks therefore decided to float a loan in London, and it was for this purpose that the Deputies had sailed for England. Blaquiere, who was primarily responsible for handling the financial affairs of the Greek Committee, had considerable difficulty in preventing various scatterbrained loan-schemes, but eventually, on February 21, 1824, a loan was floated in the City of London at a nominal value of £800,000, against the security of land in Greece. £80,000 was to be paid immediately, the balance when representatives of the London Greek Committee had satisfied themselves that the money was to be properly handled, according to the instructions of their three Commissioners of whom Byron was to be one; by a Government recognised in Greece. The actual sum raised was almost £500,000, a loan large enough in itself to justify the conclusion that the City was confident of the eventual success of the Greek cause, was sentimentally excited, and was seriously perturbed by the interruption to trade occasioned by affairs in Greece. Of this sum, when expenses had been deducted only £315,000 was eventually available.

Such sums as were sent to Greece were delayed on the way by the

Ionian Government, by the indecision of the Commissioners, and, not least of all, by the death of Byron. And when, during 1824, the money arrived much of it was squandered: 'Fanariots and doctors of medicine, who in April 1824 were clad in ragged coats . . . drew off the patriotic chrysallis before the summer was past and emerged in all the splendour of brigand life, fluttering about in rich Albanian habiliments . . . and followed by diminutive pipe bearers and tall henchmen.' (Finlay. *History of the Greek Revolution.*)

22

EARLY in the morning Gamba and I looked over Byron's papers; there were several journals and notebooks; they contained memorandums of his thoughts, not of his actions—violent invectives on the Zuliotes and others.—Italian and English letters, fifteen stanzas of the seventeenth canto of *Don Juan*, dated 8th May, several songs finished, and sundry beginnings of poems, his opinions of Napoleon's banishment, continuations of *Childe Harold*, and the *Deformed Transformed*, and other fragments. Mavrocordato came in; finally we sealed up everything. The 30 or 40,000 dollars which Byron had brought with him to Missolonghi were reduced to 5000 or 6000. Mavrocordato urged that this sum should be left with him as a loan, and that he would be responsible for its repayment. I objected to this as illegal, and insisted on the money being shipped to the Ionian Islands. The prince was exceedingly put out at this; he evidently thought my scruples arose from no other motive than personal enmity to him. The congress at Salona he considered a scheme of mine to get Byron out of his hands, and to deliver him, Mavrocordato, into the clutches of Odysseus, and he was in great terror of that chief. These things I could see engendered in his mind a deadly hatred of me. After the consummate art which this prince of Phanariotes had displayed in inveigling Byron and his dollars into Missolonghi, he looked upon him as a lawful prize, and on my efforts to rescue his victim as the height of audacity. I had no enmity to the prince, but I had a strong feeling of good will towards Byron; and never lost sight of his interest. To be brief, my plan had been simply this, to get Byron to Athens; Odysseus, whose confidence I had won, engaged to deliver up the Acropolis of that city, to put the said fortress into my hands the instant Byron promised to come there, and to allow me to garrison it with my own people and hold it; with no other condition than that of not giving it up to the Greek government as at the time constituted. There the poet would have been in his glory; he loved Athens. In that fortress with a Frank garrison he would have been thoroughly independent; he would have been safe from fevers,

THE VILLA MAGNI

From a drawing by Capt. D. Roberts, R.N.

for it is the healthiest site in the world, as well as the most beautiful. If the Greeks succeeded in raising a loan, and he was appointed to control its expenditure, at Athens he would have been in a commanding position: aloof from the sordid civil and military factions, he might have controlled them—Byron was no soldier:

Nor the division of a battle knew more than a spinster.

To carry on the war a disciplined army and an able general were indispensable. Sir C. J. Napier was the man exactly fitted for such an emergency; skilful, fearless, prompt, and decided as fate. The deep interest that great soldier felt in the cause of the Greeks was such, that he would have undertaken the war, although it would have cost him his commission in the British service, if solicited by the proper authorities, and furnished with sufficient means and power. When Byron was on his death-bed, and wandering in his mind, Napier was uppermost in his thoughts; he cursed the mercenary and turbulent Zuliotes, exclaiming: 'When Napier comes, I will have them all flayed alive.'

In one of my visits to Cephalonia, expressly to inform Napier of the state of anarchy in Greece, I told him the first duty he would have to perform would be that of shooting and imprisoning half-a-dozen of the most refractory of the leaders of factions, as well as of the Captanria.

'No,' he said, 'you shall do that; you shall be Provost Marshal. If I go there, we will raise the price of hemp; and I won't go without two European regiments, money in hand to pay them, and a portable gallows.'

'I will accept the office, and do my duty,' I answered.

To resume my story. After I had seen Byron's effects dispatched to Zanté, I left Missolonghi to return to Salona. Many of the foreign soldiers who had been in Byron's pay, now that pay was stopped, volunteered to join me. I engaged as many as I could afford to keep. I had, likewise, five brass guns, with ammunition, and some other things sent out by the English committee, which I was authorised to take to Eastern Greece. Mavrocordato opposed this order,—but I enforced it; so that I had now a cavalcade of fifty or sixty horses and mules, and about a hundred men, including the Roumeliotes whom I had brought with me. In all my motley squad there was only one who spoke English, and he was a Scot. It would have been better had I omitted that one. When I arrived at Salona, I found Stanhope and a host of others who had come to meet Byron. Stanhope had received a letter from the Horse Guards ordering him home.

I had now no motive for remaining in Greece. The Greeks were jealous of foreigners; those who had not money wandered about in rags, and wretchedness, although many of them were very able soldiers, and had greatly distinguished themselves. But I did not like deserting Odysseus; he was very anxious I should stay. He said: 'The Greeks were naturally treacherous, artful, sordid, and fickle; and that history and tradition proved they had always been so.'

The congress dispersed. I returned with Odysseus into Livadia, and we re-visited Athens and Euboea,—carrying on the war in the same inefficient and desultory way as before, un-aided by the government and abandoned to our own resources. Hitherto the military chiefs held all the real power in Greece; the territory they wrested from the Turks they considered as lawful prize: in short, they acted on

> The good old rule, the simple plan,
> That they should take who have the power,
> And they should keep who can.*

As to the government it was a mere farce, but its members knew it might one day become a reality. Their chief occupation consisted in raising money from those few spots not previously ravaged by the ruthless soldiers. The insignificant revenue thus raised they appropriated to their own uses.

They were now assembled at Nauplia. An English vessel arrived in that port with 40,000*l.* assigned to them,—this being the first instalment of the Greek loan. The rush to the diggings

---

* Because the good old rule
  Sufficeth them, the simple plan,
  That they should take, who have the power,
  And they should keep who can.
              Wordsworth. *Rob Roy's Grave*. Stanza 9.

in California and Australia, on the first discovery of gold in those regions, was partial, if not orderly, as compared with the wild and universal rush of the Greeks on Nauplia. That town was beleaguered by armed legions of robbers, frantically clamouring for their share of the spoil. Their military leaders soon found, not only that they should get no money, but that they were in imminent peril of losing their heads.

The government determined to rule with a strong hand, and to crush their military rivals. They commenced organising a force and inveigling the men from their chiefs; they attempted to assassinate Odysseus, and were plotting to seize the great Moreote chieftain, Colocotroni,—so the great captains fled to their mountain strongholds. The government ultimately arrested Colocotroni and many others.

In reading these *Recollections* it is easy to see that Trelawny's understanding of Greek internal politics was scant indeed. He had a genuine fervour for liberty, but it was as nothing compared to his love of action. Byron, he felt, had betrayed him by his prevarication, and had betrayed him even in death by not making it clear that his cloak as the leader of the British Philhellenes was to fall on the shoulders of Trelawny—who would wear it, of course, with a sword. Only Odysseus had fed him the excitement he craved, and as, at this time as always in the history of the Greek Revolution, Greece was riven to the point of civil war by the conflicting claims of the politicians (headed by Mavrocordato) and the brigand-chiefs (outstanding among them Odysseus and Kolokotrones) it was inevitable that Trelawny would side with the brigands.

For one who admired violence and despised diplomacy, for one who loved physical strength and ignored the puny, for one who loathed all aristocrats but the aristocrats of action, the choice between Odysseus and Mavrocordato was no choice at all. To him Mavrocordato was 'a mere shuffling soldier . . . a poor, weak, shuffling, intriguing, cowardly fellow'. Odysseus, on the other hand, was a noble fellow—'a Bolivar', with 'the elements to make a Washington'.

Nor, through all the bias which Trelawny releases on this subject, can the reader escape the judgment that his prejudice was not without wisdom, military if not political, for Trelawny's mind, unskilful in political logic, was quick to make tactical appreciations, and he realised, what all who know the problems of fighting in Greece will

177

corroborate, that the country is ideally suited to resistance by power-ful but isolated groups, and is remarkably unkind to all efforts at centralised control of operations.

I remained with a hundred men between Livadia and Mount Parnes. Odysseus joined me there, and gave me an account of the state of things at Nauplia.

He said: 'By stratagem and force, with my own small means, I have kept the Turks out of the Morea for three years without aid from the government. The territory we captains have dis-possessed the Sultan of, our self-elected government have sold to the Russians*; and with the money they are to get rid of us, to make way for a foreign king and foreign soldiers.'

I asked, 'What king?'

He said, they were 'divided on that subject, but the Russian party was the strongest, for they had the priests, the Phanariotes and Moreotes, with them; but,' he added, 'what puzzles me is, that England should advance money to make Greece a hospo-dariot of Russia. I never met any Greek who could understand the reason why so shrewd a nation of traffickers as the English should lend them such large sums of money, since every one must know, they said, that they neither could nor would repay any portion of it.'

---

* From the very beginnings of the Greek rebellion the revolutionaries had great hopes of help from Russia, and had based their appeals to the Tsar both on religious affinity and on the obvious enmity between Russia and Turkey. The hopes and appeals were met, at first, with scant response, but, in their efforts to stimulate the British into action, each party in Greece was apt to describe all other parties as pro-Russian. Odysseus was cunning enough to realise that Trelawny, for all his roaming, was essentially proud of his Englishness and likely to resent any suggestion that Russia was gaining advantages over England. Possibly, too, neither Odysseus nor Trelawny was capable of appreciating Mavrocordato's political wisdom, and either regarded as treachery or pretended to regard as treachery his policy of having ' connections everywhere and with everybody'.

In fact, though the Russians made a proposal in January 1824 that there should be a mediation conference at St. Petersburg, their real activities in the Greek affair did not begin until early in 1826. As a sidelight on this, it is interesting to note that Dr. Dakin, who has done more than any other historian to establish the identity of foreign adventurers in Greece, has only been able to discover two Russians among them all.

I urged Odysseus to resign his command, and with a few followers to retire to the mountains—adding that 'borrowed money in the hands of a knavish government would soon vanish.'

Odysseus said, 'This part of the country, Livadia, my father inherited from his father, who won it by his valour, and when it was lost through the treachery of the Venetians, who sold my father to the Sultan, I regained it by my wits, and have kept it with my sword.'

'And so you may again, if you are dispossessed now,' I answered, 'if you bide your time.'

How can a soldier, with nothing but his sword, defend himself against infernal machinations devised by a Prince of Hell, armed with a chest of gold? Phanariotes, like devils, work in the dark!

In one of the precipices of Mount Parnassus, in Livadia, the highest mountain in Greece, there is a cavern, at an elevation of a thousand feet above the plain. This cavern Odysseus had, with great ingenuity, managed to ascend, and convert into a place of safety for his family and effects during the war. The only access to it was by ladders, bolted to the rock. The first ladder, forty-five or fifty feet in length, was placed against the face of the rock, and steadied by braces; a second, resting on a projecting crag, crossed the first; and a third, lighter and shorter, stood on its heel on a natural shelf in the fractured stone. This third ladder led to a trap-door; the bolts and bars of which being removed, you entered a vaulted guard-room, pierced with lancet-holes for musketry. This opened on a broad terrace, sixty feet in length, screened by a substantial parapet-wall, breast-high, with embrasures mounted with cannon. The height of the natural arch spanning the cave is thirty feet above this lower terrace, so that it is particularly light, airy, and cheerful, commanding extensive and magnificent views. Ascending by steps to a yet higher terrace of solid rock, the breadth and height of the cave diminishes, until the end is reached. On the right of the great cave there is a smaller one; besides which there are many small grottoes, the size of chambers, connected by galleries. They are perfectly dry, and were used for store-rooms and magazines. One of them I converted into a chapel for an old priest, covering the rugged walls with gaudy

179

hangings, flaming paintings, and holy relics of saints, saved from the desecrated churches in the neighbourhood.

The interior of this magnificent cavern often reminded me, with its grottoes, galleries, and vaulted roof, of a cathedral, particularly when the softened light of the evening obscured its ruggedness, or by moonlight. The towering mass of rock above the cave projected boldly over its base. To make it perfect, there was a never-failing supply of the purest water, which found its way through subterranean channels from the regions of perpetual snow, filtering through fractures in the rock above into a capacious cistern built on the upper terrace.

This cavern was our citadel, and by removing the upper ladder became impregnable without the aid of a garrison. We built boarded houses within it, and stored it with all the necessaries and many of the luxuries of life, besides immense supplies of arms and ammunition.

I urged Odysseus to abide in this stronghold, saying that the borrowed money was sure to be embezzled by a government composed of arrant sharpers; and that but a small part of it would be applied to the purpose it was contracted for. Besides, Ibrahim Pasha was on his way to Greece with an immense force. Civil wars were already rife in the Morea. 'The Greeks,' I continued, 'and their country are so admirably adapted for guerilla warfare, that those chiefs who had carried on the insurrection successfully, and had shown that they alone had capacity to continue it, must be recalled from banishment to defend their country. Then you can retaliate on the government by demanding an account of their stewardship.'

'I did expose their frauds to their faces,' exclaimed the chief, 'in the National Assembly at Nauplia, and on the same night two shots were fired at me from a window opposite to the one I was sitting at. My guards seized the miscreants, and I gave them up to the police, but they were not punished. If I stay here, we shall be beleaguered by assassins, and prevented from communicating with my lieutenants and followers. Ghouras still holds the Acropolis of Athens. I cannot stay here; a stag at bay is more to be feared than a lion blockaded in his den.'

It was decided that I should remain, and he go forth. I had shared in his prosperity, and would not leave him in his adversity. As a garrison was superfluous, I reduced mine to half-a-dozen. To guard against treachery, I chose men of different countries, who were not likely to conspire together: a Greek, Turk, Hungarian, and Italian, a venerable priest, and two Greek boys as servants.

Our other inmates were the chief's son, an infant, his wife, mother, and two or three other women. I entrusted the keys of the entrance to the Albanian Turk, a resolute determined fellow.

Among the 'two or three other women' was Tersitza, half-sister to Odysseus and 'lovely as an angel'. According to most accounts she was only thirteen years old at the time, but she became Trelawny's 'wife', probably in law and certainly in fact. At least after their 'marriage' had broken up, Tersitza went through the formalities of a divorce and obtained alimony from Trelawny. The first child of this marriage, Zella, later Mrs. Olguin, lived in Brighton until her death in 1906. A second child, also a daughter, born to Tersitza soon after she had left Trelawny, was sent to him as a baby and died soon after. Her body was sent back by Trelawny to the mother 'as a punishment for [her] unfeeling conduct'.

In the mountains of Pindus and Agrafa, in Thessalia, they have the noblest breed of dogs in the world. In size and strength they are not much inferior to the king of beasts, and in courage and sagacity they are superior. When thorough-bred and well trained they are held in such estimation by their owners, that money will not buy them. We had one of these. He did the duty of a guard of soldiers, patrolling the lower terrace at night, and keeping watch at the guard-room door by day. He would not enter a room. He was best pleased in the winter snow-storms, when the icicles hung on his long brindled hair and shaggy mane. It was impossible to elude his vigilance or corrupt his fidelity; he would not take food from any other hands than mine or the Albanian's, and could not be bribed. This is more than I could say of any Greek that I had dealings with, during the three years I lived amongst them.

In addition to the small number within the cave, I had a much larger force at the foot of the ladders. They were hutted within a stone breast-work. I gave the command of them to the Scotchman whom I had brought from Missolonghi. Their duty

181

was to patrol the passes of the mountain, to collect the tithes or tribute from the neighbouring villages (these were paid in kind), to learn the news, and to keep up my correspondence with the chief and others.

The name of the Scotchman was Fenton. Thomas was, I think, his Christian name. He introduced himself to me, as I have before narrated, on my visit to Western Greece, saying he had come out expressly to join Lord Byron's regiment; that he had served in the civil wars in Spain, was skilled in guerilla warfare, that his funds were exhausted, and, as I was proceeding to the war, he begged me to take him with me.

I pointed out the deplorable condition of foreigners in Greece generally, and the peculiar state of things in that part of the country I was going to in particular, and offered to advance him money to return home. As he persisted in his wish to go with me, I reluctantly yielded to his importunity.

He was a tall, bony man, with prominent eyes and features, dark hair, and long face, in the prime of life, thirty-one or thirty-two years of age. His dress, accoutrements, and arms were all well chosen. He was restless, energetic, enterprising, and a famous walker. During the time he was with me I sent him on many missions to the Ionian Islands for money, to the seat of government to see what they were doing, and with letters to friendly chiefs, so that he was not much at the cave; and when he was, he lived in a hut below it. I supplied him with all he wanted—my purse was his. He was not squeamish on these points, but sensual, and denied himself nothing within his reach. When in my neighbourhood, he passed most of his time with me. No querulous word or angry glance ever ruffled our friendly intercourse. I thought him honest, and his staying with me a proof of his good-will, if not personal friendship, and never omitted an occasion of doing him a service.

When Odysseus had been absent three or four months, rumours reached me in January, 1825, that the government were resolved to deprive the chief of his command in Eastern Greece. To do this effectually, they were endeavouring to detach his lieutenant, Ghouras, who held Attica, from him. I despatched Fenton to Athens and Nauplia, to ascertain the truth of these reports.

23

I was told some time after this that Odysseus was corresponding with Omer Pasha of Negropont, and fearing that he might resort to some desperate measures in his present difficulties, I left the cave one night in a snow-storm, and with a trusty follower who knew the country, we descended to the plain, threading our way through the rocks and pine-trees. We mounted two swift Arab horses, galloped along a hollow valley, crossed a deep stream, the Sperchius, and proceeded towards the town of Livadia, where we arrived the next day. I was surprised to see Turkish Delhi cavalry, known at a great distance by the immense height of their head-gear, careering on the plain. On meeting Odysseus, he told me he had made a truce for three months with Omer Pasha. The only stipulation between them was that, for that period, Eastern Greece was to be a neutral territory—he said, 'It is the only way in which I could save the people from being massacred. I have written to the Athenians to say that, as the government have not only refused to give me rations or money for my troops, but are doing their utmost to induce them to desert me, I cannot longer defend the passes which lead to Athens.'

I knew it was a common practice of the military leaders in Greece to make treaties with the enemy in the provinces they governed, for especial objects, on their own responsibility—yet I saw at once the chief had made a fatal error in doing so on the present occasion. I told him that, although his family had ruled in Livadia for three generations, the Turks in the Morea had been dispossessed after four centuries of possession; that now the Greek government were strong, and would direct all their forces to crush him. If he took refuge with the Turks, they would betray him, and send him or his head to Constantinople. 'I know that,' he answered, 'I shall take care of that; they are in my power; what I have done, is only to bring the Greek government to terms.' I saw that he was anxious and perplexed, and that he repented of the step he had taken, and had been plotting to extricate himself before I arrived at Livadia. The next day we went to Thebes, and on the one succeeding followed the line of the Eubœan Strait to Talanta.

The hollowness of this armistice was apparent—Odysseus and the Ottoman Bey, suspecting each other of treachery, used every precaution to avoid being ensnared. The Turkish horse stuck to the level ground, the Greeks clung to the hills; Odysseus skirted them, his best men and swiftest runners dogging his steps, and keeping him from being cut off from his guerillas.

The Delhi Colonel was selected from the Turkish host at Eubœa, as the only soldier capable of contending in arts or arms with the wily and able Greek chief: he was the best specimen of an Eastern warrior I had seen,—calm, vigilant, and dexterous in the disposition of his troopers. Our chief knew the country better than any man in it. I urged him to give the enemy the slip, and to come to the cavern. His answer was, 'Stay, not yet!'

It was early in February we stopped at Talanta on a wet stormy night: in selecting his quarters, our chief with his usual sagacity fixed upon the ruins of a Greek church, situated as the Greek churches, chapels, and monasteries usually are, on an elevated and defensible site—the town was abandoned and in ruins. After we had supped and were smoking our pipes, some of the Greek patrols came in, saying they had captured two Franks. They were ordered to bring them in. I told the chief to make no allusion to me, but to question them through his secretary.

As they entered, one of them observed to his comrade in English, 'What a set of cut-throats! Are they Greeks or Turks?'

'Mind what you say.'

'Oh! they only want our money,' answered the other. 'I hope they will give us something to eat before they cut our throats. I am famished.'

Certainly appearances were against us. At one end of the building, Odysseus, the Greek chief, the Turkish Bey, and I sat smoking our pipes. At the other end, within the church, stood our horses saddled, ready for mounting, the soldiers lying down in clusters along the sides, with all their gear on, for neither Greeks nor Turks divest themselves of a single article of dress or arms during the night. Their hands still grasped their weapons,

184

and they slept so lightly that if in talking a voice was raised their eager wolfish eyes were instantly upon the speaker. On the strangers entering, some of the soldiers sprang up, others leant on their elbows to listen or rather to look on, for they could not understand a word. The travellers told their story,—stating that they were last from Smyrna, and had landed that morning from an English brig, at a small port in the Gulf of Eubœa, with no other object than to see the country. Neither of the chiefs believed them, nor did I; nevertheless, they were treated hospitably, had supper, coffee, and pipes, and their baggage placed beside them. They sat together in a spare corner close to us, with no arms but fowling-pieces. One of them was very ill at his ease, the other, who I learnt from their discourse was a Major [Bacon], took things as coolly as if he had been at an inn, said the cold lamb (it was goat) was the best he had ever tasted, and asked the Greek attendant, if he had no rackie (spirit), the only Romaic word he had learnt. Odysseus understanding what he wanted, told the boy to give him wine.

'If they are robbers,' exclaimed the Major, 'they are damned good fellows, so I drink success to their next foray.' Soon after, one of them lay down in a dark corner. Turks, Greeks, and all Orientals, consider it the greatest possible insult as well as an outrage on decency, for any one in public to change his garments or expose any part of his person below the waist. The major was a remarkably tall, gaunt, bony man: after finishing his wine, he set to work to make up a comfortable bed with horse-cloths, slips of carpet, a bag for a pillow, etc.; when he had done this to his satisfaction, we supposed he would lie down, as his companion had done. On the contrary, he deliberately, as if in his own barrack-room, utterly regardless of our presence, took off his boots, socks, coat, waistcoat, trousers, and shirt, folding each article carefully up and placing it by his bedside. Thus exhibiting himself in all possible attitudes stark naked, he leisurely filled the bowl of his Turkish pipe, and advanced towards us to light it at the fire.

The two chiefs at first looked on the major's novel proceedings with curiosity, as visitors in the Zoological Gardens do at the hippopotamus; but as the process of stripping advanced, they looked serious; the shirt scene took away their breath;

their pipes went out when the major advanced towards them. The Turk started up in horror with his hand on his sword. The major, supposing he was making way for him from civility, and unconscious of giving any offence, made a very polite bow to us generally; and, in a gentle and conciliating tone, said, in his own language, 'Pray, gentlemen, keep your seats, don't let me disturb you'; bent his body into a sharp angle, so as to draw a light from the burning embers. The position he stood in was so ludicrous, that Odysseus and I could not resist laughing. The major considering this a token of good fellowship, insisted on shaking hands with us, saying, 'I am sure you are both good fellows—Good night!'

I now saw by the light of the fire that he was not absolutely naked, for he had a leather waistcoat and drawers on, but they fitted as tight as his skin, and were exactly of the same colour. The major lay down and smoked himself to sleep. Odysseus went out and brought back the Turkish bey.

Expecting to be surprised by Turks or Greeks, and distrusting those with us, we could not sleep; so our chief, to conceal his own anxiety, and to wile away the time, recounted to the Turk the marvellous things he had seen done at Yanina by the Franks whilst he was serving with Ali Pasha. Odysseus then questioned the Osmanlee [or Ottoman Turks] about Paradise and Mahomet, very profanely. The Albanian Turks are by no means bigots: our bey had evidently very little faith in anything but his sword. At length we dozed as we sat.

Before daylight the major got up and went out; I followed him, accosting him in his native tongue.

'How well you speak English, my good fellow,' he said.

The frank and cordial manner of the major so impressed me with his honesty, that I hurriedly explained who I was, the critical state of things with us, and my anxiety to extricate Odysseus from the peril that encompassed him.

The major instantly and earnestly entered into my views, saying, 'The vessel we came in will remain two or three days in the port; it will take but a few hours to reach her. I will return and stop by her for Odysseus, detain her as long as I can, and go with him to the Ionian Islands.'

I told the chief our plan, he eagerly accepted the offer,—I

pledging myself to keep possession of his mountain home, and to protect his family until altered circumstances permitted him to return to Greece. Hastily making the needful arrangements, the good-hearted major departed on his mission. The chief having much to say to me, and thinking it probable I might be in danger on my return to the cave, convoyed me with his whole force. On our parting, he called some of his principal followers, and said, 'I call you to witness, I give this Englishman the cavern and everything of mine in it.' Then turning to me, he said, 'Do what you think best without referring to me.' As we sat on the turf by a broken fountain, he placed his rough hairy hand on my bosom, saying, 'You have a strong heart in a strong body: you find fault with me for distrusting my country-men,—I never doubted you. I trusted you from the first day as I do now on the last we may ever be together; though I cannot understand why you give money and risk life, to serve those who would shoot you for money, as they will me if they can.'

Either from the vigilance of the Ottomans at Eubœa, or of those with him, or from some other impediment, the chief did not reach the port he was to have embarked from until after the vessel had sailed with the major, although he had detained her as long as possible. I then expected the chief would make for the cave; we kept a sharp look-out, and posted men at the several passes; he wrote to me from time to time, but nothing definitively; and we passed months in this state of suspense. Fenton came from the Morea. I was in the daily habit of sally-ing forth to gather news, though warned against it. Early in April, when I was some distance from my den, I was startled by a shot; the red-capped Greeks were dogging me behind the rocks and pine-trees: I hastened up the steep ascent, gained the lower ladder, mounted slowly until I recovered my wind, then faster, the musket-balls whistling by me right and left—above and below. I should have come down faster than I went up, but from the great advantage my men above had, and the sharp cross-fire they kept up to cover my retreat. On my enter-ing the trap-door my assailants retreated across the mountain.

Shortly after this occurrence a large body of Greeks came to Velitza, a village at the foot of our mountain, a detachment ascended towards us; on coming near, one of them advanced, holding a green bough as a flag of truce: he said, Odysseus was with the troops below, and that he had brought a letter from him to me. It was to this effect, that he—Odysseus—was now with his friend Ghouras; he intreated me to come to him to confer on matters of great importance; saying that hostages would be given for my safe return, etc.

I merely answered, 'If what you say is true, why don't you come here? you may bring Ghouras or half-a-dozen others with you.'

Several notes of this sort were exchanged. In the last, our chief urged me to capitulate as the only means of saving his life; telling me that I might now do so on my own terms, for those with him were Romeliotes favourably disposed to him and to me; and that if I lost this opportunity, I should be blockaded by his enemies, the Moreotes, who would give us no quarter. Of course I declined, for I knew the chief was writing under compulsion: the messenger tried what he could do by tampering with my men, individually proffering large bribes; so I told one of the men to shoot him if he spoke another word. During this parley the most nimble-footed of the enemy scaled the cliffs to see if it was possible to get at us by the aid of ropes from above, or by blasting the rocks, or with shot or shell. I sent several of my people to mingle with the foe, offering five thousand dollars to those who would aid the escape of Odysseus.* On the fourth or fifth day they departed,—leaving spies to watch us, as I knew they would. I then sent all the men I could trust to follow on the trail of our chief, and wrote to all his friends. That I might not be made a target of a second time, I did not venture forth alone.

---

* Odysseus had been betrayed by Ghouras on April 6, 1825, and was confined, under torture, in the Acropolis.

24

In the latter end of May, 1825, a young Englishman named Whitcombe came to me from Racora, in Bœotia, where he had been serving with the Greek troops. At all times glad to see my countrymen, I was particularly so at that time: Fenton was especially pleased with him. They both dined and passed their evenings with me, but slept below in Fenton's hut. On the fourth day, after our noonday meal, we sat smoking and drinking on the verandah of my house on the lower terrace longer than usual.

It was intensely hot; all my people had retreated into one of the upper grottoes, where it was always cool, to enjoy their usual siesta. Fenton said, he had made a bet with Whitcombe about their shooting, and that I was to decide it. My Italian servant, Everett, then put up a board for a target at the extremity of the terrace. After they had fired several shots, at Fenton's suggestion I sent the Italian to his comrades above. Fenton then said to me, after some more shots had been fired wide of the mark, 'You can beat him with your pistol, he has no chance with us veterans.'

I took a pistol from my belt and fired; they were standing close together on a flat rock, two yards behind me; the instant I had fired I heard another report, and felt that I was shot in the back. As one of their flint guns had just before hung fire, and I had seen Fenton doing something to the lock of his, I thought it was an accident. I said, 'Fenton, this must have been accidental!' He assured me it was so, and expressed the deepest sorrow. No thought of their treachery crossed my mind. Fenton said, 'Shall I shoot Whitcombe?' I answered, 'No.' I took my other pistol from my belt, when Fenton said, 'I will call your servant,' and hastily left me, following Whitcombe to the entrance porch. The dog, growling fiercely, first stopped their flight; he had the voice of a lion, and never gave a false alarm. The Hungarian, always prompt, was quickly at his post on the upper terrace, and hearing I was shot, instantly killed Fenton. Whitcombe attempted to escape by the trap-door leading to the ladder; the dog threw him on his back, and held him as if he had been a rat. Achmett, the Turk, seized him, bound his arms, dragged him to a crane used for hoisting things from below, put a slip-knot in the rope, and placed it round his ankles to hang him. His convulsive shrieks and the frantic struggles he made as his executioners were hoisting him over the precipice, calling on God to witness that he was innocent, thrilled through my shattered nerves; he beseeched me to let him live till the morning, or for one hour, that he might write home, or even for five minutes until he had told me everything. I could not conceive it possible that an English gentleman, my guest, on the most cordial terms with me, should after four days' acquaintance, conspire with Fenton to assassinate me—there had been no provocation, and I could see no motive for the act. Fenton had never seen Whitcombe before, nor had I. If there was foul play, Fenton must have been the traitor: so thinking, I ordered the execution to be postponed until the mystery was solved. I had very great difficulty in staying the execution, every one in the cave clamouring for vengeance. His life now hung on mine, and everybody thought that I was mortally wounded. They all swore if I died, they would roast him by a slow fire: this was no idle threat, for it had been done on more than one occasion during the sanguinary war. When I was shot, I sat down on the rock I had been standing on, bending down my head to let the blood flow from my mouth, a musket-ball and several broken teeth came with it—the socket of the teeth was broken, and my right arm paralysed. I walked without assistance into the small grotto I had boarded up and floored and called my house; it was divided into two small rooms, and there was a broad verandah in front. Squatting in a corner, my servant cut open my dress behind, and told me I had been shot with two balls between my shoulders, near together, on the right side of my spine, and one of them close to it. One of the balls, as I have said, its force expended on my bones, dropped from my mouth without wounding my face; the other broke my collar-bone, and remained in my breast—it is still there. No blood issued from the places they had entered at. We had no surgeon or medicines in the cave; the air was so dry and pure, our living so simple, that this was the first visit sickness or sorrow paid us. Nature makes no mistakes, doctors

ODYSSEUS' CAVE

do; probably I owe my life to a sound constitution, and having had no doctor.

The morning after I had respited Whitcombe, my servant brought me the following letter from him, which he read to me, though he could not speak English:

'For God's sake, sir, permit me to see you, if it is but for five minutes conversation; it will save my life. In the fulness of contrition I yesterday told Favourite (Everett) my crime, and through misconstruction, or some other cause, he has interpreted it to Camerone, so as to cause my death. They all declare to me they will kill me and burn me. Camerone knocked me down and has thrown me in irons. For the mercy of Almighty God, let me see you; instead of augmenting, my explanation will palliate my offence. I wish not that it should be alone. I wish also that Camerone and Everett should be by, to question me before you, and to endeavour to implicate me if they can. I wish only to tell you all the circumstances which I told Everett. Camerone declares that I have plotted all the evil for Ulysses (Odysseus). For God's sake let me explain myself immediately, and do not let me be murdered without a word of explanation. O God! my misery is already too great; they care not for what you tell them; they want to tie me up by my irons to the beam of the room, and cut my head off.'

I refused to see him: he then wrote an incoherent account of what took place between him and Fenton—the latter accusing me of having usurped his place, as Odysseus wished him to have the command during his absence; saying that Odysseus had sent a messenger to him at Athens to that effect, and that on his return he should take possession of the cave; that there were beautiful women in it, and stores of gold; he would man it with English, clothe his followers with rich dresses and jewels: there would be a row first, a scene of blood, but that all he wanted was a friend to stand by him. By Whitcombe's account—too rambling and absurd to transcribe—his feeble brain was worked up to a state of homicidal insanity; he used the gentle term of infatuation. He persisted in his asseveration that Fenton shot me, and his only crime was not warning me of my danger. The only thing his writing proved, was that he had a very feeble intellect, and that Fenton had taken advantage of his weakness.

o

He was now mad with terror, he screamed and shrieked if any one came near him, he was in irons and chained to the wall, with no other food than bread and water. I resolved on the twentieth day of his imprisonment to set him free, which I did. When restored to life and liberty he wrote me the following letter:

MUCH-INJURED SIR, I cannot express to you what I feel for your unmerited kindness to me for your releasing me from an untimely death; other release it is not in the power of man to procure for me, my internal misery and shame being complete. May you never feel the half that I do. May you never be like me, reduced by an acquaintance of four days with a villain from the smiling circles who loved me, and had pleasure in my society, to the solitary wretched outcast which I am now become. I have now no home, no family, no friends—and all I regret is that I have still the gnawings of a conscience which makes me prefer life a little longer, with all my former enjoyments cut off, to an ignominious and untimely end. I can say no more, perhaps now I have troubled you too much.

That God may send you a speedy recovery, and turn every curse which falls upon my head into a blessing upon yours, is the prayer of the wretched W. G. WHITCOMBE.

He subsequently addressed one of his friends as follows:

CAMP, *August* 11, 1825

MY DEAR SIR, You will, perhaps, be astonished at my addressing you, when from the unhappy circumstances into which my fatality has immersed me, I ought only to calculate on your discarding all converse with a being whose sin has placed between him and society a gulf fitter to be removed by any hands but his. But I cannot, cannot bear so sudden a transition into exquisite misery and shame without a line which may give palliatives to my offence. Scan it with a dispassionate eye; my only motive for begging this last favour of you is, that you may rather hold me the weak unsuspecting tool, than the practised unprincipled villain. Others played that part; others saw my easy nature, and thought me a fit instrument for the furthering of their grand speculations and enterprises. They discerned rightly—they have entailed the curse upon me; they have made the villain of me that they wished; but yet shall that curse be retaliated upon them. One is dead: the other still lives, and has left behind him many little interesting traits of character which will tend well to the blazonment of his fame, and conscience, if not warped by constant meannesses, shall by its sweet recollections requite him for the rest.

Charmed by Mr. [Capt. W. A.] Humphreys' account of the excessive intrepidity, honour, romantic situation, etc., etc., of his friend Fenton, added to his good-nature and *bonhomie*, I was induced by the repeated, by the urgent entreaties of that Mr. Humphreys, added to a letter (expressing the most pressing invitation from Fenton, addressed to Humphreys, with many dark mystic expressions, known only, I presume, to himself)—I was induced, I say, to pay that visit to the cave. On my arrival I was beset by Fenton's utmost talents of duplicity (in which never mortal man has excelled him). Touched by his mournful tales of wrongs, rejection, deprivation of right, viewing him only as the romantic, the injured, the generous hero he had been represented by Humphreys, I swore to stand by him on his resolution to recover his rights or die. He worshipped me for it, and being too good a discerner of character to disclose further the nature of his designs, at the idea of which he knew I would revolt, he nailed me to the spot and moment of action, and by not giving a minute's time to recover from my infatuation, he precipitated me into that hell of guilt and shame which had long yawned for the wretched adventurer as his meed, but which, without arraigning Providence, might still, methinks, have been withheld from me. But where misfortune ever exists, there am I sure to get acquainted with it. And because such a villain survived in the same land, I, without holding with him a shadow of previous connection, without one thought in the whole association of our ideas, which brought with it the slightest similitude, whereby to enable me to account by a harsh destiny, for my being coupled with the memory of such a villain's fate, am nevertheless doomed, solely because such an one exists, to connect myself, and all my happiness and honour, irretrievably with his fate. I am now a wandering outcast, a being whose very claim on society is departed, and would not

193

now wish to renew those claims, from the recollections of dependence which would necessarily hang on that renewal.

But it is not for myself that I am wretched. No—I can roam to far distant regions, and amidst other scenes and other inhabitants, commence a new career, unembittered by the past. It is for my family, a family who had boasted that, through all their branches and connections, it had never had a spot to sully it. That that family should, through my faults, be disgraced, is more than I can bear. My mother is a parent who loves me to distraction. I received a letter a few days ago from that quarter. She has been dangerously ill, and the only reflection that contributes to her recovery is that of seeing me return crowned with laurels. They will be laurels!

Now view the reverse. It has been reported that I was dead. That report, with aggravated causes, will reach the ears of my family; my mother, I know, will not survive it. And all this for me.

I only regret that being too great a coward to put an end to my existence, I cannot cut off the miseries of anticipation.

But I have troubled you too long with subjects about which you can feel but little interest. Only one word more. Should an opportunity present itself, for God's sake let not accounts reach England that I am killed.

With hopes that you will excuse my long and selfish letter, and with many kindest remembrances to Mrs. Alison and all your family, I remain, Your sincere though unfortunate friend, (Signed) W. G. WHITCOMBE.

PS.—I sincerely regret that, by the most untoward circumstances, both the letters which you have been good enough at different times to send me, have been lost before they reached my hands; the one by the lies of that rascal Charlilopulo—the other by Dr. Tindal,* amongst his other things.

---

* Tindal was Millingen's assistant, and the two were responsible for the dispensary in Missolonghi. The sins of Charlilopulo and his very identity are now obscure.

25

FOUL plots have been devised, and fit instruments found to
execute them in less than four days. I was much more astonished and humiliated at the retrospection of my idiotic infatuation when, by Fenton's papers and other evidence, I discovered
that I had been his dupe from the first—a blind man led by
a fiendish cur—no more. He was foisted on me at Missolonghi,
to act as a spy on Odysseus, and had done so for a whole
year.

My credulity was such that I not only told him all I knew,
but employed him in many important transactions. Not a
shadow or doubt of his honesty ever crossed my mind from the
first day of our meeting until his death. I was a fool, and deserved my fate. Fenton, a mercenary bungling ruffian, in the
hands of a professor of the black art.

To cut short this disagreeable subject, I extract from Gordon's* always fearless and generally accurate History of the
Greek Revolution [1833], his brief notice of the affair:

'On taking the field, Odysseus deposited his family in his den
on Mount Parnassus, which he confided to the guard of Trelawny (who had lately married his youngest sister), with a
handful of men, for that singular cavern is impregnable, and
when the ladders that gave access to it were removed, neither
armies nor artillery could make any impression. It is a perpen-
dicular height of one hundred and fifty feet from the bottom of
a precipice, and sheltered above by a lofty arch. In front were
natural and artificial bulwarks, concealing the interior and a
portal cut in the rock, to which the flights of ladders gave
access; within were houses, magazines stored for the consumption of years, and a fine spring of water.

'An attempt was made to murder Trelawny by two of his
own countrymen, one of whom, Fenton, a determined villain,
having accepted a bribe from the government, seduced the

---

* Thomas Gordon was Trelawny's next-door neighbour at Zante. A
careful historian, he later became a Major-General in the Greek Army,
Governor of the Peloponnese and A.D.C. to King Otho.

other, a crack-brained young man, into complicity by extravagant tales, and the perpetual excitement of potent liquors. Although pierced through the back with two carbine balls, fracturing his arm and his jaw, the wonderful vigour of his constitution enabled Trelawny to recover. In the midst of his agony, he had the magnanimity to dismiss, unhurt, the unhappy youth who fired at him; as for Fenton, the prime assassin, he was instantly shot by a Hungarian soldier.

'In the same month, on the 17th of June, the rising sun disclosed the lifeless body of Odysseus stretched at the foot of the tower that had been his prison; it was said, that a rope by which he was lowering himself had broken, and that he was killed by the fall; however, no one gave credit to this story; it was supposed that he had been strangled, and then thrown from the top. Ghouras subsequently felt remorse for the death of his former patron; heard with pain the mention of his name, and occasionally murmured, "In that business I was misled." There can be no doubt that Mavrocordato was at the bottom of these tragical events, instigated fully as much by private revenge as care of the public weal. Odysseus was undoubtedly a tyrant and a traitor; Trelawny in open rebellion, and suspected of tampering with the Turks, who were very anxious to get possession of the cave; but all this might have been forgiven, had they not previously been the personal foes of the Director-General of Western Greece.'

It is surprising that Trelawny allows these charges to pass unchallenged, and even compliments their author on his general accuracy. Much that Gordon implies about Odysseus is true, though the extent of his 'treachery' was his animosity for the central Government and an intention to make a three-months' local truce with the Turks (no uncommon occurrence at that time) in order to give himself time to settle, to his own satisfaction, his disputes with Mavrocordato. But Trelawny had gone out of his way to dissuade Odysseus from dealing with the Turks, an action which he felt to be both unworthy and unwise.

For the first twenty days after being wounded, I remained in the same place and posture, sitting and leaning against the rock, determined to leave everything to nature. I did not change or remove any portion of my dress, nor use any extra covering. I would not be bandaged, plastered, poulticed, or even washed; nor would I move or allow any one to look at my wound. I was kept alive by yolks of eggs and water for twenty days. It was forty days before there was any sensible diminution of pain; I then submitted to have my body sponged with spirit and water, and my dress partly changed. I was reduced in weight from thirteen stone to less than ten, and looked like a galvanised mummy. I was first tempted to try and eat by seeing my Italian eating raw ham of a wild hog which I had shot and cured; by great effort I opened my mouth sufficiently to introduce a piece of the size of a shilling, notwithstanding the agony of moving my fractured jaw, and by degrees managed to devour it, and from that time gathered strength, I suppose from the affinity of our Saxon nature to hog; excepting coffee, I refused all wishy-washy or spoon-food and stuck to wild boar, which in turn stuck to me; it spliced my bones and healed my flesh, excepting my right arm, which was shrivelled up and paralysed.

In three months after I had been wounded, my hurts were healing, and my health returning, but my right arm was painful, withered, and paralysed, my only hope of regaining the use of it was to get the ball extracted; and for that purpose a surgeon was indispensable.

Ghouras had been nominated to the command of Eastern Greece, as the stipulated payment for his treachery to his former chief, but the Turks held all the plains. So we were environed with foes and closely watched, but my trusty and zealous friends the Klephtes were always on the alert; nestling with the eagles amongst the most inaccessible crags by day, and coming down with the wolves at night, they supplied us with fresh provisions and kept us informed of everything that took place around. They even brought me a Klephtes surgeon, stipulating to kill him if he did not cure me; he made an incision with a razor under my breast-bone, and poked about with his finger to find the ball but in vain; the Klephtes then proposed to escort me to any place I chose to go to for a Frank doctor, or to kidnap one at Athens, and bring him to me, and to leave their families as hostages. I had perfect faith in their probity, but lingered on hoping for a change. [News of Trelawny's plight reached the outer world, and Canning was asked to intervene on his behalf, but refused on the grounds that to interfere would give 'the Turkish government reason to complain of the assistance given by British subjects to the Greeks and sanctioned by the King's government . . .'] Soon after this, Zepare, one of their leaders, brought me news at night that his men were on the trail of a Frank, and they would bring him to me: he said a medico, for they believe all the Franks are more or less so, from their habit of carrying and giving medicines. The next morning a party of soldiers arrived escorting the Major who so astonished Odysseus and the Turkish Bey at Talanta, by his eccentricity. I was even more surprised now than then at meeting him. It appeared he had never lost sight of me. When he heard I was in peril, he made several unsuccessful attempts to come to me; he then took a cruise in search of the Commodore on the station, Hamilton, and stated my case. Hamilton, always prompt in acts of humanity, insisted on the government's not only permitting the Major to have free access to me, but that I should have liberty to embark in one of his ships, if I chose to do so. After some days of deliberation and consultation with Odysseus' widow, and the inmates of the cave, I reluctantly agreed to take advantage of this favourable occasion; my trusty crew promised to remain at their posts until my return, or until the enemies of their former chief, then in power, were ousted, and then to be guided by circumstances. No sooner had I left than Ghouras closely invested the place. The eagerness of both the Greeks and Turks to possess the cave, arose from the stories current in that land of lies, of the fabulous treasures it contained. The cupidity of the Greeks was lashed up to frenzy; every stratagem their subtle wits could devise was tried; crouching behind every rock and tree, they kept up a continual fusillade; they might as well have fired at the man in the moon, as at the men in the mountain— if they came too near, the Hungarian stopped them with a shower of grape from the cannon. Some months after, when men and things were changed, the inmates of the cavern came to terms with some of the old friends of the late chief, who had always used their influence to protect the cave, as well they might, since much of the plunder they had accumulated during the war was deposited within it. If the Hungarian Camerone had served in any other country than Greece in a time of war he would have ranked high, for he was a well-trained warrior, skilful, resolute and modest; he had been nearly two years in Greece, when I fell in with him at Missolonghi, serving without pay or promotion: noted he certainly was, for his valour had been conspicuous in many battles.

26

Late in 1825 Trelawny with Tersitza and her brother was taken aboard the 'Sparrowhawk' commanded by Captain Stewart. They were later transferred to Commodore Rowan Hamilton's flagship, H.M.S. 'Cambrian', and from her to H.M.S. 'Zebra' which took them to Cephalonia. He wrote to Roberts: 'My shattered hulk no longer sea-worthy was towed into port. . . . I have been damned near going down, two shots between wind and water, all my timbers carried smack away, standing and running rigging cut up—to wit, two balls entered my back, broke my jaw, breast bone, cut all the nerves of my right arm and in short all but did my business . . .'

In May 1826 Trelawny moved to Zante.

WHEN the Muses deserted Parnassus, the Klephtes, *i.e.* outlaws, took possession of their haunts, and kept alive the love of freedom and the use of arms. They were the only Greeks I found with any sense of honour; they kept their words and fulfilled their engagements; I protected and fed their families, and they escorted me in all my expeditions; I was continually in their power, yet they never attempted to betray me. The Klephtes were the only efficient soldiers at the commencement of the insurrection; and their leaders maintained the war for three years, so successfully that the Greek government were enabled to borrow money. The government then resolved to divide the forces of the Klephtes, to appoint their own partisans as leaders, and to conduct the war themselves; they raised forces and imprisoned the former military leaders, wasted time in disputing about their plans of campaigns, and the nomination of the commissioners to see that they were carried out. In two scientific campaigns carried on by civilians, the Greeks lost all the territory the former arbitrary chiefs had won; and of the foreign loan, 2,800,000*l.*, there remained only five shillings in bad money at the close of those campaigns. If there had been any place of refuge, the insurrection would have ended by the flight of the leaders and submission of the people. The members of the government sent away the money they had embezzled, and the Primates and other rich rascals attempted to escape with their families, but they were stopped by the populace.

In February 1825, a Turkish force from Alexandria landed in Greece, and, after a long and bitter campaign, invested Missolonghi early in 1826. Heavy loss of life on both sides—only two thousand Greeks survived out of the twelve thousand inhabitants and garrison —resulted in the complete destruction of the town. Only three houses remained standing; one of them the house in which Byron had lived and died. Revisiting this place next year, Trelawny wrote that the 'house loomed like a lonely column in the midst of a desert'.

After the fall of Missolonghi the Turks concentrated their attention on Athens, which fell without much resistance, in June 1827. A small and heroic band held out in the Acropolis.

Greece was reconquered; the vanquished Christians sat in sullen groups round the walls of their only remaining fortress in the Morea; death, or to resume the Moslem's chains, their only alternative. At this critical period a messenger arrived from Navarino, proclaiming, in the words of our great poet:

'News, friends; our wars are done, the Turks are drowned.' *
The people now sprang up frantic with joy.

For six years all the Christian states had been standing looking on at the bloodiest insurrection on record, sympathising with the unbelieving Ottomans. At the twelfth hour, the three great maritime Leviathans turned round, and, falling unexpectedly upon their ancient allies, annihilated them.

The responsibility for Britain's official attitude to Greek affairs lay principally in the capable but tiring hands of George Canning. To ardent Philhellenes like Trelawny Canning's activities were shamefully indecisive but, both as Foreign Secretary and in the few months before his death in 1827 when he was Prime Minister, Canning was working for Greece. Already in 1825 he had described his policy as a desire 'to save Greece through the agency of the Russian name upon the fears of Turkey, without a war', and to that end had sent the Duke of Wellington to St. Petersburg.

Various statements by Greek leaders, and particularly by Mavrocordato, led him to believe that such action would not leave Greece a Russian satellite. In order to make this doubly certain Canning went himself to Paris to persuade the French to support any action he might take.

---

* Shakespeare. *Othello*, II. i. 205.

A treaty between the Three Powers was signed on July 6, 1827, whereby, under the mediation of Russia, France and Britain, Greece was to be established as an autonomous state within the Turkish Empire. The Turks refused this mediation, and accordingly Allied Fleets were ordered to impose a 'peaceful blockade' upon the Turks in Greece. The English, Russian and French admirals informed the Commander of the Turkish Fleet in Navarino Bay that no ship would be allowed to leave, and when the Turks opened fire, battle was joined and the Turkish Fleet destroyed on October 20, 1827.

Mopping-up operations continued. In April 1828 Russia abandoned ambiguity and declared war. Turkish domination was now over, and the struggles that followed were more diplomatic than military. Whatever Trelawny may say to the contrary it is a justification of Canning's policy that when eventually Greek Independence was acknowledged, in September 1829, by the Treaty of Adrianople, a monarchy was established independent of Russian influence, and against the machinations of the temporary President, Capodistrias, whose previous career in the Tsarist service made him suspect, if no more, of pro-Russian leanings.

The policy of the crafty Muscovite is intelligible. He wanted to possess Greece and cripple his natural enemy, the Turk. He did both at little cost; the Ottoman fleet was destroyed, and Greece converted from a Turkish into a Russian Hospodariat. The policy of France and England is inexplicable; it is one of those inscrutable diplomatic mysteries devised by heaven-born ministers, which men of women born cannot comprehend.

From the beginning to the end of the insurrection in Greece, Commodore Rowan Hamilton and Colonel C. J. Napier were the only English officers in command who acted justly and generously to the Greeks. Sir Thomas Maitland, and his successor, Sir Frederick Adams, High Commissioners of the Ionian Islands, from their natural sympathy with tyranny, favoured the Turks on all occasions. Napier was high-minded and independent in his opinions, which is always a disqualification in the eyes of officials. His general popularity and superior influence with the Ionians mortified Sir Frederick Adams excessively; he did all he could in his official capacity to thwart Napier; he gave vent to his rancour in the most trivial matters; he even sent an official letter to Napier on the impropriety of his wearing moustachios. The Colonel was very much amused

202

at this despatch; he instantly obeyed the mandate by cutting them off, and enclosing them in his reply to the Lord High Commissioner, who, no doubt, forwarded this important correspondence, with the enclosure, to the Commander-in-Chief. If these emblems of war are preserved amongst the trophies at the Horse Guards, the hair may be used as the lion's beard is by the Indians—they burn it, and swallow the ashes, believing it will give them the strength and courage of the lion.

It was particularly revolting to the mind as well as feelings of Napier, to witness the war as waged in Greece,—without a plan, combination, system or leader; every man frantic with excitement to kill and plunder on his own account. Napier, as I have before said, would have undertaken the war when he was solicited by the Greeks to do so, if they had complied with the terms he considered indispensable to their success, which were that he should have uncontrolled power over the army. Whilst the Greek government were treating with Napier, a distinguished French officer, Colonel Fabvier,* volunteered his services without any stipulations, and was accepted. Napier having no other object than the success of a just cause, pointed out to me on the map the strategy and tactics he should have used at that juncture, had he commanded the Greek forces in the Morea. I asked him to write his plan, as the art of war is so little studied by our military men. I transcribe a campaign on scientific principles, as improvised on the exigency of the moment, by the great master of the art; the general principles laid down by so skilful a commander are applicable to any other locality in all times, especially in defensive warfare, and it requires no prophet to foretel there will be many such wars ere the lamb lies down with the lion.

Napier's letters not only exemplify the skill of the soldier, but show the frank, generous, manly character of the man. Byron, in a letter to the Greek committee from Cephalonia, in 1823, speaking of Colonel Napier, says, 'Of his military character, it is superfluous to speak, of his personal, I can say, from

---

* Fabvier, a veteran of the Napoleonic Wars, had arrived in Greece under the name of Borel. Accompanied by some of his former subordinates, it was his original intention to found an agricultural colony.

my own knowledge as well as from all rumour or private report, that it is as excellent as his military; in short, a better or a braver man, is not easily to be found; he is our man, to lead a regular force, or to organise a national one for the Greeks,—ask the army—ask any one.'

The following letters are addressed to me by this great General:

26*th May*, 1826

Circumstances must decide in war, speaking generally, but frequently they may be commanded by able arrangements; instead of waiting to see what an enemy will do, he may be often forced to do that which we want him to do. I think this may be now accomplished by the Greek troops, should Ibrahim Pacha [Commander of the army from Alexandria] besiege Napoli di Romania.* In this event, I conclude he will have about 15,000 men, and that he will draw his supplies from Navarin or Modon, a distance of about eighty miles; and have an intermediate depôt at Tripolitza, which is about twenty-five from Napoli. These roads pass through the mountains, and great difficulties will arise in marching his convoys, both from the nature of the country itself, and the exposure to constant attacks.

I also conclude that the Greek forces will amount to about 6000 regulars and 10,000 irregulars, exclusive of the garrison of Napoli, in which I would leave only irregulars, the best to be had; taking the worst, with the whole regular force, to Monemvasia, into which place I would throw in as much provision as possible; and leaving this fortress with the smallest possible garrison picked from the irregulars, but (as well as Napoli di Romania) with the most *resolute governor and engineers*, I would issue forth and throw the whole regular and remaining irregular force on the communications of the besieging army.

The point at which I would cut them must be *determined* by local circumstances, viz., the force of the enemy; the distribution of that force; the nature of the country; and the exact knowledge of distances, or rather *times of march*. By this, the Greek army would oblige the Egyptian army to *raise the siege*,

---

* Nauplia.

or to *send a force able* to *clear the road of the Greek army*, or he must go without provisions; if he raises the siege, such a failure, besides its actual cost, would have an immense moral effect to his prejudice, and enable the Greeks to take more bold measures; in short, it would be, what they have yet not seen, a victory produced by sound principles of war.

If he prefers the second way, viz., to send a force which he thinks capable of clearing the road, and re-opening his communications, what is the consequence? His army must be so weakened that the siege cannot be continued with vigour; and the detached force will either be fought and defeated by the Greeks, or they would retire before this force into Maina, and even to Monemvasia. The moment this was done, this detached force would again march to join Ibrahim before Napoli; and would be followed up by the Greek army, which would again occupy its old position on the communication. This might be repeated twice or three times; but it is impossible that Ibrahim could continue this game long, and the moment he ceased to play it, he would be obliged to raise the siege. It seems difficult to say how this plan could fail, unless the Greek commander allowed the force detached against him to cut him off from Monemvasia, or from wherever he drew his subsistence.

As to the third choice, it is evident that he could not adopt it, as, although his Egyptians may live upon little, yet that little they must have; he would therefore try to receive his supplies from Patras; and although there would, perhaps, be more difficulty still, the Greek general might play the same game on that line of operation, as he would on the line with Navarin. He might occupy the *last* with his regulars, and detach his irregulars on the first. A Turkish force could hardly venture against the Greek irregulars, having their left flank exposed to the regular army of Greeks. I do not know whether I have clearly explained my meaning; but I am sure that if the Greek government will do what they ought, viz., give Colonel Fabvier the full and uncontrolled direction of the war, or do this with Colonel Gordon, both those gentlemen will see what I mean, and that this plan is formed on sound strategetical principles.

It is impossible to believe that any force which Ibrahim could detach would be able to force six thousand regular Greek

205

soldiers through the passes of the Mainiote country back upon Monemvasia. I have only supposed the *worst* in supposing that they would do this, but in point of fact I imagine the Greek regular force could occupy some strong position in which it would force the troops detached against it to give battle under every disadvantage; and should the Greeks be defeated, that they might rally at and defend a multitude of defiles in the strong country between Tripolitza and Monemvasia—all these things are details of the execution, which depend on the talents of the commanders. If this commander is Colonel Fabvier with Colonel Gordon supporting him, there is no doubt in my mind of its success; if the Greek force, on the contrary, is commanded by the Greek General-in-Chief, Colocotroni, it must inevitably fail, as he is incapable of even comprehending, much less of executing such a campaign.

In regard to the number of forces that I have supposed on each side, it is not very material that I should be exact, because the principle will hold good as long as the disproportion between the opposed armies is not *so great* as to put an end to all opposition, and this is a disproportion so vast that in such a country as Greece I can hardly conceive possible. Supposing that the Turkish forces receive their provision by sea, then they would not perhaps detach a force against the Greek army coming from Monemvasia, which might attack Tripolitza at its leisure: this, I suspect, would quickly produce the desired results! And last, though not least important, one has everything to expect from Lord Cochrane, who will not allow this provision to arrive by sea so easily. Are we to suppose that one of the greatest men of the age, for such he decidedly is, will be unable to effect anything against the enemy? Lord Cochrane's whole life has been a series of proofs that he possesses all the qualities of a great commander.

DEAR TRELAWNY, When I returned from my ride, I wrote down what I said;—if you think it would be of any use, send it to Gordon. Not but that both he and Fabvier could form this plan as well or better than I, but my own opinion may have some weight with the Greeks, in support of those held by these two officers. For my own part, I would try this plan had I but *one* thousand men and *one* cannon! so convinced am I that it is a sound one; and that if executed with skill, activity, and courage it would make Ibrahim lose his game.   Yours, C. NAPIER.

I dare say this is full of errors, for I wrote as fast as I could scribble; keep it, for I have no copy. I wish you to give me one.

Cephalonia, 20th June, 1826

DEAR TRELAWNY, Many thanks for your note dated 12th, which I have only this morning received. I hear Hastings has reached Napoli, which I hope will help Gordon to make arrangements. I hear that Ibrahim Pacha has taken and fortified Sparta.—If he can occupy Leondari and Sparta with strong detachments, he may render the execution of my plan difficult; but if he divides his forces with such numerous garrisons, the question arises, whether or not he can keep the field? However, he would greatly embarrass all operations by fortifying Leondari and Mistra (Sparta). These posts are, at this moment, the real points of 'strategy' for the defence of Napoli; and his seizure of them denotes a good military head. Were I in Gordon's place, supposing him master of his movements, I would make them keep their *vigils* in Sparta. That garrison should have no sinecure; but my fear is, that at Napoli they are all in such a state of confusion and ignorance, that he will not be able to make any movements at all. However, all I can say is, that the loss of any strong post demands that the Greeks should act upon the same principle against those posts, that would have been acted upon against the original positions of the Turks. The general principle remains the same, but is applied to a different locality. For example (take your map).—When Mistra is held by the Turks, the Greeks can no longer throw themselves on the line of communication between Tripolitza and Navarin. They must then change their *object,* and throw themselves on the line between Mistra; and from wherever the garrison draws its provisions, Mistra becomes the object instead of Tripolitza. How this is to be accomplished, God knows. The war is, in this instance, on too small a scale to judge by a map, as I could in a large movement acting against Tripolitza; but military talent, in a country like the Morea, finds ways to do what it wants. The grand secret in *mountain* countries is to *isolate* the enemy, which obliges him to abandon *his strong* position, and attack you in *yours*. It is not to one so well acquainted with the country as you are, that I need say what it would be to attack a good position in Greece, even without fortifications, much more with them.

It is in the art of forcing an enemy to fight you on your own chosen ground, that military genius consists, and few things are more difficult in practice. It unites so much theory and so much practice with great fearlessness of character, no timid man will throw himself into those decisive positions which produce great results. Yours truly, C. NAPIER.

Cephalonia, 1st August, 1826

MY DEAR TRELAWNY, Pray do not let Mr. Ruppenthal* say that I made proposals to him, without contradicting him, because I did no such thing. I think I know what he is; but be he what he may, he can make nothing of my letters that can do me any harm, supposing he should be a bad one. When one has *no secrets* it is hard to discover them!

I hope Gordon has made port. I do not understand Fabvier's movements. I dare say they are not voluntary. I give no man credit for doing what he likes—what is wise—in Greece; until I hear that he has 2000 good European drilled soldiers at his back, and 100,000 in his pockets, and a gallows with his advanced guard. I think were I there with the only power that would tempt me to go, I should raise the price of hemp 50 per cent in ten days. What has become of Lord Cochrane? all hands say *he comes*—but he comes not! With kind regards to Gordon if he is with you, believe me, Yours hastily, C. J. NAPIER.

I wish to God something may be done for the Greeks, for our orders are positive not to admit fugitives, and really though I think the rules laid down by the government are just, it is very distressing to execute them,—at least to me it is so.

---

* Ruppenthal, the banker.